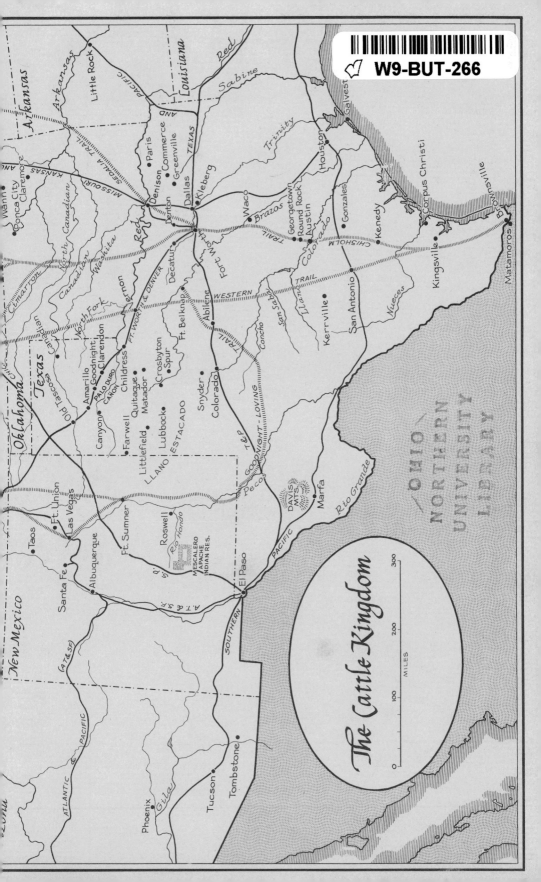

The Cattle Kingdom

iction has overwhelmed and obscured
history of
```
```
n battles, but the cattleme
v and order, even vigil
rly days when court
few and ineffect

Lewis Atherton, author of *Main Street on the Middle Border* and *The Pioneer Merchant in Mid-America,* among other works, is Professor of History at the University of Missouri. He served as chairman of the history department at Missouri from 1944-1950, was made director of the Western Historical Manuscripts Collection in 1952, and was the first recipient of the University's Distinguished Faculty Award in 1960.

He was awarded a Guggenheim Fellowship in 1940, was a Newberry Library fellow in 1950-51, and received a Rockefeller grant in 1953. THE CATTLE KINGS was written with the aid of a grant from the Social Science Research Council. Mr. Atherton has served on the editorial board of the *Journal of Southern History,* and is currently a member of the editorial board of the *Mississippi Valley Historical Review.*

(New Mexico State Tourist Bureau)

THE CATTLE KINGS

by Lewis Atherton

INDIANA UNIVERSITY PRESS

BLOOMINGTON

Contents

Illustrations

Introduction

AMERICANS display an avid interest in Western history but few take it seriously. Every schoolboy knows Davy Crockett, Daniel Boone, and Buffalo Bill; adults watch television shows and motion pictures based on Western themes. Rodeos rival baseball and basketball in spectator appeal, and Wild West literature continues to find a ready market. Nostalgia, an interest in the colorful, episodic, and romantic, and a desire to escape from the constant pressure of contemporary problems help keep such interest alive. In popular and scholarly thinking alike, however, the West becomes more and more divorced from twentieth-century realities.

This puzzling situation can be explained more easily than it can be rectified, for much historical insight must prevail before Western history gains the serious as well as the leisure-time attention that it deserves. One difficulty lies in the antiquarian and local nature of much that has been written in the field. Too many monographs record details without seeking to relate them to any over-all pattern of meaning. Too many local and amateur historians assume that every fact about the early history of their communities will intrigue others as it does them.

Another difficulty lies in the debate that has raged over the relative importance of environment and heredity in shaping American civilization. Frederick Jackson Turner's rebellion against the one-sided approach of teachers who wanted him to believe that American democracy could be traced to meetings of tribesmen in the forests of Germany stimulated him in 1893 to produce his famous essay on the significance of the frontier in American history. Intended to suggest and illustrate the possibilities inherent in a study of American environment, his essay became in reality an intellectual declaration of independence from European origins on the part of many of his disciples. Even Turner, tempted no doubt in part by the spirit of the occasion, assured the graduating class of the University of Washington in 1914:

American democracy was born of no theorist's dream; it was not carried in the SARAH CONSTANT to Virginia, nor in the MAYFLOWER to Plymouth. It came out of the American forest, and it gained new strength each time it touched a new frontier. Not the constitution, but free land and an abundance of natural resources open to a fit people, made the democratic type of society in America for three centuries while it occupied its empire.

Such unguarded enthusiasm invited rebuttal, and many scholars contributed to showing the imitative, ephemeral, and unrewarding aspects of Western history. The attack proved so devastating that many American historians shifted their attention to other approaches and assumed that the West had little to offer in the way of a serious understanding of our culture.

Still another difficulty lies in the industrial-urban nature of our contemporary civilization and our growing interdependence with other nations. Today, six out of every ten Americans live in one of the 174 metropolitan areas of the United States and many more reside in smaller urban communities. Population experts predict that two-thirds of the expected large increase in population by 1975 will occur in the heavily urbanized centers, thus adding to the preponderant influence of that way of life. Americans are concerned with urban problems and international difficulties, not with our agrarian, frontier past, and until they understand its meaning they will continue to show an interest only in its superficial aspects.

For the moment, Americans are still engaged in cutting their cultural strings to the past. Like the adolescent child, they must rebel before they can be free. The American West contributed greatly to the rationale used to justify our cultural declaration of independence from Europe, and was taken more seriously as a result. It became necessary, however, for urban-industrial society to repeat the process and to further free itself from the restraining bonds of the preceding agrarian-western age. To do so required a challenging of earlier American values, a virtual denial of their validity for the present. Nevertheless, once sure of its independence, the new age will acknowledge its debt to the temporarily repudiated historical past, and there are signs that such a time has arrived.

In this book I have concentrated on the role of the Western cattleman in American culture. I believe that ranchers were far more important than cowboys in shaping cultural developments, and, incidentally, were far more exciting as well. As hired hands on horseback who compromised with their environment at relatively low levels, cowhands exerted little influence on the course of American history. On the other hand, ranchers tried to dominate their environment, and at least succeeded in modifying it. I have examined source materials in various libraries but have drawn heavily on reminiscences and published biographies of individual cattlemen. It seems to me that the time has come to consider the dominant personalities on the various frontiers in terms of group characteristics. What were cattlemen really like as a whole? For what did they stand? Such an approach should make it easier to repress the episodic and ephemeral in favor of the more enduring and more meaningful aspects of the cattle kingdom.

Although I owe a debt of gratitude to many individuals, libraries, and foundations for advice and aid in the preparation of this book, I am especially indebted to the Social Science Research Council for a faculty research grant; to Dean Henry E. Bent and the Research Council of the University of Missouri for a summer research professorship; to Dean W. Francis English of the Arts College of the University of Missouri for reading an early draft of the manuscript and making suggestions; to Mr. and Mrs. Phil Viles of Claremore, Oklahoma, for arranging interviews with early-day cattlemen; to Mr. Tom White of Roswell, New Mexico, for information and the loan of material in his personal possession; and to various scholars and staff members along the way who gave me more consideration than was my due: Miss Llerena B. Friend of the Barker Texas History Center, Austin; Dr. William Martin Pearce of Texas Technological College at Lubbock and its Southwest Collection; Mrs. Laura A. Ekstrom, Assistant Librarian, State Historical Society of Colorado, Denver; Dr. Gene Gressley, Director of the Archives in History, University of Wyoming at Laramie; Miss Virginia Walton, former librarian, State Historical Society of Montana at Helena; and Dr. Dale L. Morgan at the Bancroft Library in Berkeley. My wife, Louise Webb Atherton, has been of great assistance in helping locate and transcribe material.

LEWIS ATHERTON

University of Missouri

ONE

Change and Continuity

THE cattle kingdom of the American West developed rapidly. At the close of the Civil War enormous herds of buffalo still ranged the Great Plains, a region constituting a fourth of the United States. Many Americans still thought of it as "The Great American Desert," suitable only for the wandering bands of Indians who found a home there. Twenty years later, the buffalo herds had virtually disappeared, the Indians had been pushed aside, and the cattle kingdom seemingly reigned supreme. Cowboys and cattle kings characterized the region, a remarkable transformation.

A combination of economic factors in the post-Civil War period sparked the change by greatly increasing the competitive advantage of the Great Plains region in beef production. Opening of the public domain provided cheap land for grazing, extension of the railroads into the high plains and invention of the refrigerator car lessened the difficulties of moving beef to market, and modifications in British corporation laws in the direction of investment trusts stimulated a flow of capital into Western ranching. Increased consumption of meat in America and abroad, the rise of world markets, and the growth of great packing centers encouraged ranchers to extend their activities into frontier regions. Men could well be optimistic as to the future of the industry.

As a result, entrepreneurs from many foreign countries and from virtually all the older American states came west to engage in the cattle business. Abilene, Kansas, the first of the railroad cowtowns, illustrated in microcosm the nature and meaning of that migration of men and capital. When Joseph G. McCoy selected Abilene in 1867 as the site for his venture in bringing Texas trail drivers and eastern buyers together at one point, it was only a small village of log huts. By 1870 Abilene had grown to some seven or eight hundred people and was a roaring cowtown at the height of the shipping season. Its inhabitants represented some twenty-seven different American states and thirteen foreign countries, with Ireland, England, Canada, Germany, Sweden, and Scotland furnishing most of the foreign element.[1]

Of course, one could expect a trading point like Abilene to attract people from a distance, but the same diversity characterized the cattle kingdom as a whole. Representatives of the historian Hubert Howe Bancroft, for instance, interviewed fifty-three "typical" cattlemen in Wyoming in 1885. Forty were Americans and thirteen were foreign born. The native Americans came from sixteen of the thirty-eight states—ten from New York, five from Virginia, four each from Pennsylvania and Ohio, three each from Massachusetts and Missouri, two from Iowa, and one each from New Jersey, Delaware, Rhode Island, Wisconsin, New Hampshire, Vermont, Illinois, Indiana, and Maine. Six of the foreign born came from England, two from Ireland, and one each from Canada, Scotland, Germany, France, and Russia.[2]

Even the Texas rancher, who in the public mind runs to type, displayed the same geographical variety of background. Texas drew more heavily than did the more Northern parts of the cattle kingdom on the older Southern states, such as Virginia, Mississippi, Alabama, and Tennessee, but it had a considerable number of ranchers from Pennsylvania, New York, Rhode Island, and other Northeastern states also. There, too, one found foreigners engaged in the cattle industry—from England, Scotland, Ireland, Canada, Alsace-Lorraine, and Germany.[3] Individuals from Massachusetts, Pennsylvania, Kansas, Colorado, Texas, Canada, and England participated in opening the Texas Panhandle ranching frontier in the 1870's.[4] The cattleman's frontier definitely had an international flavor.

Occupational backgrounds were even more diverse. Most of the fifty-three Wyoming ranchers interviewed in 1885 by Bancroft agents had followed many different occupations before concentrating on cattle raising. A considerable number listed mining, law enforcement, or freighting as earlier work, all of which may have been helpful to them in adjusting to a ranching environment. Some had participated in trail driving, stage driving, the piloting of steamboats or the guiding of immigrants. They too may have benefited from their previous work. Former railroaders, blacksmiths, painters, and plumbers perhaps found their previous trades of limited value when they turned to ranching. At least, however, their previous occupations seemed no further removed from cattle raising than did the backgrounds of their fellow cattlemen who had formerly been army men, politicians, bankers, teachers, or hotel-keepers.[5] As in Chouteau County, Montana, in 1884, where interviews with fifty-six cattlemen revealed that only four had previously been engaged in the cattle business, lack of previous ranching experience seems to have deterred few from entering that occupation.

The cosmopolitan nature of the ranching frontier was also accentuated by the variety of classes represented. Rich and poor, nobleman and commoner alike participated in its development. Teddy Roosevelt and Dan Casement came from prosperous, even wealthy, Eastern families and had attended Ivy League schools. George Miller and George W. Littlefield traced their ancestry back to the plantation class of the Old South. Richard King came off the streets of New York City. English nobility made up a sizable part of the European contribution. Gregor Lang and Murdo Mackenzie represented substantial British middle-class backgrounds. Pierre Wibaux's family belonged to the French bourgeois textile manufacturing group, the Baron de Bonnemains and the Marquis de Mores to the French nobility. Conrad Kohrs and Henry Miller came from the lower German middle class. Few places and periods have witnessed such a mingling of classes, cultures, and backgrounds as did the days of the cattle kingdom.

Years later, John Clay recalled the variety of personalities that frequented the Cheyenne Club, a luxurious social center for cattlemen, when he joined it in 1883. There he met cautious Scots, exuberant Irishmen, careful Yankees, confident Bostonians, worldly New Yorkers, chivalrous Southerners, and delightful Canadians, as he characterized them.[6] These men were products of their backgrounds, not a uniform type because of their participation for the moment in a common occupation.

The assemblage within a few years of so varied a group of men, bound only by a common interest in the cattle industry, demanded some dramatic explanation to satisfy public curiosity. As usual, promotional agencies had no trouble in providing an answer so appealing in its simplicity and novelty as to find ready acceptance in the public press. According to them, a freighter crossing the plains late in the season found himself stormbound and his team of oxen unable to move his heavy cargo. In desperation, he turned them loose and made his way on foot to the nearest habitation. The following spring he returned with a new team of oxen, hoping to recover his abandoned wagon. To his great surprise, he found his old team, fat and sleek, grazing nearby.[7] Thus, by accident, men learned that the Great Plains provided fine grazing conditions for cattle, and the great boom got under way.

Supposedly, too, ranchers crowded the open range of the Northern plains with vast herds of cattle and without giving thought to the possible necessity of supplementary feeding in severe winter weather. For several seasons all went well, and then the hard winter of 1886-1887 decimated herds to the point where owners were bankrupted almost overnight. And thus open-range ranching terminated as abruptly as it had begun. Since the cattle kingdom grew and changed with remarkable rapidity through the efforts of colorful and diverse personalities drawn from all over the world, it naturally gave rise to dramatic explanations for its beginnings and its vicissitudes. Even though the hard winter of 1886-1887 only served to stimulate changes already under way and brought no abrupt transition in ranching techniques, change did constitute a major characteristic of the cattle kingdom.

An emphasis on change alone, however, accentuates the abrupt, the colorful, and the episodic to the point of concealing the essenial continuity of the cattle kingdom with the past and with the future. Those who participated in shaping its course recognized its historical antecedents and took pride in them. When Joseph G. McCoy published his *Historic Sketches of the Cattle Trade of the West and Southwest* in book form in 1874 he commented: "We deem it time idly spent to further show, what all men must acknowledge, that the vocation of live stock is not only ancient, but of old, as now, altogether honorable in the highest degree."[8] McCoy had read and pondered the Bible stories of old. To him, it was no accident that herdsmen upon the hills of Judea were selected first among men to hear angelic tidings of "Peace on earth and good will to men." Theodore Roosevelt, who played at ranching in the Dakota Bad Lands, also noted the long traditions of that occupation. American ranching reminded him of the life of vigorous, primitive, pastoral peoples and had little in common with the humdrum, workaday world of the nineteenth century. In their manner of life, ranchers showed more kinship to an Arab sheik than to a sleek city merchant or tradesman.[9] Similarly, the noted English historian, Arnold Toynbee, suggests that a pastoral, nomadic life actually began to emerge in the West and that its essential continuity with the past has been obscured by modifications resulting from the Industrial Revolution.[10]

Although ranching developed rapidly on the Great Plains, it constituted no sharp break with pre-Civil War conditions. The Texas longhorn cattle and methods of handling them traced back many decades into Southwestern history, and white men knew the possibilities of cattle raising on the Great Plains long before the story of the stranded trader made its appearance.

Nevertheless, emphasis on continuity with a primitive, pastoral society can obscure the capitalistic-commercial nature of the cattle kingdom, which employed every known Wall Street device of organization and financing available at the time. It has, in fact, contributed to the popular idea that the cowboy represented medieval ideals of chivalry and escaped the humdrum restrictions of nineteenth-century commerce. It has focused popular attention on the cowboy rather than the cattleman, who built and directed the cattle kingdom. McCoy saw all this clearly, as well as the existing continuity, although Roosevelt gave freer reign to his own romantic concepts of the West. Toynbee's conception of an emerging pastoral, nomadic life cut short by an industrial revolution could well be reversed, with emphasis on Commercial and Industrial Revolutions creating, rather than terminating, ranching as a pastoral occupation, enabling it to pass rapidly from a herding to a highly organized, profit-centered regime. But ranching maintained a continuity with the future as well as with the past.

As a matter of fact, expansion of population into the world frontier as a whole following the great geographical explorations of the fifteenth and sixteenth centuries depended upon market outlets for the products of frontier settlements. In treating frontier expansion in South Africa between 1652 and 1836, S. D. Neumark has pointed out that the famous "Great Trek" occurred primarily because the participants considered ranching economically more profitable than a wine or wheat culture. They did not feel cramped for land or room in their old location nor did they move with the idea of pursuing a self-sufficient economy. A quest for knowledge through exploration motivated only a small minority. Love of adventure appealed to a larger number, if, according to Neumark, the phrase is defined as "a spirit of enterprise," but economic improvement constituted the universal motive. There, as on the American ranching frontier, markets for beef and its by-products largely regulated the degree and timing of advancement into new lands.[11]

American cattlemen drove their herds to market until commercial transportation became available. As Teddy Roosevelt pointed out, the rough rider of the plains was a first cousin of the backwoodsman of the southern Alleghenies. The term "round up" had exactly the same meaning for early-day mountaineers in Kentucky, Tennessee, and North Carolina as it did in the post-Civil War cattle kingdom.[12] Even in the better lands of the East, driving of stock to market was a common practice long before the Civil War. Daniel Drew, of unsavory Wall Street fame, began life as a drover and also operated a tavern for their accommodation.

Farm boys from east of the Mississippi River understood and applied such marketing methods when they turned to ranching on the Western frontier. George W. Briggs, early Colorado miner and rancher, for instance, assisted in driving a herd of cattle to New York City while working as a farm hand in his native Ohio in the late 1840's.[13] John W. Iliff, Colorado's first cattle king, the son of a well-to-do Ohio farmer who specialized in raising fine stock near Zanesville, grew up in the cattle business. For more than forty-five years cattle were driven from that region over the Allegheny mountains to seaboard markets and some of his father's stock very probably were included.[14] At least, when Iliff began his rapid rise in the livestock business in Colorado in the late 1850's he was no stranger to marketing problems. Similarly, Joseph G. McCoy, whose father migrated to Illinois by way of Tennessee and Ohio before the War of 1812, grew up in a region noted for its beef cattle and engaged in transporting stock overland, by rail, and by steamboat before undertaking his famous venture at Abilene, Kansas, in 1867.[15]

Nor did Texas cattlemen wait until railroads began to penetrate the High Plains to start their drives to distant markets. After the annexation of Texas by the United States in 1845, cattle raising expanded greatly there. During the 1850's, travelers, agricultural papers, and the local Texas press publicized the advantages of the state for ranching. They pointed out that cattle multiplied rapidly, with net increases running to 30 per cent a year; that expenses of feeding and wintering were negligible; that Texas had excellent grazing lands, and that labor costs could be held to a minimum. In short, raising cattle in Texas constituted a sure way to wealth. Texas drives to Missouri and to New Orleans took place before the Civil War. Some Texas longhorns even reached New York City by 1854, although in small numbers. By 1855 Missouri had passed a law against the entry of diseased cattle, through fear of the Texas tick fever, and the territorial legislature of Kansas enacted a similar restriction in 1859.[16] Quite obviously, Texans began to seek distant markets for their cattle well before the Civil War and had learned much concerning the problems and difficulties involved.

In the same period, ranchers in the Great Plains region to the north of Texas found sufficient market opportunities to justify their maintaining small herds of cattle. The ranching industry of the High Plains began as a result of the needs of emigrants along the Oregon Trail. Movements of these people to California and Oregon in the two decades preceding the Civil War encouraged traders at Far Western posts to build bridges and ferries on emigrant roads. They also supplied forage for the stock of emigrants and exchanged fresh oxen for worn-down work cattle at a profitable ratio. Mining camps constituted still another market for early cattlemen. During the 1860's army posts, erected to grapple with the growing Indian problem, and camps of workers engaged in building railroad lines expanded opportunities for marketing cattle. As one historian has put it:

Thus, by the close of the sixties, there existed in the northern section of the High Plains and in the adjacent mountain valleys, herds of considerable size, recruited from the stock of the emigrant and gold seeker, from the work animals of the freighting companies, from the Mormon herds, and from the herds of Oregon and California. Their owners were making good profits in supplying the local markets of mining camp, section crew, and military post.[17]

Granville Stuart, pioneer prospector and rancher, recorded the names and activities of some of the early cattlemen who successfully exploited marketing opportunities on the ranching frontier. In 1850, for instance, Captain Richard Grant and his two sons began trading along the emigrant road in Utah for footsore and worn-out horses and cattle. Rest and a little care restored them to usefulness. The Grants spent their summers along the emigrant road between Fort Bridger and Salt Lake but wintered their stock at other points where forage and protection from winter blasts could be found. In 1856, Robert Dempsey, John M. Jacobs, Robert Hereford, and Jacob Meek began a similar business, and wintered six hundred cattle and horses in Montana near the Grants' range. When Stuart went to Montana in 1858, Jacobs and the Grants possessed herds of several hundred cattle and horses, which they fattened on native grasses on the open range in preparation for the spring trade with emigrants. Ranges in the Beaverhead, Stinkingwater, and Deer Lodge valleys became increasingly popular. By the time of the gold discovery at Alder Gulch, ranches were well established and ready to profit from that additional market. In 1864-65 the territorial legislature found it advisable to pass a law regulating marks and brands, and in the spring of 1866 Nelson Story of Bozeman drove the first herd of Texas cattle into Montana.[18]

The color and charm of those early times appeal to modern-day urbanites, but the industry even then was strictly market centered. Quite obviously, ranchers probed the Great Plains preceding the Civil War and realized that they could supply still larger markets. When these opened up, ranchers filled the region with cattle so rapidly that observers thought of their activities as something startlingly new.

Moreover, ranching continued on beyond the bonanza days of open range and high speculation. Large ranches still exist today. Some portions of our country seem suited only for grass, and in many places a considerable acreage is still needed to carry even a small herd of cattle. It is estimated, for instance, that around 60 per cent of Texas will always be cattle range.[19] Of course, like the Indian, the open-range rancher had to give way when others wanted his land for more intensive cultivation. The grazing of cattle demanded relatively large acreages and returned less per acre in those places where crops could be grown. But, rather than disappearing from the American scene, ranching became more selective of land location.

This changing but long-continued economic role parallels and perhaps reenforces the distinctive cultural role assigned to the cattleman. The American public today recognizes a rancher by his dress more quickly than they can identify almost any other American type. Even the organization man in his gray flannel suit is less conspicuous than the rancher in his boots and Stetson hat. As early as the 1880's the rancher's role in matters of dress was pretty well defined. Moreover, the American public knows the "code" of the West, which is most intimately associated with the ranching industry, better than that of any other American group. A violent murder in Iowa brings no report that the "Code of the Cornbelt" sparked the incident, but a similar happening in ranch country will evoke a great deal of such comment.

In 1948 the Rockefeller Committee at the University of Oklahoma commissioned Charles L. Sonnichsen to make a report on the contemporary status of the American cattleman. For several months he traveled extensively in the cattle country, observing and interviewing ranchers and their families. His report constituted an interesting, broad-gauged analysis of the modern cattleman's way of life. In his travels, Sonnichsen noted that the cattleman still held to a code and a uniform as in earlier days.

In 1948, as in the heyday of the cattle kingdom, ranchers dressed in cowboy boots, Stetson hats, and other distinctive clothing on public occasions, a uniform which indicated that they thought of themselves as a group apart from the rest of mankind. Trousers might be pink, blue levis, or border on the gray-striped garment more commonly seen in cities, but they must have the appearance and cut of riding breeches. Shirts could vary from a Hollywood sports model to blue denim, providing they carried a distinctive outdoor flavor. Open vests, once a common feature of the cattleman's costume, had virtually disappeared, but otherwise the uniform still showed its close connections with the history of the industry.

Such a uniform owed much to convenience and utility in the days of open-range ranching, and modern-day cattlemen occasionally still justify wearing it on such grounds. Sonnichsen quotes a cattleman on the subject of hats:

Most cowmen always wear Stetsons. . . . Mine has never blown off. They shade your eyes, keep the rain from running down your neck, and keep you from being beaten to death with hailstones. They make the best eyeshades in the world—for reading, playing poker, or what have you. That is why cowboys wear them in the house. These high-school kids who go without hats puzzle me. I wonder why they don't protect their brains, if they have any—why they wear slickers in the rain, but no hats. They go out in these convertibles and rain runs down their necks so they have to sit in it. I'd feel like a baby that needs to be changed.[20]

One would be more inclined to accept such an explanation for the popularity of the uniform were it not for the fact that it is worn on dress-up occasions more than at work. When going about his regular duties on the modern-day ranch, the cattleman's attire sets him apart from others much less sharply than when he appears in town or on some public occasion. In Sonnichsen's opinion, the uniform marks a preferred status in the scale of American values, so much so that outsiders like to dress in the same manner. On dude ranches such imitation can be tolerated, but in parts of Texas anyone caught wearing the regalia may find himself dunked in a horse trough unless he actually owns at least one cow.[21]

In 1948 ranchers were equally emphatic concerning their code of values. In a speech to the American Livestock Association that year, Dan Casement, a leader in the cattle industry, told the group:

You do not represent a business system or a political organization. You are a social class, typifying a way of life, a fraternity of ideals, that preserve the best in American lore, that unify in a single code of citizenship the traditions of our forefathers for freedom, independence, opportunity, resourcefulness, and rugged individuality.[22]

From interviews and personal observations Sonnichsen concludes that the rancher's code involves courage, cheerfulness, and a willingness to settle problems through one's own powers and without undue recourse to others. It emphasizes high respect for womanhood. It places a premium on loyalty—loyalty to one's own outfit and to the brand burned in the hides of the stock for which the individual is responsible—and on honesty—a man's word should be as good as his bond. It extols the love of horses. It demands reticence with strangers, unwillingness to pry into the affairs of others with personal questions, but hospitality to all in need.

Of course, it is changing because of the impact of new influences. The rancher, and especially his wife, has begun to find that a reputation for hospitality can lead to serious impositions. Strangers may take advantage of it to enjoy free food and lodging at a ranch home when good highways and automobiles could quickly carry them on to commercial accommodations at a nearby town. Ranchers are beginning to distinguish between invited and uninvited guests to protect themselves from such abuse. Nevertheless, the code remains a part of their social inheritance and they respect it.[23]

And yet, Sonnichsen doubts if the ranching code rests on solid foundations. He calls attention to a "myth" about the cattleman, a tradition based on an idealized version of the past and created more by outsiders than by ranchers themselves. As captives of that myth, modern-day cattlemen feel called upon to act in accordance with its concepts. In actuality, their predecessors varied so greatly as to lack unity of outlook. After surveying the diversity of backgrounds among early-day cattlemen, Sonnichsen concludes: "What could the individuals in such an assortment as this have in common? Not much, probably, except for the qualities needed for survival on the frontier. . . ."[24]

Does the cattleman's code rest on so flimsy a foundation? If change rather than continuity dominated his occupation, then he had little chance to develop a role grounded otherwise than in myth. Perhaps, however, an interest in the colorful and the episodic has done less than justice to more enduring aspects of the cattleman's occupation. If so, his scale of values can be understood best of all by looking at his way of life in all its manifestations.

Why Be a Cattleman?

POWERFUL and varied motivations kindled the rush to the Great Plains ranching frontier. Some people came primarily for reasons of health, believing that the "champagne" air of high altitudes or a strenuous life in the open would heal them of chronic illnesses. Colonel O. W. Wheeler of Connecticut, for instance, educated himself for a business career but fell prey to tuberculosis. In hopes of finding renewed health, he made an ocean voyage to the Pacific Coast. Too weak physically to work in the placer mines upon arrival in California in 1851, he clerked briefly in a store at Sacramento, but turned to trading in worn-out cattle with emigrants as a means of getting outdoors. Within a few years he amassed considerable wealth, his health no longer barring him from long and strenuous trips to all parts of the cattle kingdom.[1] And, of course, all know the story of Teddy Roosevelt's strengthening his constitution by life on a Dakota Bad Lands ranch. According to Michael Slattery, general manager of the Waddingham Ranges and Cattle Raising Associations in New Mexico in 1885, there was a real danger of overstocking the local range because virtually every Easterner with a few thousand dollars and the consumption wanted to enter ranching.[2]

Many expected ranching to enable them to live a gentleman's life. Until the hard winter of 1886-1887 definitely proved otherwise, such people considered ranching a seasonal occupation in which owners needed to be present on the home range only a few months each year. Supposedly, they should put in an appearance at spring and fall roundups to check on increases in their herds and to consult with their foremen on the few simple policies needed. Moreover, ranching involved claims to range rights over thousands of acres of land and herds of cattle. Under such conditions a man could make money and still think of himself in terms of feudal overlordship, well removed from the bourgeois world of commerce and industry. In addition, wild game was plentiful and the hunting excellent.

In giving his reasons for becoming a rancher, Baron de Bonnemains expressed the convictions of this class as a whole. Born in France in 1851, he served as a captain in the French army and spent several years in Paris before migrating to New York and "fixing" himself up in business. A trip to Montana to hunt wild game introduced him to the possibilities inherent in ranching, and by 1883 he was in the cattle business. He did not know the size of his range but estimated it at some "thirty-two miles in extent." The cattle just "ran around" winter and summer, increased rapidly, and losses were very small. As a matter of fact, the Baron considered ranching almost all pure profit. He had cattle, horses, and sheep on his range but had reluctantly decided that the climate was too cold to add ostriches as an additional source of income. If he could raise more capital in France, he intended to remain in ranching, for Montana was the finest cattle country in the world. The Baron left his ranch by the middle of October, there being so little to do during the winter months that his partner could easily look after things, and did not expect to return until March. During the winter he enjoyed the pleasures of San Francisco, and obviously felt free to move around as he pleased for several months.[3] Land, flocks and herds, easy money, good hunting, and time to visit metropolitan centers—what more could an aristocratic young man wish?

Sons of well-to-do Eastern families succumbed to the same appeal. When Richard Trimble of New York City visited his former college friends at the famous Cheyenne Club in the 1880's, he readily observed the paper profits that they had in the making. In letters to "Dear Momie" and other members of his family, he spoke of the stimulating companionship and the financial returns which such a life offered. Horseback rides and invigorating champagne air, roundups, wild game, cowboys, and a multitude of novelties impressed him. On one occasion some of his friends had to leave the comforts of the Cheyenne Club to help with a roundup. They were accompanied by a chap named Wister. Of course, Trimble did not know that Owen Wister was gathering material which would make him famous through his writing of the great cowboy novel, *The Virginian.* Had Trimble known, it probably would have occasioned little surprise, for to him the West represented romance as well as easy money. He remembered vividly his first night at a roundup. A full moon lighted up the scene, coyotes wailed in the distance, and just across a stream from the camp two cowboys circled a herd of cattle all night long.[4]

The cattleman's frontier also furnished an opportunity to prove one's self. Those addicted to the "strenuous life," of which Teddy Roosevelt was so fond, could find it in abundance on the plains and in a form peculiarly suited to the needs of youth. Because of this appeal to youthful vigor, Roosevelt selected a quotation from the poet Browning to preface his book *Ranch Life and the Hunting Trail:*

> Oh, our manhood's prime vigor! No spirit feels waste,
> Not a muscle is stopped in its playing nor sinew unbraced.
>
> . . . .
> How good is man's life, the mere living.

In Roosevelt's opinion, no matter how intellectual a man might be, he could not succeed in the West without possessing the ruder, coarser virtues and physical qualities.

The same spirit of adventure appealed to common men who came from less economically favored homes. Although they lacked financial means to go where they pleased in seasons of slack work, the ranching industry offered them opportunities to move about. Texas farm boys watched the trail herds of longhorns move past their homes on the way to distant markets at Abilene, Kansas, or on the Northern plains, and by their middle teens signed on as hands to accompany the herds. At their destinations, they found every conceivable form of commercialized vice, if they wished to indulge; and at least they saw and participated in a rugged and picturesque life. As seasoned hands, they could drift from ranch to ranch, certain of finding work at spring and fall roundups when additional help became necessary.

The wandering cowboy was no myth. Records of the famous Spur Ranch of Texas show that it never lacked for a supply of hands in busy seasons during the period 1885 to 1909, except for the year 1888, when the manager sent a wagon to Abilene, Kansas, and Colorado to recruit help. Usually, letters of application for spring employment began to arrive as early as December, and many cowboys simply put in an appearance just before the busy season opened. Among them were overgrown country boys in their teens looking for adventure, and the manager frequently received letters from anxious parents inquiring about their sons and asking that they be sent home. Ranch records document the high rate of sickness and accidents, about the only hazards that could have made the work seem adventurous, but still the men came. Of the 901 different hands employed between 1885 and 1909, only 3 per cent worked as many as five seasons and 64 per cent remained only for one.[5] A desire to try a different ranch or a different part of the cattle kingdom accounted for much of the high turnover in the labor force.

Joseph G. McCoy declared that the drovers and dealers continued to risk their money and personal safety on the long drives, even after achieving financial prosperity, because their occupation offered a change in climate, country, scenes, men, and circumstances. Risk and excitement, both personally and financially, exerted a fascination which caused them to hang on year after year, and to expand until some circumstance beyond their control brought disaster.[6] They, too, like the cowboy, found the open road to their liking.

An opportunity to live in country as yet unspoiled by man ex-

Above, cutting out a cow from the roundup herd on Shoe Bar Ranch, Texas.

At left, cowboy stopping at a waterhole to drink from his hatbrim. (Both photos from Erwin E. Smith Collection, Library of Congress)

The Mill Iron Rawhide: Roundup near Missouri River in Montana. Famous old brands shown in picture include Pierre Wibaux's W Bar. (L. A. Huffman photo)

Above, cowboy heating the branding irons. (New Mexico State Tourist Bureau)
At left, Harry Campbell, son of the first manager of Matador Ranch, branding a calf on the range. (Erwin E. Smith Collection, Library of Congress)

Bringing a calf to the branding fire. The lookout rider on the left checks the mother's brand, so that the calf will bear the same mark. (L. A. Huffman photo) erted a strong appeal to many ranchers. In the Dakota Bad Lands, Gregor Lang's son, Lincoln Lang, along with the many-sided Roosevelt, deeply felt the charm of their surroundings, and both, characteristically, grew bitter over the later abuse of land and resources by settlers. Although Roosevelt hunted game in the Bad Lands with great enthusiasm, he also loved its virgin nature. His home ranch, stretching along both sides of the Little Missouri River, separated him by ten miles from his nearest neighbor. As a result, he could enjoy the rapidly changing landscape without interruption on early morning rides. Only the sounds of nature were evident. During the hot, lifeless summer day he listened to the soft, melancholy cooing of mourning doves; at night, he heard the "whip-poor-wills," and noted that only the last two syllables of their call could be distinguished, unlike their breed in the East. He thrilled to the coyote's wail, to the strident challenge of a lynx, to the snorting and stamping of deer that lived in the brush only two hundred yards from the ranch house.[7]

Fresh from his home in Northern Ireland, Lincoln Lang first saw the Dakota Bad Lands as a boy of sixteen in the early summer of 1883. In the course of a few weeks the entire current of his life changed. He felt closer to earth, closer to truth than ever before, as if he had answered the call of his inheritance. He resented the application of the term "Bad Lands" to the region where he found a peace of mind that passed all understanding. He reveled in the wealth of color—in the birds, in the tints of flowers and foliage, in the sunrises, in the moonlight, and in the soil: "A wild romantic rock-garden of the Gods where in peace and security the wild and untamed revelled in the exalted atmosphere with which nature had surrounded them."[8]

Nor did one need to come from strikingly different environmental background to appreciate the natural beauties of the West. Granville Stuart's parents took him to Illinois from their Virginia home in 1837 when he was three years old. A year later they moved on to Iowa Territory, where he attended a country school. Later in life he remembered from those days Webster's famous spelling book, with its discouraging frontispiece of a lightly clad young man weakening halfway up a mountain. On top stood a cupola, bearing in large letters the word "fame," toward which a rough-looking female was ordering him to climb. Stuart blamed her constant look of contempt for so impressing him with the difficulties of becoming famous that all hope of it died within him.

In reality, he was born a dreamer and a philosopher, a student of books and of nature, a lover of all creation. During a stay in the California gold fields in the 1850's, Stuart took great pleasure in the magnificent virgin forests and in the setting of his primitive cabin. His mind photographed the landscape: sugar pines, yellow pines, fir, black oak, cedar, dogwood thirty feet high and covered with glossy leaves and enormous white blossoms, flowering bushes. Although a covey of quail ranged near his cabin, he preferred eating less appetizing squirrel meat to killing them. He would remember forever the deep canyons with their rivers of clear water dashing over boulders, the azure sky, and the variety of wild animals. His consciousness of flowers, of birds, of everyday beauty, of being vitally alive meant more than placer gold, and it remained with him throughout his later business and public career in Montana. Others made more money out of mining and ranching but Stuart found his greatest rewards in other ways.[9]

The career of Charles Goodnight, who spent a lifetime in the ranching business, provides an interesting example of the subtle variation in motivations among ranchers. An almost perfect illustration of the cattleman, Goodnight impressed many as a person of limited feelings. Gruff and less articulate than Stuart, he lived an intensely active life and seldom spoke of basic convictions. Although adventures came his way in sufficient quantity and variety to document the most exciting television Western, something more than a love of adventure for its own sake marked his colorful exploits. Nor was he a nature lover in exactly the same manner as a Roosevelt or a Granville Stuart. Seemingly less complex than many of his contemporaries, he surpassed most of them in the delicate shadings of his basic drives.

When Goodnight blazed the famous Goodnight-Loving Trail to Colorado by way of New Mexico in 1866, his difficulties with

Indians and the hazards of the harsh country through which he traveled tested him to the fullest. At one stage of the journey he and his men drove their cattle eighty miles without water, and Goodnight had no sleep for three consecutive days and nights. Some of the animals stampeded when they smelled water and others had to be left bogged down in quicksand or otherwise inaccessible. The journey was a nightmare for all involved, but Goodnight proved that cattle could be driven across a region that long bore the reputation of being the cattleman's graveyard.

Financially, the trip was highly profitable. At Fort Sumner in New Mexico Territory the partners received twelve thousand dollars in gold for cattle to feed reservation Indians. Goodnight's partner, Oliver Loving, drove the remaining stock on to Colorado while he and three cowboys returned to Texas for more cattle. Goodnight packed a mule with provisions and the gold, and he and his companions rode only at night, lying in concealment during the day, in hopes of arriving home safely. At one stage of the trip the pack mule, frightened by some unexplained cause, bolted, leaving the men vulnerable to hunger and even to murder by lurking Indians. They recovered the gold, but not the precious food. The crisis impressed Goodnight deeply:

Here you are with more gold than you ever had in your life, and it won't buy you a drink of water, and it won't get you food. For this gold you may have led three men to their death—for a thing that is utterly useless to you.[10]

Years later, Goodnight told his biographer that he had always remembered the seriousness of that moment and thereafter never worshiped money. The death a few months later of his partner from wounds inflicted by Indian raiders strengthened his realization of the human costs involved in driving cattle to market. Love of adventure for adventure's sake would have seemed rather silly to Charles Goodnight. He found more than he wanted without seeking it out. Satisfaction to him lay in skill in planning to avoid difficulties and in meeting them successfully when they arose, not in foolhardy escapades as such.

Much the same attitude marked his outlook on nature. By experience he learned its harsh and implacable but harmonious system of action as it applied to frontier existence. It challenged his ingenuity. If one studied and applied its rules, disaster could be averted. By understanding it, its virtues became clear. Goodnight lived in harmony with nature because of his constant study of its operation. To his wife, the incessant winds of the plains meant constant irritation; to him, they served a useful purpose in cattle raising. By facing into the wind, cattle found a measure of protection from dust, heat, and flies.

As a young scout with the Texas Rangers, Goodnight acquired a fund of lore that casual observers would have ignored. For instance, he was always "mighty glad" to see a mesquite bush. On the dry plains it seemed to spring up only from the droppings of an animal. Since the wild mustangs were the only animals that ate mesquite beans on the frontier lying beyond established ranches, and since they rarely grazed out from water for more than three miles, the sight of a mesquite bush indicated to Goodnight that he could find water nearby. If he saw a herd of mustangs strung out and walking steadily, he knew they were headed toward water; if they were scattered, and frequently stopped to graze, they were returning. Goodnight also observed closely the distance that various kinds of birds ranged from water for the survival value such knowledge had for human beings traveling across the plains.[11] In preferring the country to city life, and in sensing his own identity with nature, Goodnight typified those who found an enormous satisfaction in ranching that stemmed from something more elemental than a so-called "love of nature."

Perhaps the word freedom came closest to encompassing any nonmaterial, common element among the motives that attracted men to ranching. Many of the rank-and-file liked the freedom with which they moved from ranch to ranch or from ranch to cowtown with herds of longhorns. Aristocrats came and went on the supposition that ranching was seasonal in nature. They enjoyed the pleasures of sophisticated society during the winter months and returned to enormous ranges in the spring, where they escaped from irksome restraints of elders and tedious social conventions. Some enjoyed the solitude of nature and felt freer in open country than in cities. All of them enjoyed pitting their personal abilities against the hazards of open nature in situations where the protective forces of organized society could not easily rescue them if they came to grief. Some were merely young and reckless; others understood the odds against them, but all sensed the freedom of action possible on the ranching frontier.

Only a few seem to have defined that freedom more narrowly in terms of political or social democracy. John Clay explained his first trip to America in 1872 on the grounds of having inherited radical views from his parents and a dislike for the caste system in Scotland, which, in his words, smothered ambition, neglected ability, and gave a silent, sarcastic repression to any forward movement.[12] One hunts in vain, however, for any proof of Clay's radical ideas during his long career as manager of cattle corporations and owner of a livestock commission firm. Social and economic opportunities appealed to him, but in America he represented political conservatism, if a man so heavily involved in economic activities can be labeled at all in the political field.

On the other hand, Scotch-Irish Gregor Lang, who grew up in an archconservative family, dreamed of America as a land of free institutions long before he moved to the Dakota Bad Lands. Lang read Tom Paine and other radical philosophers, named his son Lincoln after America's great president, and undoubtedly cherished the liberal tradition in American democracy. As a Democrat, he argued violently with his friend Theodore Roosevelt while the two occupied neighboring ranches, and he insisted on applying democratic ideals in social relations. In some respects, he surpassed the general run of Western Americans in devotion to liberal ideas, as in his friendly and just dealings with wandering Indians. He gladly served in various political capacities, believing that all citizens should participate actively in government.[13] As an old man, Lang returned to Edinburgh to die at the home of a daughter, but life in America still appealed to him because of his hopes for democracy. In spite of his violent arguments with Roosevelt on political theories, they held similar views on society and government, and Lang was no revolutionist. Nevertheless, he found the ranching frontier an appealing place because of his political and social ideals.

Undoubtedly, except for many of the rank-and-file cowhands, economic opportunity ranked first among motives that drew people to the cattleman's frontier. Eastern and European aristocrats and commoners alike expected to make money, and many of them expected to make it very fast. Even Gregor Lang came to America to represent a Scottish aristocrat who was interested in investing in large-scale ranching. In the days of open range, a rancher often purchased or homesteaded a quarter section of land as a base for his operations and then grazed his cattle freely on thousands of acres of the public domain. He started his herd at minimum cost from Texas longhorns and needed only a few hands to handle several thousand animals. Increasing demands for meat in metropolitan centers stimulated market prices, thus providing seemingly ideal conditions for making astronomical profits. No wonder then that so many either engaged directly in ranching or invested in companies and corporations devoted to cattle raising.

The boom got under way shortly after the close of the Civil War. During that conflict Texans found it more difficult than ever to sell their cattle. With markets virtually closed down and so many men in military service, cattle were allowed to run wild in much of the state. When Charles Goodnight returned home after service with the Texas Rangers during the War, his herd had increased to some seven thousand cattle. In the later 1860's he and others began to collect and drive to market considerable herds, with profits so favorable as to encourage rapid expansion of the trade.

Texans now began to emphasize ranching and trail driving more than ever before. George W. Littlefield, for example, used that means to restore family prosperity. When Littlefield first returned home from the War on crutches, he concentrated on cotton production, but a drouth, two floods, and the ills of Reconstruction hampered his efforts. He then shifted to merchandising and to driving cattle to outside markets, a program that made him a wealthy man within a few years.[14] The same pattern appears often in biographical sketches in the *Trail Drivers of Texas:* of men who found themselves in poverty at war's end, who tried to restore their fortunes by farming, and who turned to trail driving as a more rewarding occupation. Many failed to achieve a success comparable to that of Goodnight or Littlefield but, like them, they became ranchers and trail drivers for economic reasons.

New arrivals on the plains saw how rapidly the early drovers and ranchers had established themselves. In 1869, Joseph M. Carey, recently appointed United States District Attorney for Wyoming, wrote to a brother in Philadelphia concerning local opportunities. He was thinking of inviting some member of his family to come to Wyoming to engage in cattle and sheep raising. Carey knew of nothing else that could so speedily and surely lead to fortune, and cited as proof a local man who in two years acquired considerable wealth through use of borrowed capital. According to Carey, anyone with some capital and a willingness to stick for five years would with ordinary luck be worth one hundred thousand dollars.[15] Time proved him right insofar as his own family was concerned. The Careys achieved economic prosperity and the offices of governor of the state of Wyoming and United States senator as well.

Foreigners, too, learned of success stories involving fellow countrymen, and were thus encouraged to invest in ranching. John George Adair, prominent Britisher and owner of a large estate at Rathdair, Ireland, was trained for the diplomatic service but preferred business instead. In 1866 he established a brokerage house in New York City and prospered by placing British loans in America at high interest rates. About 1869 he married a remarkably attractive and venturesome New York widow, Cornelia Wadsworth Ritchie, member of a family prominent in American public life. Both Adair and his wife possessed a fair share of sporting blood, and in 1874 they staged a buffalo hunt on the Kansas prairies. Although on that trip Adair managed only to shoot his saddle horse in the head, he became greatly interested in the West, and in 1875 moved his brokerage firm to Denver. A loan of fifty thousand dollars at the rate of 18 per cent a year to Charles Goodnight by one of his agents, and information concerning Goodnight's abilities, led Adair in 1877 to form a highly profitable partnership with him. Another Britisher, Moreton Frewen, came to America to hunt big game and through Adair learned how profitable ranching could be.[16] Frewen played a prominent role as manager of one of the big British cattle corporations during the heyday of the cattle kingdom. Information from family members or personal friends undoubtedly stimulated investments in ranching for it had the ring of accuracy and sincerity, inadequate as it may have been at times for making sound business judgments.

In keeping with the age-old American urge to grow rapidly in population and wealth, county and territorial immigration commissions trumpeted the virtues of their localities for ranching. In their efforts, they found ready allies among the railroads seeking to expand traffic. As soon as the Union Pacific Railroad completed its lines, it began to promote the cattle industry. Dr. H. Latham, Union Pacific surgeon, wrote numerous articles seeking to attract increased business for his road. Latham cited letters from successful stockmen to document his case. For instance, he quoted John W. Iliff to the effect that cattle could range in the open both winter and summer without being fed, thus limiting costs of operation to the hiring of a few hands.[17] Similarly, the Santa Fe railroad published a prospectus in the middle 1880's stressing the high profits from ranching in New Mexico. Included were figures furnished by the immigration commissioner of Colfax County in the northeast corner of the territory. According to him, $6,450 invested in 510 cattle, and an additional outlay of five hundred dollars for ranch, corrals, horses, and equipment, would in five years yield a net profit of $17,052.50. Even this seemed mild in comparison with the report of a New Mexico cattle corporation, issued from its Boston office, listing profits of 9 per cent for the past year and possibilities of annual dividends of 46 per cent for the next five.[18] As early as 1870, J. S. Foster, in his *Outlines of History of Dakota and Emigrant Guide*, described stock raising in what later became

South Dakota as a "very remunerative business" in which investments usually returned 50 per cent annually.[19]

Seemingly never before had it been so easy for promoters to bring prospective investors face to face with frontier opportunities. In 1875 the growing city of Denver sponsored railroad excursions to watch cowboys at work on the plains. In mid-June, 1875, William Holly, secretary of the Colorado Stockgrowers Association, organized and managed an excursion of six hundred guests on a Kansas Pacific train to the roundup at Wilson's Ranch in Elbert County: "Newspapermen, business men, dudes and debutantes, attended the barbecue and danced to music of a string band on the moon-lit prairie. At night they slept under the cottonwood trees in blankets and buffalo robes."[20] Such promotional stunts enabled railroads and local agencies to reach a wide audience.

Eastern and Midwestern promoters began to take options on range rights and herds of cattle in hopes of selling them to newly formed cattle corporations financed by Eastern and foreign funds. They too added to the speculative mania. In 1884, for instance, in spite of poor returns from some existing companies, Tait, Denman and Company of New York City, brokers in ranches and land, published a brochure, *The Cattle Fields of the Far West*. The pamphlet asserted that previously organized companies were in good shape, and quoted a Scottish newspaper's estimate that profits should run to 50 per cent annually. Land tenure in the West was secure; the cattle business could not be overdone; and the United States offered exceptional opportunities to small capitalists and younger sons of wealthy Europeans.[21] Such promoters had less success than the agents who first introduced investors to the cattle kingdom but they did keep the pot boiling.

In 1881 General James S. Brisbin published a book, *The Beef Bonanza: or, How to Get Rich on the Plains*, which was of more significance for revealing the frenzied claims made by promoters than for actually stimulating additional investments. Brisbin's book reflected the feverish hopes of many who were expecting enormous dividends from cattle companies and the arguments to which they had succumbed. He had lived in the West for a number of years and claimed to have ridden over most of it on horseback. There, as he phrased it, professional young men, flying from the over-crowded East and the tyranny of a moneyed aristocracy, could find honor and wealth. There, the young politician could free him-self from the machinations of corrupt rings and rise to position and fame. The West promised land for the landless, money for the moneyless, briefs for lawyers, patients for doctors, and, above all, "labor and its reward for every poor man who is willing to work."[22] Presence of railroads in the West would enable a man to do for himself what it took his father fifty years to accomplish in an earlier day.

Brisbin included the American plains in his list of the five great grazing regions of the world, all of which put together could no more than keep pace with the increasing demand for beef. In chap-ters labeled "Estimated Fortunes," "The Money to Be Made," and "Millions in Beef," Brisbin included examples of previous suc-cesses of cattle companies and individuals. According to him, the high rate of profit explained why so many Southwestern ranchers were wealthy men in spite of having started out poor. Although he warned readers of the necessity for hard work, sobriety, and will-ingness to face exposure and hardship, he omitted other and more important requisites for success. Moreover, his numerous illustra-tions encouraged people to invest their money and leave the drudg-ery to others. A long appendix to his book contained an advertise-ment by Judge David W. Sherwood of Connecticut, who offered investors an opportunity to become rich by buying stock in a new cattle corporation. According to Sherwood: "The profits are enor-mous. There is no business like it in the world, and the whole secret of it is, it costs nothing to feed the cattle. They grow without eating your money. They literally raise themselves."[23]

Four years later, Walter Baron von Richtofen, a jovial, bearded immigrant from Breslau who had built a castle on the sagebrush plains east of Denver, published still another enthusiastic promo-tional work on the cattle kingdom.[24] Since the cattle boom was already beyond its peak, Richtofen's book appeared too late to attract significant additions of outside capital. His illustrations and arguments were emphatic and optimistic, but the public by now was familiar with their conclusions if not their content. True to breed, however, the promoters hoped to prolong the boom indefinitely.

Since the West possessed many advantages for ranching, investors found it difficult to differentiate between sheer propaganda and truth. This was especially true in England, where farmers dreaded competition from new lands on the world frontier. Britain was importing part of her beef before the Civil War period. During the 1860's anthrax ravaged local herds, thus contributing to a rise in cattle prices. Although some American cattle were shipped to Britain on the hoof in spite of difficulties occasioned by quarantine regulations, refrigeration contributed most of all to an increasing market for American beef. British investors and farmers, as well as American livestock producers, quickly saw the implications of the new technology. Not knowing how limited American production of cornfed beef actually was, British farmers feared that they would be driven wholly out of the home market. When prices of cornfed beef sagged, the prospects were discussed everywhere— in Parliament, in drawing rooms, and in public. In the spring of 1877, an Edinburgh newspaper sent James Macdonald, an expert on animal husbandry, to America to determine the extent of production and its possible competitive effects. Although Macdonald concluded that beef from the plains region could not compete directly with English and Scottish meat, he warned that range herds could be bred up to the point where they might threaten disaster to British cattle raising.

Excitement occasioned by the Macdonald report caused England to establish the Royal Commission on Agriculture in 1879 and to send two assistant commissioners, Clare Read and Albert Pell, to America to investigate. They reported that the "Great American Desert," as described in English schoolbooks, actually was stocked with thousands of cattle. Texas served as a wonderful breeding ground; range was free for the taking to owners of adjacent streams and springs; and no immediate prospect existed of settlers paying $1.25 an acre for land worth only 12½ cents an acre without water. When the country settled up, some difficulty might arise on that point, but at the moment the stockman had control. He had no expense save that of herding his cattle eight months of the year and trifling local taxes. No wonder then, said the commissioners, that stockmen made an enormous profit:

It is generally acknowledged that the average profit of the stockowner has been for years fully 33 per cent. No doubt this is by far the most remunerative branch of American farming, but to secure the greatest return a large amount of money must be employed. . . . .With regard to cattle, for the present the American stockman in the West is possessed with singular advantages; land for nothing, and abundance of it.[25]

On the basis of such seemingly well-authenticated conclusions, Englishmen rushed to invest in Western ranches. They could not know that open range would pass rapidly away and that the hard winter of 1886-1887 would prove to even the most rabid promoter that winter feeding of livestock was necessary to prevent periodic decimation of herds.

Quite obviously, however, the matter was one of economics, of comparative advantage in factors of production, and, except for the few who looked strictly to adventure, a quest for more economical means of producing beef. Leadership in ranching, as in all other economic activities on the world frontier, came from men with acquisitive instincts. The dangers and risks involved kept out or eliminated the timorous, it is true, but those who stuck with the business did so fundamentally because of profits and not through sheer love of adventure. Even in motivation, therefore, a common pattern emerges among those who developed the cattle kingdom.

THREE

Code of the West

A RECENT study of the American cowboy suggests that ranching alone among American
businesses has evoked a literature, a mythology, and a graphic
symbolism of its own.[1] In sociological terms, the cattleman's role
has etched itself more indelibly on the public mind than that of
any other class in American history. Although this has stemmed
from interest in the cowboy, ranchers share the fame of their more
romantic employees and wear the same uniform. Undoubtedly,
many aspects of the role are more mythological than real and have
obscured more basic patterns of thought and society in the cattle
kingdom.

Of course, popular impressions coincide with realities in some
aspects of ranching. For instance, the public pictures the cowboy
as an active, happy-go-lucky type who bothers himself little, if at
all, concerning the meaning of his way of life. In his book on the
cowboy, Philip Ashton Rollins has the cook, Steve Hawes, comment on the low regard for abstract ideas:

Such things, they don't bring no facts to nobody. The feller that's a-goin
to do the talkin' he just natcherally begins by pickin' out a startin' pint
that rully ain't nowhars at all. He brands that startin' pint "Assoomin'
that," so he can know it if he runs acrost it agin. Then he cuts his
thinkin' picket-rope, and drifts all over the hull mental prairie until he
gits plumb tuckered out. And when he gits so dog-gone tired that he

can't think up no more idees to wave around and look purty in the wind, he just winds up with "Wherefore it follows." Follows. Hell! It don't follow nothin'. It just comes in last.[2]

To a considerable extent cowboy and cattleman alike agreed with the cook's comments. Active and concerned with things rather than ideas, few of them expressed reasoned convictions about their over-all role in the scheme of life. When Joseph G. McCoy wrote his *Historic Sketches of the Cattle Trade*, he laid no claim to literary merit, pointing out that it had been his lot in life "to do, to act, and not to write."[3]

The same active practicality characterized George W. Little-field's approach while serving on the governing board of the University of Texas. Littlefield had a real interest in the University's welfare. University president Robert E. Vinson noted, however, that Littlefield's outlook differed markedly from that of R. L. Batts, his chief rival on the board. Batts was a scholar by instinct. He read widely—Isaiah, Darwin, Spencer—and meditated on their writings daily. Any conversation with him soon turned in the direction of the origin and meaning of life, and of its destiny. But Major Littlefield lived and died in the world and work that he loved. Darwin and Spencer were only names to him, if even that. Batts was primarily a man of thought; Littlefield a man of action. When Batts spoke of the University of Texas, he emphasized the word *university*; when Littlefield spoke of it, he stressed the word *Texas*. Batts concerned himself with the policies of the institution; Littlefield thought in terms of the people served. Their only common interest lay in the welfare of the university.[4] When Littlefield filled out a questionnaire on his life at the request of the historian Hubert Howe Bancroft, he limited himself almost wholly to straight, factual reporting. Even in commenting on the relative advantages of certain regions for ranching, he concerned himself with things rather than abstract ideas.[5] Littlefield did not lack a philosophy— he simply thought it queer that a man should ponder such a thing instead of putting it into operation. And the large majority of ranchers agreed with him.

This constituted no unique role for cattlemen since most businessmen elsewhere were doers rather than philosophers. And some ranchers were interested in abstract ideas. Nevertheless, as active businessmen, the great majority conformed to a common role. They spoke the language of business, not that of the mystic enamored with the great open spaces. Attuned to nature though he was, Charles Goodnight endeared himself to Eastern and European capitalists because he understood the business point of view and believed that the West must have an adequate flow of capital to develop its resources. In short, it should occasion no surprise that the rancher must be understood primarily in terms of what he did rather than from well-reasoned explanations on his part.

Although the modern-day rancher likes to think of his inherited code as one of manners rather than murder, and rejects popular impressions of the Old West as a lawless, godless place, lawlessness remains an essential ingredient of the Western, no matter in what media of entertainment it is presented. Moreover, it can be documented for short periods in the early history of many Western communities even though the better elements displayed remarkable speed and efficiency in terminating it.

A number of factors contributed to lawlessness in those places where it managed to rule briefly. For one thing, in the early days ranching was a man's world, and of young men at that. Biographies and comments in the *Trail Drivers of Texas* reveal that many of the hands who made the long drives to cowtowns were boys not yet out of their teens. That, and the hazardous nature of the drives, placed an accent on courage, daring, and high spirits. Over and over, one notes a recognition of the scarcity of women and the youthfulness of the men. Within the limits of Billings County in the Dakota Bad Lands in 1884 there were 122 men but only twenty-seven women.[6] In 1885, when Alexander Mackay visited America to inspect ranching property, he noted that most cowboys were in their twenties, and that the bosses, the chief men who ran the business, as he put it, looked to be in their thirties.[7] Young men devoid of the companionship of respectable women took their pleasures where they could, and prostitutes in cowtowns found

ready patronage. In such places, youngsters escaped the social dis-
approval that would have been visited upon them by respectable
elements in home communities.

A second factor contributing to lawlessness lay in the distance
of new frontiers from courts and law enforcement agencies. When
Charles Goodnight established his ranch in the Texas Panhandle,
he was 250 miles from a railroad base of supplies and one hundred
miles from his nearest neighbor. For a time, the nearest court of
law was some two hundred miles southeast of Goodnight's ranch.
The country soon began to fill up, but as late as 1880 the Panhandle knew almost nothing of the sovereignty of Texas. Goodnight imposed a type of law and order on his region, but it involved such expedients as dividing up the country on occasion
with outlaws as a necessary preliminary to pushing them completely off the plains.[8] Similarly, the Langs and Teddy Roosevelt
immediately became involved in a struggle to establish impartial
and legal agencies of law enforcement when they entered the Dakota Bad Lands in the early 1880's. Until that could be done, they
had to rely on distant courts, nonresident law enforcement agents,
and threats of retaliation against desperadoes by the better element
locally. Respectable people even hesitated to try to organize a
county government for fear that the lawless element would gain
control. Montana lay just to the west, Wyoming offered a haven
to the south, and Canada was within easy reach of desperadoes
who found local conditions temporarily too hot for them.[9] Almost
everywhere within a few years such handicaps to orderly life disappeared, but lawlessness did have its brief day in many spots.

Moreover, many impressionable individuals read the dime novel
type of literature so popular everywhere in the early days of the
cattle kingdom. If they lived on the frontier, they felt a special
obligation to emulate the deeds of crime and valor that the pot-
boilers assured them were characteristic of the West. In describing cowboys in 1874, Joseph G. McCoy spoke of their tendency
to read nothing but blood-and-thunder stories of the most sensa-
tional types.[10] A decade later, Teddy Roosevelt participated in the
capture of three "ruffians" who had stolen a boat from him. Among

Abilene in its glory, in the year 1874. (From Joseph G. McCoy, *Historic Sketches of the Cattle Trade*)

"DANCE-HOUSE."

Above, dance house, 1874. (From Mc-Coy, *Historic Sketches of the Cattle Trade*)

At right, Spur cowboys celebrating shipment of cattle to Kansas City. (Erwin E. Smith Collection, Library of Congress)

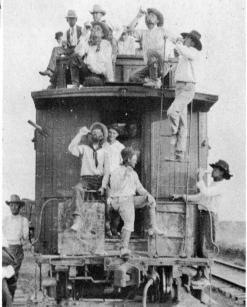

Granville Stuart, 1885. (L. A. Huffman photo)

Mrs. Pierre Wibaux. (Historical Society of Montana)

Pierre Wibaux. (Historical Society of Montana)

Marquis de Mores, 1886. Shown below is his residence at Medora, North Dakota. (L. A. Huffman photos)

their possessions were a supply of dime novels and the inevitable "History of the James Boys," which, according to Roosevelt, could be found along with the *Police Gazette* in the hands of every putative ruffian in the West.[11] Although their influence cannot be measured precisely, the hack writers undoubtedly stimulated violence by prating of the code of the West.

Nor did the West escape the general letdown in moral fiber that characterized the post-Civil War period. Shoddy standards throughout the nation in an era that historians have variously labeled "The Great Barbecue," "The Tragic Era," "The Gilded Age," and other derogatory terms, found expression in the cattle kingdom as elsewhere. During the Civil War Texans neglected to brand cattle on the open range, thus creating confused claims to ownership. In the Reconstruction era they complained of favoritism to Union men on the part of carpetbag courts in adjudicating property disputes. A resulting general disregard for the property of others gave rise to stories that were told all over the cattle kingdom for the next two decades, and with sufficient truth to make them more than a mere jest. Why should a cattleman eat his own beef when he could just as easily kill a wandering steer from a neighboring ranch? Cattlemen enjoyed the story of the rancher who invited a neighbor to dinner, promising him something to eat that he had never tasted before. When the guest sat down to the usual ranch-country meal he saw no exotic food until his host ended his puzzlement by telling him that he was eating his own beef for a change! There was also the story of the widow who assured her cowboys that she would as soon eat one of her own children as beef killed out of her own herd. Similarly, ranchers on the Northern plains recognized grim truth as well as humor in the universal story of the stranger who arrived in a community leading a steer from whose progeny he rapidly developed a whole herd of cattle. In spite of constant efforts to stamp it out, cattle rustling plagued ranchers for many years.

Abilene, Kansas, first of the railroad cowtowns, exemplified the results of such lawless forces during its brief heyday as a shipping point. There one found numerous saloons, billiard tables, tenpin alleys, and gambling devices, every known way of obtaining money honestly or dishonestly. As soon as cowboys delivered a herd of cattle in Abilene they turned their thoughts to other things. They visited a barbershop for a haircut and a bath, and a clothing store to buy new suits, hats, and boots. Thus beautified, they began a round of barrooms, theaters, gambling spots, dance halls, and bawdy houses. In 1871, the Alamo, the most famous saloon and gambling resort in Abilene, maintained a well-lighted room opening directly on the street as a means of attracting patronage. Its bartender looked like a divinity student but the general atmosphere tingled with excitement. Crowds lounged around the gambling tables to watch the play, seemingly unconscious of the music coming from violin and piano on a raised recess at the side. Faro and monte ranked first in popularity, and Mexican cowboys played the latter for hours, indifferent to their mounting losses.

An observer commented that few wilder, more reckless spectacles of debauchery could be seen than a dance house in "full blast" in a frontier town. Participants danced wildly and in an abandoned manner, putting even the French cancan to shame. At such times, the eyes of cowboys lighted up with excitement, liquor, and the lust of the dance. As the tempo speeded up, they swung their soiled doves completely off their feet, and uttered occasional demoniacal yells like Indians. Between dances they took their girls to the bar for drinks costing fifty cents each, on which their partners received a percentage from the house.

Abilene tried hard to curb the vicious activity. Its most famous marshal, "Wild Bill" Hickok, lived to finish out his appointment, but some were less fortunate. By ordinance on May 20, 1870, the town expelled owners and inmates of brothels, but the lewd pack simply shifted to the banks of Mud Creek, a mile northwest of town, where they occupied shanties until their cowboy patrons departed in September. During the winter months the women plied their trade elsewhere but returned in greater numbers than ever the following spring. A petition from respectable local women caused the creation of a segregated district southeast of Abilene. A contemporary description of it spoke of houses literally covering the ground, some of them one hundred feet long. Beer gardens, dance halls, dancing platforms, saloons, and cribs vied with one another for the patronage of cowboys avid to visit this "Devil's Addition to Abilene," which could be reached easily from more respectable parts of town by hacks day or night. By the end of 1871 Abilene ceased to be a cowtown, and the carnival of corruption moved on to another location, leaving respectable people in control.[12]

In spite of the patina of romance cast by time, obscenity rather than glamor characterized such activities. Shopworn women and rutting cowboys reduced sex to an animal level. Joseph G. McCoy praised the many creditable exceptions among the cowboys, men who refused to patronize such districts, but blamed the group as a whole and Northern renegades with bringing the whole personnel of the Texas cattle trade into disrepute and with filling many graves in Abilene, Newton, Wichita, and Ellsworth as the carnival followed the railroad west. Dodge City, Kansas, Tascosa, Texas, and other cowtowns witnessed the same kind of life for short periods of time. Red-light districts in mining camps also added to the opportunities for cowhands to engage in vice.

Joseph G. McCoy's book indicates that the pattern of lawless play was already somewhat stylized by the early 1870's, even as to matters of dress. Cowboys wore sombreros, boots, and spurs; loved to play practical jokes on their comrades; and delighted in impressing greenhorns with their ferocious ways. Mounted and drunken, they charged wildly through the streets, shooting up the town as they went, or rode directly through the swinging doors of saloons to demand drinks at pistol point.[13] Very early, then, those who played at being cowboys had a code of reckless action ready-made for them to emulate. More serious individuals who entered ranching in the late seventies or early eighties found this code humorous or irritating, depending upon the seriousness with which its devotees applied it.

Around Medora in the Dakota Bad Lands in the early eighties respectable ranchers like the Langs and Teddy Roosevelt faced a criminal element attracted by the weakness of law enforcement agencies. Wittingly and otherwise, this lawless group received a measure of support from the actions of individuals who arrived from other parts of the world seeking adventure or who thought it impossible to curb rowdyism on the frontier. In that highly cosmopolitan society, butchers and cowboys, carpenters and laborers, adventurous young college graduates, and younger sons of English nobility drank and gambled and shot up the town in keeping with Wild West traditions. They rode into saloons on horseback to demand free drinks and to wreck walls, floors, and furniture with their six-shooters. They lassoed and upset privies at respectable homes. As a means of showing their status as real Westerners, they occasionally shot at the boots of greenhorns to make them dance. Dudes on passing trains gaped at corpses being carried out of front doors of hotels, periodic volleys of gunfire preceding the appearance of several "cowboys" lugging out the body of still another victim, with the same individual playing the part of the corpse on each trip and hurriedly returning by the back door for a repetition of his act before the train could move out of sight.[14] Of course, the boys paid for property damage resulting from their pranks, being willing to suffer reasonable financial penalties if only the code of the West could live on, even in the form of make-believe.

But the code had a more serious side. The Marquis de Mores named the new town of Medora after his beautiful titian-haired wife, a daughter of the wealthy New York banker von Hoffman, whose money financed his numerous projects for making a large fortune in the Bad Lands region. A poor judge of men, the Marquis employed a number of questionable characters to aid him, and seems to have felt that lawlessness could not easily be curbed in frontier regions. So long as his own property remained unmolested, he gave only token support to movements to end depredations. In the same period, a young college man, A. J. Packard, started the first newspaper, *The Bad Lands Cowboy*, and used its columns to support law and order, insisting that drunkenness should not excuse a man for killing another.[15] Although such views gained acceptance rapidly, those who delighted in portraying the code of the West gave unwitting support in the interval to others who found it a convenient cover for their serious illegal activities.

Writers began to glamorize the role of the bad man very early in his career. Mark Twain, for instance, spent two years as a reporter on the *Territorial Enterprise* at Virginia City, Nevada Territory, beginning in 1862. His experience there provided background for his book, *Roughing It*, which appeared in 1872 and helped to launch his literary career. Virginia City was a mining center, but bad men moved easily back and forth from ranching country to mining camp. According to Twain, such men stalked the streets in long-tailed frock coats, shiny stump-toed boots with jingling spurs, and with their slouch hats cocked at an angle to proclaim their fighting instincts. People deferred to them through fear of the six-shooters flapping under their coat tails, but their prestige rested on still deeper foundations. In a society where many aspired to saloonkeeping or a reputation for having killed their man, "chiefs" who "kept their own private graveyard," as the phrase went according to Twain, represented success. Desperadoes like "Fighting Sam" Brown, Billy Mulligan, Farmer Pease, Sugarfoot Mike, and El Dorado Johnny were acclaimed by lesser fry for their murderous exploits. Twain pictured them as brave and reckless fellows who traveled with their lives in their hands. They did their killing principally within their own circles, for what credit could they gain by murdering someone "not on the shoot?" They seldom molested peaceable citizens. Among themselves they killed on the slightest provocation and they hoped and expected to be killed themselves. They thought it shameful to die with their boots off.[16] Such was the professional bad man according to Twain.

When Owen Wister gave concrete expression to the cowboy legend in his famous novel, *The Virginian*, in 1902, his story reached its peak of intensity in the hero's classic gunfight on his wedding night in a little frontier town. Everyone in town knew that the code of the West compelled him to meet his mortal enemy, Trampas, the bad man, face to face, and that he who was quickest on the draw alone would survive. Citizens concealed themselves behind protective barriers to watch the duel; deathly stillness reigned as the two men stalked forward in the open street to their rendezvous with death. With a movement fast as lightning, the Virginian beat his opponent to the draw, and thus showed the courage and skill necessary to survive under the code of the West.[17]

Both Twain and Wister found avid readers for such exciting accounts, but those who depicted gunmen more realistically lacked an audience. While working on the Virginia City *Enterprise*, Twain became a close friend of its senior editor, Dan De Quille, who spent many years on the paper. Twain encouraged De Quille to write a factual and accurate account of Virginia City mining, which appeared under the title *The Big Bonanza* in 1876. Although praised for its authenticity, and reprinted as recently as 1957, the book never provided sufficient income to permit De Quille to relinquish a full-time newspaper job in favor of a writing career. The public continued to prefer Twain's exciting portrayal of the bad men to De Quille's more sober but realistic account.

Although De Quille agreed with Twain as to the dress and reputation of the bad men, he judged them much more harshly. In his opinion, their bravery contained a measure of cowardice, and they enhanced their prestige by cheap killings. "Fighting Sam" Brown illustrated his point. Brown arrived in Virginia City in the spring of 1860 with a reputation already established all over the Pacific Coast. As a "big chief," his entry into a saloon caused the lesser chiefs to hunt their holes. To maintain his reputation, he soon picked a quarrel in one of the local saloons with a man too drunk to know what he was saying, and proceeded to rip him up with a bowie knife. The murder completed, Sam wiped the blood from his knife on the leg of his pantaloons, strolled over to a bench, stretched out, and went to sleep. He now had some fifteen murders to his credit, most of which had involved little danger to himself. But Fighting Sam erred in taking a shot at a barkeeper in a station maintained by a rancher in Carson Valley. Learning of the incident, the rancher armed himself with a double-barreled, heavily loaded shotgun, mounted a fast horse, and started in pursuit of the desperado. Knowing that an enraged rancher surpassed fellow desperadoes in danger, Sam began firing as soon as his antagonist came in sight. The rancher waited until he could bring Sam within range of his shotgun and then tumbled him from his saddle, riddled with buckshot, at the edge of the town of Genoa. "Thus died 'Fighting Sam Brown'—died with his 'boots on,' an end which all 'chiefs' dread."[18]

Undoubtedly, the riffraff preyed on one another with considerable impunity in the early West. Respectable people stayed away from their haunts and considered the killing of one of them good riddance. They filled most of the graves in "boot hill" cemeteries that tourists visit today, and cowhands seldom shared their final resting places. During the first year after the Santa Fe railroad reached Dodge City, Kansas, in 1872, twenty-five men died with their boots on in the brawling activities of that cowtown, but only one was a cowboy. The rest came from the gamblers, toughs, and desperadoes who made a point of following new frontiers.[19]

Although some respectable people met violent deaths, few if any of these could be traced to the code of the west. On the basis of his own experiences in the Dakota Bad Lands, Teddy Roosevelt concluded that people needed to fear murder in the West little more than in the East if they minded their own business and stayed out of barrooms. Roosevelt agreed with many other observers that revolvers were nothing more than foolish encumbrances except in the hands of skilled marksmen.[20] In a way, De Quille's story of the killing of "Fighting Sam" Brown by an enraged rancher armed with a double-barreled shotgun filled with buckshot contains in microcosm the truth of what actually happened on the frontier. The "good" man did win out, and in a surprisingly short time. In doing so, he preferred the most lethal weapon of all, a shotgun with a scattering pattern of shot that could scarcely miss the target, or, if not that, a Winchester rifle. Nor did men march openly to meet their enemy, disdaining any cover. In killing at close quarters in saloons, the riffraff had no intention of giving their opponents an equal chance. For all concerned, good and bad alike, the fighting code of the West consisted primarily of the rule that one must not shoot an unarmed man. Such a killing added no prestige to a gunman and placed anyone guilty of it in jeopardy of lynching.

In truth, then, modern-day ranchers have every reason to consider their inherited code as one of manners rather than murder. Their predecessors in the early days of the cattle kingdom knew that lawlessness disrupted the normal conduct of business quite apart from any matter of ethics. D. W. Barton, for instance, one of the first Texans to make a drive to Dodge City, recalled in later years a peaceable assemblage of cattlemen in that town in 1883 to form an organization to promote their welfare. According to Barton, the ranchers made Dodge City; the gunmen and gamblers only gave it notoriety. By special resolution, the cattlemen urged their foremen to discourage cowboys from carrying firearms "except where absolutely necessary."[21] Since ranchers seldom had trouble in finding a supply of cowboys, the threat of being discharged for carrying six-shooters exerted considerable influence for good. Those who refused to obey could easily be replaced by other hands.

Moreover, rules against carrying guns made good sense. The six-shooter was a heavy, cumbersome instrument, which, along with the gun belt and ammunition, added several pounds of weight around a man's waist, an uncomfortable addition to his dress. Since the code of the West proscribed shooting an unarmed man, it was wiser to go unarmed unless positive and specific danger decreed otherwise. Murdo Mackenzie, perhaps the most successful, and certainly one of the best-paid managers of cattle corporations on the plains, never carried a gun for protection. In old age he explained his reasons at some length. He avoided gun toting for the simple reason that gunmen killed themselves off:

I thought the matter over and decided that if I did carry a gun, I wouldn't last long. If anyone picked a fight with me and it came to shooting, he would get me first. For me to tote a six-shooter would be a provocation and an excuse to others. I didn't believe it was necessary, anyway. So I didn't buy any pistols. . . . The men who went more than halfway to meet trouble found it waiting for them, and plenty of it; *just as they do to-day, anywhere and in any occupation.*[22]

Many native-born ranchers agreed with Mackenzie's point of view. J. W. Iliff, Colorado's first cattle king, traveled widely on the open range but took a Winchester rifle along only when accompanied by his young son.[23] John Chisum, early New Mexico cattle king, never carried a gun, although tradition insists that he hired thugs to do his fighting for him.[24] J. P. White, Sr., Littlefield's nephew and range manager on the New Mexico frontier, never packed a gun, according to his son.[25] Shanghai Pierce, who transported large sums of gold everywhere to buy cattle in the early days of the Texas drives, went unarmed throughout his career except for his *opéra bouffe* quarrel with "Colonel" Miller of the famous Oklahoma 101 Ranch.[26] Illustrations could be extended, and perhaps they should be, for the tradition dies hard that everyone connected with ranching went constantly armed.

Mari Sandoz's recent book on the cattlemen recognizes that important men like those mentioned above found greater safety in going unarmed, and quotes John Chisum to the effect that "Only halfwits and greenhorns pull down on a man of any substance," that is, propertied men. According to her, only outsiders failed to realize that Western gunmen avoided shooting important people because retaliation would surely follow. Moreover, she feels that ranchers often contributed to violence visited on less prosperous individuals. Certainly, they disliked her father, Old Jules, because he helped farmers locate homesteads on the open range. In addition, one of her uncles was murdered during a period of ill will between cattlemen and farmers over land. She has much to say of Print Olive, who shot only "unimportant" people until he met death at the hands of a little man. Usually, however, in her opinion, the "little fellow" fell prey to gunmen or big cattlemen, not the reverse.[27] But Print Olive was not typical of the ranchers as a whole. His insane temper and disregard for life by her own admission forced him to leave his native Texas for new ranching frontiers. As she suggests, there were too many ways to strike back at such characters other than employing gun play to necessitate putting up with them as neighbors indefinitely. Prairie fires could be set, cattle herds stampeded, and help in times of sickness and acci-

dent denied in ways other than outright refusal. And so Print Olive
moved on from frontier to frontier until his fortune disappeared,
eaten up in legal fees necessary to defend himself against charges
of murder; and in the end he met a violent death, as did those of
his sons who disregarded the rights of others. Indeed, his career
exemplifies Mackenzie's axiom that gunmen killed themselves off.

Many cattlemen and little men did avail themselves of the protection afforded by going unarmed. Some spent a lifetime in the
cattle kingdom without seeing a gunfight, and many others never
witnessed violence in the classic manner of gunfighting so popular
in legend. Recalling his career of almost sixty years as a cowman
on the high plains of Texas, John Arnot said that even on the long
drives cowboys kept their six-shooters rolled up in their blankets
more often than at their hips. Arnot never once saw gun play, although he lived for a time in Old Tascosa, a town noted for its
violence. Arnot seldom carried a gun because people needed one
then no more than at the present time.[28]

Survivors among the old-time cowhands consider the modern
TV Westerns highly unrealistic in their emphasis on gun play.
Homer Grigsby, who spent seventy-four of his ninety years on the
Arizona-New Mexico range, comments: "These modern writers
would have people believe that most of the oldtime range riders
were all gunslingers and no-goods. . . ." He never saw a gun drawn
except when some greenhorn came west "filled up with ideas from
those novels written back in Chicago." Most cowboys carried
weapons only for defense against snakes and animals.[29] W. F.
Friend, a member of the Oklahoma cowboy "Hall of Fame," participated in the long drives and then became an independent
rancher. Like Grigsby, he saw few signs of violence during his long
career.[30]

Some cowboys needed no urging to avoid gun play because they
abhorred killing or preferred to concentrate on getting ahead in
the world. Branch Isbell's autobiographical sketch in the *Trail
Drivers of Texas* bears the exciting title "Days that were Full of
Thrills" but contains an explanation of why he chose to go unarmed. He frankly disliked guns. As a youngster he saw several

men killed in a saloon brawl and also remembered vividly being assigned to unpleasant duty of shooting newborn calves that could not keep up with the herd on one of the long drives.[31] Gordon Hampton Scudder, owner of the JH Ranch on Coon Creek near Wann in modern-day Oklahoma, recalls no violence as he looks back on a long life spent in ranching. Scudder worked for one man for sixteen years, leaving his pay to accumulate for him, although he was authorized to write a check on his employer at any time. At the end of sixteen years, he drew out the four thousand dollars saved from his small monthly wage and married a neighbor woman who held title to some Indian land. Such was the genesis of the JH Ranch.[32] Scudder was simply too busy to visit saloons and other spots where he might have seen violent action.

For those of less steady nature, employers invoked rules of order in the interest of good business. Charles Goodnight insisted that cowboys who worked for him on his early-day, hazardous drives to distant markets must keep their differences under control. His warning that the outfit would immediately hold a trial and hang any member guilty of committing a murder was sufficient to prevent such incidents on the trail.[33] At trail's end the men could settle their differences as they pleased. Less typical but not alone in their attitude, the early-day firm of D. H. and J. W. Snyder rested their hands and herds on Sunday and forbade employees to drink, play cards, gamble in any way, or to swear.[34] Their devoutly religious outlook and stern moralistic code proved no barrier to finding plenty of cowboys to drive their herds to market.

Even on the home ranch cattlemen recognized the value of discipline, and the more successful of them had little patience with any nonsense. Contrary to popular views, says James Evetts Haley, historian of the range country, many ranches west of the 100th meridian adopted severe moral regulations. Goodnight enforced three rules on his ranches: no gambling, no drinking, and no fighting. He, S. W. Lomax, and H. H. Campbell, managers respectively of the great Spur and Matador holdings, mutually agreed not to employ cowboys discharged elsewhere for theft or drunkenness. Goodnight went further. With the help of neighboring cattlemen he declared all the country south of the north fork of Red River under prohibition, with no liquor whatever to be allowed. Goodnight played no favorites in disciplinary action. He downgraded the son of his employer's wife for permitting gambling and discharged his own brother-in-law for a similar offense while managing a ranch under Goodnight's over-all supervision. Such unpleasant duties led him to comment "I am heartily sick of men and ranches," but he enforced his rules nevertheless.[35] On the gigantic XIT Ranch in western Texas only the slender fence erected by its owners separated it from the wilderness that lay beyond. Since cattle stealing plagued the ranch in its early days, the management hired two former Texas Rangers, "Big Ed" Connell and Wood Saunders, to eliminate lawless elements. Their supervisor, Ira Aten, another former Ranger, expected to be killed when he took over the job of protecting the ranch. He doubled his life insurance before starting the task and carefully avoided following the same trail twice in his rounds of inspection. For ten years he "controlled with fear" those elements that otherwise would have preyed on XIT property.[36]

As the story of the XIT makes clear, problems of maintaining law and order extended beyond the open-range period. Specialization in handling the matter developed rapidly, however. XIT cowboys, for instance, worked at routine ranching operations while the ex-Texas Rangers took care of troublemakers. In 1888 owners of the ranch instituted twenty-three rules to govern the conduct of cowboy employees. Under these they were forbidden to keep horses of their own on ranch property or to chase mustangs and antelopes while using XIT mounts. No longer were horses to be ridden so recklessly as to endanger them. Cowboys also were forbidden to drink, gamble, or carry six-shooters.[37] Records of the Spur Ranch for the years 1885 to 1907 referred to employees as "hands" not as cowboys, and the work performed by them justified the terminology. No one at the ranch thought of such work as unusual or heroic.[38] Thus the cowboy who actually handled cattle very quickly came to feel the hand of authority governing his daily routine and morals, and his only escape lay in joining forces with renegades who lived a precarious and often very short existence.

Efforts to establish a type of order conducive to efficient ranching operations did not result in perfect justice to all concerned, nor did ranchers and their foremen escape threats to their lives when they assumed authority for policing their domains. Until impersonal law, regular courts, and an adequate police force came into being, one could expect a personalized, somewhat arbitrary, and fluctuating type of justice to prevail. All this is documented in the early days of ranching.

Charles Goodnight, for instance, definitely preferred a reign of law to one of disorder. Only a man of great personal courage could have operated on the frontiers where he located, however, and he had to assume responsibility for keeping order until regularly constituted agencies could be created and brought to bear. He could not afford to wait for others to protect his herds against Indian raids and desperadoes. Goodnight's biographer grants that he acted in an arbitrary manner at times during his early days in the Texas Panhandle, such as condoning the hanging of thieves without court trials.[39] Mari Sandoz pays tribute to Goodnight's fine qualities in spite of her general dislike for cattlemen, but also recognizes the arbitrary manner in which he acted occasionally. In 1869, when some Coloradoans tried to turn back a Goodnight herd for fear that the Texas longhorns would infect their stock with cattle fever, Goodnight loaded his shotgun with buckshot, armed his cowboys with Winchesters, and, riding in the lead of his herd, warned the men who stood in his way, "I've monkeyed as long as I want to with you sons of bitches."[40] In such a manner he forced his herd through to its destination.

Richard King used equally forceful methods to protect his ranching empire near the Mexican border in Southwest Texas. King was no gunfighter, preferring his fists to other weapons when a brawl developed. Nevertheless, as late as the 1860's disorganized conditions—created by the Civil War, Reconstruction, and long-standing troubles with Mexico—made it necessary for him to go well armed on his numerous business trips between Corpus Christi and Brownsville. On such occasions, King generally traveled by coach.

He established corrals at twenty-mile intervals along the way, which enabled him to change teams frequently and to travel rapidly in the interest of greater safety. King carried a shotgun loaded with buckshot, and four or five vaqueros rode at the side of his coach. Since he frequently carried large sums of money on such trips for payrolls or land purchases, he presented a tempting challenge to desperadoes. Although they never successfully ambushed him, they did shoot at his coach, and on one occasion killed the driver.[41]

Both Goodnight and King possessed great personal courage. Neither of them would have gone unarmed simply to obtain the protection afforded to unarmed men by the code of the West. They did prefer to leave law enforcement to regularly constituted agencies. Where these were inadequate, they knew the advantages of shotguns and buckshot, or of Winchesters, and refused to give criminals or opposing factions an opportunity to shoot them down treacherously while stalking such foes openly on the streets of some cowtown.

Not all Texans were so touchy about their personal bravery, however. Shanghai Pierce went unarmed frankly because it afforded him the greatest measure of protection. Like a good many other ranchers—King and Iliff, for example—he preferred to travel by stage or buggy rather than on horseback, but he differed from most of them in boasting of his willingness to escape gunfire. Supposedly, he broke and ran in the face of danger, and then joked himself out of his embarrassment. His military service in the Confederacy had consisted largely of acting as "regimental butcher" for his cavalry unit, since he understood the art of acquiring beef. When a friend teased him about his military record, he supposedly replied, "By God, Sir; I was all the same as a major general: always in the rear on advance, always in the lead on retreat."[42]

Still later, when he quarreled with "Colonel" George W. Miller of the 101 Ranch over a cattle deal, the latter supposedly threatened to kill him if they met again. Shang took a shotgun along on his next Pullman trip through Miller's part of the country. As the story goes, when Miller started up the Pullman steps at a train stop near his ranch, Shang fired a shot through the Pullman roof, much to the alarm of other passengers. Miller is said to have beaten a hasty retreat, leaving Shang in control of the field. On his next trip, Shang hired a bodyguard armed with a Winchester rifle for protection. Although he loved such stories too well not to fabricate or embroider many of them, here was one early-day cattleman who delighted in making a mockery of the code of the West. All exaggeration aside, he did go unarmed, even when carrying large sums of money. Shrewd and determined to avoid dangerous situations, he protected both his life and his money without resorting to serious gun play.

At times, of course, danger could not be avoided. As a supervisor for large foreign cattle corporations, Murdo Mackenzie occasionally had to deal with disgruntled employees. At least twice in his career he faced down men who had threatened to kill him. On both occasions he used persuasion and logic instead of firearms to achieve his purpose.[43] John Clay, another ranch manager, handled dissident elements in much the same way during his long career. On only one occasion did he think it advisable to carry a gun. In the fall of 1887, incorrigible cowhands ran off the local manager of a ranch under Clay's supervision, thus making it necessary for him to assume direct control. While visiting the ranch to plan the winter's work, he carried a shotgun and was accompanied by a guard armed with a Winchester rifle. In the spring he hired a manager "who would rather hunt a thief than eat" and whose past record in handling desperadoes insured a return of peaceful conditions.[44]

Even in regions where lawlessness held temporary sway, people could find safe and respectable accommodations. Abilene, Kansas, typified most cowtowns in having its respectable district on one side of the tracks and its dives on the other. Churches, courthouse, newspaper office, and the respectable citizens occupied the north side; on the south lay Texas Abilene, with its invitation to every form of corruption.[45] Similarly, although Old Tascosa, Texas, remained a cowtown from its founding in 1877 until it disappeared in the middle 1890's, its disreputable element was largely segregated. Most of Tascosa's lurid history was made in "Hogtown," some half mile from the town proper, where dance halls, saloons, and prostitutes entertained visiting cowhands.[46] When Lincoln Lang arrived in the Dakota Bad Lands as an impressionable teenager, the town of Medora was beginning to attract prospective dive-keepers, prostitutes, and gamblers. To Lincoln's disgust, his father immediately put him to work on a ranch in the country, where he stayed for six weeks while his father located a permanent site for the family. Instead of being able to loaf in a questionable environment, Lincoln helped stack hay in temperatures approaching one hundred degrees daily, but gained weight and muscle at the same time from the plentiful supply of milk, sourdough bread, garden truck, and venison which graced the ranch table.[47]

As in all societies, one found what he looked for. Murdo Mackenzie became a wealthy, prominent, and respected manager of cattle corporations. One of his sons graduated from Princeton University and then joined his father as a start toward a successful managerial career of his own. Another son, "Dode," looked after some of his father's duties on the Northern range. Less steady in nature than his father or brother, he began to associate with some of the cowboys who loafed around the wild Missouri river towns during the slack season of work in the dead of winter. Bud Stevens, a former employee of Dode's father, tended bar in Lebeau. Out of respect for Mackenzie he took a personal interest in the son, but the youngster became increasingly unmanageable. After a night of drinking and carousing, Dode ordered Stevens to serve him another drink, but the latter was reluctant to comply. Enraged, Dode pulled his gun and threatened to kill the bartender, who shot him fatally in self-defense. When bystanders examined Dode's gun, it was empty of shells and had been for a long time![48]

The Kenedy family of Texas experienced the same kind of tragedy. Mifflin Kenedy, Richard King's early partner in steam-boating and ranching, practiced the tenets of his Quaker faith and became a successful rancher and citizen. One of his sons, "Spike," turned out badly, however. He became involved in a shooting scrape in Dodge City in which a dance-hall girl was killed and he permanently lost the use of his right arm. His father brought him home to Texas, where he learned to shoot lefthanded, killed a man face to face, and died the same way at the hands of another.[49]

Environmental factors alone do not explain the lives of such individuals. Charley Siringo, whose accounts of his own exploits and those of other free-wheeling cowboys have been called classics by some, invariably headed for the Red Lights when he hit town, be it Chicago or Tascosa, Texas. Naturally, when he accompanied a carload of cattle to Chicago, he expected to celebrate in his usual manner. And he was not disappointed. His first night in Chicago he managed to dispose of all of the two hundred dollars in his pockets.[50] Significantly, he made no mark in ranching, relying instead on writing Western thrillers that became gorier and gorier over the years to satisfy his market. Serious ranchers who set the real code for their occupation had no time for or patience with such characters. J. P. White, Sr., New Mexico rancher, well expressed ranching opinion of Siringo and others of his kind. He had employed Siringo on his ranch for a time, and his opinion was well founded: "He was no cowhand, and there was not a damn thing to him anyway. He was always hard-up, and I still have a note from him for about a hundred and fifty dollars."[51]

Ranchers, sheriffs, and marshals found themselves in agreement with the riffraff on one point—when fighting had to be done, the code of the West should be left to greenhorns and romanticists whose lives were not at stake. George W. Littlefield, for instance, killed one man during his lifetime. The dispute arose in Reconstruction days when Littlefield was preparing for a cattle drive and planned to take along a Negro boy for whom he had legal papers as guardian. Although the youngster wanted to accompany him, a neighbor laid claim to guardianship at the request of the boy's mother. The argument led to gun play, but certainly not in the classic manner. Guns misfired during the duel, both men took cover, and Littlefield killed his adversary while the latter was peeking around a tree behind which he had taken shelter. Moreover, Littlefield gave bond for appearance in a regular court before starting on his drive, stood trial on his return, and was acquitted.[52]

Sheriffs and marshals used much the same tactics. Sheriff Pat

Garrett shot "Billy the Kid" from concealment, and only misguided romanticists have insisted that he should have exposed himself to needless risk in performing his duty. "Little Black John" Slaughter, who was elected to clean up Tombstone and surrounding Cochise County, Arizona, in the early nineties, used a double-barreled shotgun in his work. Nor did he give his adversary any advantage. According to one story, he shot a desperado while the man slept, being too kind-hearted to awaken him, as frontier humor phrased the incident.[53] Captain Burton C. Mossman, who organized and commanded the famous Arizona Rangers for the first few months of their existence, ordered his men to use any method necessary to protect themselves and to kill their opponents. In old age, Mossman boasted of stabbing a Mexican murderer to death without giving him a chance to defend himself and at a time when Mossman had no legal rights on Mexican soil. He even claimed to have hanged murderers when it was inconvenient to bring them in for jury trial.[54] In spite of his prowess and his personal bravery, his account of his exploits as a duly appointed peace officer revealed an alarming willingness to take the law into his own hands.

By careful planning and avoidance of mock heroics, Nathaniel K. Boswell proved that officers could greatly reduce the hazards of their occupation. Born in New Hampshire and educated in Vermont, he joined the Colorado gold rush in 1859 as a boy of nineteen. Mining did not pay well, and by 1867 he was operating drugstores in Cheyenne and Laramie, Wyoming. Beginning in 1869, he served as a sheriff in Wyoming Territory for a decade and also doubled as Deputy United States Marshal at Laramie from 1869 to 1883. In the latter year he became chief of the detective bureau of the Wyoming Stock Growers Association, with thirty or more men working under him. Boswell found plenty to do, having in jail at one time thirty-seven prisoners, of whom fourteen were accused of murder or robbery. Nevertheless, he claimed never to have received a scratch in line of duty, although he was wounded once by Indians. He seldom found it necessary to shoot a man in making an arrest, and fatalities were fewer still. Boswell used all available help in capturing desperadoes, preferred a double-barreled shotgun above all other weapons in dangerous spots, and did not hesitate to conceal himself in order to take culprits by surprise. He claimed that he never failed in an attempt to arrest a man and never let one escape.[55] Respected as brave and resourceful, he, and many fellow officers, proved that the shotgun surpassed the six-shooter as a weapon of law enforcement, and that success and honor came to men who ignored the stylized type of gunfighting, supposedly a characteristic of the brave, in favor of more effective methods.

In spite of their desire to support impartial agencies of law enforcement, ranchers occasionally bypassed them in favor of extralegal methods. In many communities, cattlemen found it difficult to obtain convictions of thieves in jury trials, since the criminal elements, and even those inclined to sympathize with the "little fellow" as against the "cattle baron," tended to vote for acquittal when serving on juries. As a consequence, even the finest of ranchers resorted to other methods to achieve results. Speaking in later years, Murdo Mackenzie claimed that cattle thieves could not be convicted legally at certain times and places. Therefore, a kind of gunfighting became necessary, an extralegal action for the defense of property and life. Although Mackenzie denied that he was ever personally involved in killing cattle thieves, he admitted that he had sanctioned such action, and justified it on the grounds of necessity. In his estimation, it involved not the truculence of one man but an organized struggle against disorder.[56] Such an attitude seems startling in view of Mackenzie's Scottish background, education, and admirable record in so many ways. Although representing foreign corporate wealth, he has generally been praised, even by writers otherwise critical of cattlemen for their arrogant disregard of the rights of the settlers. Mari Sandoz, for instance, calls Mackenzie one of the finest cattlemen in the world, and praises him for sound conservation principles and willingness to help shape government policy in the interest of the small settler and the homeseeker.[57]

Extreme provocation, of course, lay behind most extralegal action. In the Texas Panhandle, for instance, Alfred and Vincent

Rowe, cultured English gentlemen, owned the RO Ranch. Their manager, John Petrie, was a college graduate and an able cattleman. Such men ordinarily would have favored law and order. Nevertheless, the local cattlemen's organization obtained proof that Petrie was rustling cattle and asked the Rowes to dismiss him from his job. Unwilling to believe the evidence, they refused to cooperate with the other ranchers. An indictment against Petrie led to trial in 1883, but a gang of toughs rode in from Tascosa to overawe the judge and thus obtain an acquittal. Charles Goodnight and his fellow cattlemen furnished armed protection to the judge and made it clear that men of Petrie's stripe must face court action. Under the circumstances, those indicted agreed to leave the country in return for the charges being dropped.[58] In this case no one could claim that farmers were being persecuted since ranchers alone were involved. Presence of armed men in court to see that justice prevailed scarcely squared with American concepts of orderly legal procedure but the outcome lay in that direction.

Unfortunately, such methods could lead to abuse, even when instituted by men of fine reputation. Granville Stuart, whose motivations and record demonstrate his liking for peaceful, orderly government, headed vigilantes who cleaned out rustlers in eastern Montana and western Dakota. Seemingly, a loose organization of ranchers furnished him with funds and designated responsible men in each roundup district to whom subordinate bands of "stranglers" reported for orders. Each subordinate band operated independently, district leaders being unaware of the names of those in charge elsewhere. Possibly at least one band that originally served under Stuart's direction turned to the hanging of small farmers. Vigilantes could easily settle personal scores or eliminate farmers who dared to homestead land on open range.[59] And yet, in purpose, and generally in action, Stuart's vigilantes sought to establish order and the protection of life and property for all honest citizens.

Of course, the classic debate as to whether cattlemen wanted law and order on anything but their own terms revolves around the famous Johnson County War in Wyoming in the early 1890's. Articles and books have discussed the conflict at length, but interpreters still disagree as to where justice lay. In its broad outlines, the story is a simple one. Local ranchers and their supporters hired a group of Texas gunmen to help them stage a lynching raid on people accused of rustling livestock. Local inhabitants and the elected officials of Johnson County surrounded the invading force, compelled it to surrender, and obtained indictments against many of those involved. Undoubtedly, the cattlemen overstepped their legal rights, and their action directly challenged the authority of established legal agencies. Farmers had entered the county in considerable numbers, however, thus reducing the amount of range available for ranching activities. Some very probably only played at farming, that being a useful front to cover their thievery. Beyond this, the story becomes involved in controversy.

In her recent book on the cattlemen, Mari Sandoz condemns John Clay for instigating the raid, and claims that it occurred because ranchers wanted to eliminate small settlers. She and Clay differ markedly in their characterizations of actors involved in the drama, even to those eliminated prior to the raid. Sandoz defends James Averill, a homesteader who took up a claim near the village of Bothwell, a gathering place for big ranchers and cowboys. Averill opened a store and saloon, and displayed a peaceful and friendly attitude in personal relations with all groups. Nevertheless, he wrote fiery letters to newspapers denouncing big cattlemen as range tyrants and grabbers of the public domain. Many agreed that he possessed no cattle and was never accused of rustling. Ella Watson, commonly called "Cattle Kate," lived nearby. She may have been Averill's wife, and perhaps used her own name in order to homestead additional land for the family. She "entertained" the cowboys and was said to take cattle in trade. A strong, husky woman in her twenties, she washed and ironed for the cowboys in addition to her so-called entertainment. Gradually her homestead became stocked with cattle, some forty to eighty head, with more having been marketed. Both she and Averill went unarmed. Why shouldn't they, when men like John Chisum did so? But for them there could be no protection. When Averill contested possession of some land desired by the cattlemen, both he and Kate were hanged by the ranchers' henchmen. Sandoz comments that this action looked very bad in a region just admitted to statehood, and especially so in one that had boasted of giving women the suffrage while still a territory twenty years before.[60] From her point of view the conflict represented an arrogant disregard for the rights of the little fellow from its inception to the end.

Averill and Kate bear decidedly different reputations in Clay's account. According to him, Averill operated a roadhouse and a saloon, and represented a disreputable element in society. Cattle Kate was a low-class prostitute who was willing to accept a branded maverick or two if her cowboy patrons were short of cash. Since ranchers could not obtain court convictions, they resorted to repeated warnings to Kate and Averill, and, finally, one morning in the summer of 1889, hanged both of them. It was horrible, of course, but could ranchers only stand helplessly by and see their property stolen?

According to Clay, the cattlemen had suffered tremendous losses in the hard winter of 1886-1887, were financially hard pushed, and yet could not obtain convictions of rustlers in Johnson County courts. Defenseless against theft of cattle, they were driven to desperate measures. Apart from the hired gunmen, the raiders of 1891 were a band "of the best, bravest men who ever lived." The group did include some honest and respectable cattlemen of long standing, like E. W. Whitcomb, and such exotic members of the ranching fraternity as the Harvard-bred H. E. Teschemacher and Fred de Billier, who owned a villa in France. In defending the group, Clay asserted that although one might cry out against violence, the complexity of the world would still make it difficult to decide where law ends and individuality begins. Great reforms flow from revolutionary methods—the Boston tea party and the victories of George Washington represented protests against a Teutonic dictatorship. In spite of calling on sacred American traditions to justify the raid, Clay took no credit for planning or financing it, claiming that he was as innocent of the charge as "an unborn babe" and that his absence in England at the time proved him so.[61]

Unfortunately for the cattlemen's reputation, the raid was so arrogant and so threatening to the safety of honest settlers that it clouded the ranchers' undoubted efforts at earlier times and places to create an environment favorable for respectable men and women of all occupations. Moreover, their defeat in the Johnson County War accelerated the decline of the cattleman's power. It contributed mightily to the popular conviction that the code of the West did involve murder rather than manners, a wealth of evidence to the contrary notwithstanding.

FOUR

Live and Let Live

ON THE cattleman's frontier men followed a rule of live and let live because it fitted their needs and circumstances. Pouring in from all parts of the world and from all social classes within a brief span of years, they could not hope to establish uniformity even if they so desired. Moreover, they were young and hopeful of economic success, not social theorists who wanted to create a Utopian order. Few women and children accompanied them. Needing large quantities of land to maintain their herds, they located at widely scattered points, and the hand of authority rested lightly on them in the absence of courts of law. All these things contributed to the wisdom of applying the principle that men could live as they pleased, so long as they recognized the right of others to do likewise and refrained from trying to force their personal convictions and habits of living on mankind at large. Since necessity and inclination alike made the rule effective, one need not seek its sources in any innate, mystic influence of the frontier. When the Mormons migrated to Utah, they took with them a single code of conduct to which their people must conform, and they were highly successful in enforcing it from the very first. But the ranching frontier exemplified a high measure of tolerance and individuality.

On the larger ranches the basic social unit consisted of an "outfit," which included the manager and sufficient hands to look after the herd of cattle. At spring and fall roundups several outfits worked together, and additional hands were employed to supplement the regular force. Those who stayed on the year round thus found themselves associated with considerably enlarged groups of men at roundup time and with smaller numbers in periods of routine activity. Whatever the season, they worked by the sun and not by the clock, with Sunday seldom observed as a day of rest. This basic pattern shaped the nature of society even beyond frontier days.

Major W. A. Towers, one of the cattle kings of the Northern range, described the layout of his ranch in terms that illustrate the over-all pattern in microcosm. His ranch house was fifty miles distant from a railroad station on the Northern Pacific. It consisted of a large log house, notched at the corners, and plastered inside and out with alkali mud. The roof consisted of poles covered with a layer of brush and on top of that a layer of mud mortar three inches thick, the whole topped off with a covering of soil a foot deep. A huge fireplace kept the house warm in winter, a necessity since heavy snows kept the men indoors for several days at a time. It took three days to make the trip to the railroad station, the nearest village, which contained a grocery store, several saloons, and a section house for railroad hands. The ranch hauled its foodstuffs of flour, meal, bacon, coffee, and dried apples, prunes, and peaches. During the winter season six to eight men looked after the ranch, but during the summer the number increased to twenty-five, most of whom lived directly on the range to oversee the herds of cattle.[1]

Of course, the type of construction used in ranch buildings varied according to the climate and the wealth of the owner, but all were highly utilitarian. Writing in 1897, Emerson Hough mentioned ranches in the South that looked much like vast and partly tilled farms, with white buildings dotting the landscape. More typical of early days, there were also one-room structures similar in appearance to the cabins occupied by hill dwellers in mountainous sections of the Southeast. On the Texas coast, ranch houses had large, airy rooms and a band of cottonwood trees for protection from the heat. In the Southwest they were built of adobe, and the

interior walls were whitewashed with gypsum. Another building
served as kitchen, dining hall, and quarters for the men. The two
buildings often were joined by a covered runway which provided
convenient storage space for the cowboys' equipment. In the North,
the ranch house might be a simple dugout toward the east in cold
Dakota, a hut in some high mountain valley, or a sod house standing on a wide bleak plain.[2] Whatever the type of construction,
ranch hands everywhere lived as members of the outfit and followed a common routine, thus enabling them to move from ranch
to ranch without feeling that they were entering a different world.

Since they lived in a man's world, they ordinarily felt no need
for elaborate manners. At the bunkhouse they ate rapidly and generally in silence, often with their hats on, a habit acquired from
spending so much of their time outdoors. When Lincoln Lang first
arrived in the Dakota Bad Lands, he was astounded at the speed
and silence with which people consumed their food.[3] Charles
Goodnight dined quickly and silently, even in his later years, and
then left the table. To do otherwise after having eaten so many
meals in the open made his stomach hurt. Like most cattlemen, he
preferred a diet of meat and coffee and was fond of smoking.[4]

Monotony rather than thrilling stampedes, Indian fights, and
gun battles characterized the cowhand's workaday life. To enliven
matters, he resorted to all sorts of practical jokes on his associates.
Owen Wister based one episode in his famous cowboy novel on
this proclivity. During a community dance, the Virginian and his
cronies changed the clothing around on a sleeping row of babies
so successfully that parents departed for home carrying the wrong
children. Since most ranches provided no organized social life for
their hands, the latter continued to play pranks to relieve the monotony long after open range had given way to more modern practices. On the Spur Ranch in Texas men worked seven days a week.
At the Christmas season they received three or four days off, but
were more bored than pleased by being released from work without
having some form of recreation to fill the void. Occasionally they
took a day off in July or August for a picnic, with a political speech
serving as entertainment. Most of all, they enjoyed hunting, since

game remained plentiful and could be pursued as a part of their regular work. Some of them took two- or three-day trips to muddy streams to fish all night long for catfish. They liked to attend court to testify in trials, the only change from routine in which they received pay for their time. Occasionally they had the opportunity to attend a wedding. Although they liked dances most of all, Spur Ranch records for the period from 1885 to 1907 mention only one such affair being sponsored by the management.[5]

In the early days of open range cowboys looked forward eagerly to spring and fall roundups as social occasions in spite of the hard work involved. An element of competition permeated the day's activities as men from different outfits rode side by side in carrying out their assignments. At night, campfires served as focal centers for visiting and entertainment. And what a variety of men gathered on those occasions! College graduates and illiterates, paupers and millionaires, noblemen and commoners, Europeans and Americans joined forces for a brief time in a common effort. And all knew that to be accepted they must follow the rule of live and let live.

The Dakota Bad Lands of the middle 1880's illustrate the process. Perhaps the most colorful of all its exotic inhabitants was the Marquis de Mores, French nobleman, graduate of the military school of St. Cyr, army officer, and aristocrat. A magnificent figure of a man, with black, curly hair, upturned mustaches waxed to needle points, heavy eyelids, and cool, arrogant eyes, the Marquis wore the widest sombrero and the loudest neckerchief in the region. He lived sumptuously in a private railroad car while his mansion was under construction and enjoyed the luxuries to which he was accustomed elsewhere. As a dreamer who hoped to re-establish the French monarchy, his ideas verged perilously close to expecting others to give way to his "rights" and privileges. Gregor Lang, a devotee of Tom Paine, never cared for him. Some claimed that the Bad Lands accepted him only because he spent money freely, and that helped, for he could stand treats at a bar in a most democratic manner. Moreover, he seemingly tried hard to conform to the prevailing code of respect for differing scales of value.[6]

In spite of various handicaps, Teddy Roosevelt succeeded even better than the Marquis in adjusting to the new community. He could not throw off the influences of his upbringing in upper-class Eastern society nor his physical limitations. He and Gregor Lang were the only men locally who found it necessary to wear glasses, and Roosevelt was called "four eyes" by some who lacked that handicap. His cultured language seemed strange to many, as when he urged greater speed on a roundup by calling out "hasten forward quickly there," a phrase that cowboys humorously repeated on similar occasions. Somewhat of an eccentric in any society where he lived, Roosevelt was bound to strike people as odd. Nevertheless, he gladly adopted the one basic code of his new community: a man must not try to force his own views and values on others. That alone was sufficient to win acceptance by others in the Bad Lands.

Wherever he went, however, Roosevelt wanted still more. He must have status among his associates, and he gained it by proving himself equal to the problems at hand. When hunting, he insisted on dressing out game killed by him to show his ability. On round-ups, he insisted on drawing lots with his own cowboys for the selection of horses, although he could have selected the gentler and finer mounts, as his ownership of the outfit entitled him to do. When one of the horses which had fallen to his lot staged a bucking fit, Roosevelt stayed in the saddle, although he had to grasp both saddle horn and cantle to retain his seat. In doing so, "he pulled leather," as the phrase went, thus failing to meet the standards of professional bronc riders who disdained to hold on when fighting a bucking horse. Although he had ridden to hounds in the East, and was not totally inexperienced, he suffered a severe jolting and lost both hat and glasses before subduing his pony. But he kept from being thrown, and in so doing achieved status in the eyes of bystanders. Others liked him not simply because he respected their right to do things their own way; he obviously valued their accomplishments sufficiently to want to emulate them. Partial success in such efforts elevated him to a status where his hands and many others addressed him as "Mr." Roosevelt and also extended their appreciation to his own peculiar way of doing things. One of the local characters, Bill Jones, had a reputation for profanity and foul stories, which he delighted in exhibiting in front of self-right-eous individuals. Knowing Roosevelt's dislike for such language, and respecting him as well, Jones refrained from it when in his presence.[7]

Moderation and consideration for the other fellow's point of view were certainly necessary during the first general roundup in the Medora community in the spring of 1885. Since many of the participants knew little about rounding up and branding cattle, they appointed an experienced and forceful Texan as captain of the group. Gregor Lang's outfit illustrated the types of men with whom he had to work. It consisted of ten men, some of whom were new hands. The son of Lang's benefactor, Sir George Pender, and three other visiting scions of English nobility also tagged along with Lang's outfit. Within a few days young Pender was complaining that the cowboys showed no respect for him and refused to call him "Mr." Trouble also developed over the cooking device which he had brought along for use in preparing food for him and his friends. Since the cook considered this an implied insult to his methods of cooking, and also loved intoxicants in any form, he began to drink the alcohol needed to operate Pender's equipment. To conceal his actions, he watered the remaining alcohol each time he raided the container, and before long the supply was too diluted to serve any purpose whatever.

But other novelties lessened attention to Pender's difficulties. On the third day of the roundup someone found a pair of boxing gloves at the Three Seven R Ranch, and with these Roosevelt and a young English aristocrat staged a boxing match at the day's close. Pierre Wibaux's ranch lay on Beaver Creek in the roundup dis-trict. This son of a wealthy, bourgeois French family and his cul-tured English wife were favorites locally. When the roundup crew reached Beaver Creek, Mrs. Wibaux rode out to visit, electrifying the men by her beauty and poise. She invited them to an open house at the Wibaux ranch, where she served beer, wine, and cigars to en-hance the occasion. Texans, Easterners, Englishmen, Frenchmen, and full-blooded American Indians participated in that roundup, and most of them thoroughly enjoyed their associations.[8] They had youth and hope and health, and gladly subscribed to the one role that let them operate effectively: recognition of the right of others to do and think and believe as they pleased. Young Pender alone seems to have objected to the role, and he soon left for his homeland.

Years later, old-timers remembered the exotic birds of passage who enlivened early days on the ranching frontier. Around 1879, for instance, three Englishmen, Kenny Smith, Ernest Lee, and Tom Carson, drove a herd of cattle from the Nebraska sandhills to a spot near an Apache reservation in Arizona. There they found kindred spirits in St. George Creaghe, an Irishman; John Swinburne, nephew of the great poet of the same name and an amateur ornithologist; and Clement Hull, a prominent English tennis enthusiast. From profits amassed in ranching, Carson later made several trips around the world and settled down to a life of ease in England. Smith and Lee also finally returned home, although with less wealth than their more successful countryman. Swinburne lost his life fighting in the Boer War in Africa, and Hull moved on to California to raise lemons for a pastime.[9]

In New Mexico, William French, nephew of the English general, played at ranching for a time but took greater interest in recording his experiences with Apaches and bad men. His range foreman, an Irishman named Louis Lloyd, astounded the cowboys in the surrounding country by taking early morning shower baths under a ten-foot wooden water tower, no matter how cold the weather. Lloyd's marriage to the sister of a neighboring English rancher when she visited the region perhaps accounted for his decision to return to Ireland to live as a country gentleman. Three English brothers, the Manbys, ranched in northern New Mexico for a time around the 1890's. One of them moved to Canada, a second entered the livestock commission business, and the third established a ranch near Taos, where he could enjoy the companionship of a local artist's colony. Farther south, an Englishman, Jack Culley, ran a sheep ranch and devoted his spare time to composing music. Another Britisher, Dick Walsh, managed the JA

Ranch in Texas after Goodnight terminated his partnership with the Adairs, but finally moved on to ranching in Rhodesia, South Africa.[10] The presence of such diverse personalities, even for short periods of time, emphasized the need for tolerance of all cultures.

Dan Dillon Casement well represents the Eastern college-boy element in the early cosmopolitan days of ranching and the ease with which they found congenial companions. Dan attended Princeton, where he made the second team in football, became class president, and established the friendships that he considered the greatest benefit from his college education. Tot Otis of Cleveland attended Yale during the same period. Both went on to Columbia to study law, where they became close friends. Their fathers acquired a Colorado ranch during that industry's boom period, and there the boys lived for several winters beginning in 1891.

Although Casement insists that they took ranching seriously, their primary interests seem to have centered on other things. Their foreman was better known as a hunting guide than as a cattleman. Each fall they went to New York for the annual Yale-Princeton football game and they visited freely among the other upper-class people in their region. Phil Sherrard, younger son of an English family, owned the nearby SK brand. Phil had two gray horses, "Irish-you-son-of-bitch" and "Jock you bahstard," the names by which he usually addressed them. Although he gracefully accepted the rough life around him, Sherrard spent much time reading a London paper devoted to sports and finally returned home. "Pate" and Jim Smith, one a Swarthmore graduate and the other from the University of Pennsylvania, operated another nearby ranch, thus adding to the opportunities for visiting. One Christmas a college friend and his new wife visited Otis and Casement at the ranch. To celebrate the occasion, the bride donned a year-old Paris gown, the men put on tails and white ties, and they dined on turkey and champagne. Although Grand Junction lay some thirty-five miles distant from the ranch, the boys visited it frequently, and loafed at the Windsor hotel or the more exciting "Bucket of Blood" saloon. Grand Junction was quite cosmopolitan. The banker was an Exeter graduate and the real estate broker an alumnus of the Boston Latin School. In spite of their liking for ranch life with so much variety, Tot departed after his marriage, and Casement also turned to more serious activities with increasing age and marriage.[11]

Although a few of the cosmopolites remained permanently in the cattle kingdom, the departure of so many of them to other parts of the world reduced their long-range significance in the development of local society. They undoubtedly hastened economic growth by their heavy investments and they stimulated the movement toward improving breeds of cattle. They could afford to buy blooded stock and knew something of its advantages from observations made in the course of trips to older communities. By adding to the cosmopolitan nature of local society during their stay, they contributed to the need for tolerance of all viewpoints and classes.

Most of all, they introduced plush living to self-made ranchers who wanted to demonstrate their affluence. Along with the promotional fraternity that benefited business-wise by maintaining an air of prosperity, they furnished examples of how one could spend money on something more than cows and land. Ranchers like Shanghai Pierce and Cap Mossman enjoyed displaying the fruits of their wealth and liked to be seen in company with sophisticated people.

Social clubs catered to this urge on the ranching frontier. In 1880, for instance, twelve charter members established the famous Cheyenne Club in the frontier town of Cheyenne in Wyoming Territory. The founders and early members were wealthy young cattlemen, most of whom depended upon family money to underwrite their activities. Invitations to membership read:

We shall have rooms for a limited number, a good restaurant for all, billiard room, reading rooms, etc. Phil Dater is President. The members are limited to 50 to the end that they may be selected with great care. The entrance fee is set at $50 and annual dues at $30. . . . We expect to furnish to members a substitute for and an improvement on the Old Railroad House where the butler has lately been promoted and the sprees of the Jones family are growing inconveniently frequent—in short to have a good clubhouse. . . .[12]

Above, Library of the Denver Club, 1902. (Colorado
State Historical Society)
Below, Cheyenne Club. (University of Wyoming Library)

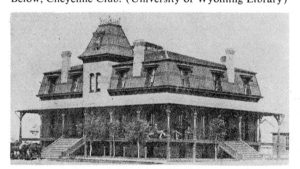

Montana Club before the fire of 1903.
(Historical Society of Montana)

Mr and Mrs. George W. Miller and the White House on their 101 Ranch. (Oklahoma Historical Society)

Left, interior of an old-time ranch house. (University of Wyoming Library)

Below, manager of Hat X Ranch and his family on Timber Creek, Montana, 1902. (L. A. Huffman photo)

At bottom, nester family at Three Block line camp, New Mexico, about 1908. (Erwin E. Smith Collection, Library of Congress)

In time, the initial membership fee was raised to one hundred dollars and as many as two hundred men could belong at one time. In addition, visitors from a distance were granted temporary residence if recommended by some regular member. Nevertheless, the club tried to retain its exclusive nature. Applicants for admission had to be sponsored by a member in good standing, their records were carefully examined, and even then they could be blackballed in the final balloting by club members. Quite obviously, a man could think of himself as a gentleman if he won acceptance by so meticulous a group.

Special rules forbade drunkenness to an offensive degree, profanity, and obscenity. A member guilty of striking another within the clubhouse was subject to discipline. There could be no betting on cards in the public rooms, and cheating at play was strictly forbidden. Members and guests could not smoke pipes in public rooms or tip servants who waited on them. Expulsion penalized any member guilty of an act "so dishonorable in social life as to unfit the guilty party for the society of gentlemen." Club records show that the rule was enforced. In October, 1888, the governing board censured those guilty of gambling and of admitting improper persons to the premises, and ordered its decision to be posted where all could see it. In 1882, the board suspended C. M. Oelrichs for thirty days for striking the bartender, Oelrichs admitting that he was "full" at the time. For intemperate language on the same occasion, his brother Harry was censured. When the Oelrichs refused to take their penalties properly, the club ousted them. As one of the founders, C. M. Oelrichs had been very active in building up the organization. Undoubtedly, the club lost two of its most colorful members by its disciplinary action. The Oelrichs often traveled in style to their ranch, some seventeen miles from Cheyenne, using a coach-and-four with the proper footmen on occasion. Harry made newspaper copy from coast to coast by pursuing the actress Lily Langtry in one of her triumphal journeys across the continent. But the brothers were something more than playboys. Both achieved considerable success in the field of speculative finance before trying their hands at ranching. Such escapades as striking the bartender and kicking a club servant down the stairs for refusing to hold the reins of Harry's horse could not, however, be tolerated by the Cheyenne Club.[13]

The Club itself was a frame structure, its dormer windows, large veranda surrounding the second story, and glass-enclosed observation platform on top giving it a measure of individuality. In 1888 members paid two dollars to reserve the private dining room for an evening, five cents a cue for pool, and sixty cents an hour for billiards. All such games were forbidden on Sundays, as was smoking of any kind in the dining room from seven in the morning to seven-thirty in the evening, as a regular policy. The first president, Phil Dater, was out of place as a rancher but graced his office well. Tall, fine-looking, Bohemian by nature, keen in satire but kindly, he was the beau-ideal. Women found him irresistible. He loved the good life in a morally fragile sense, and age failed to dim his charm and grace. The third president, H. E. Teschemacher, was the son of an Englishman, a Harvard graduate, and a frequent visitor to France, where his parents maintained a home.

The Cheyenne Club impressed boys from wealthy, sheltered Eastern homes when they came west to enter ranching. Richard Trimble stayed there in the 1880's. He reported back to "Dear Momie" that Teschemacher told him of having reviewed nearly all of his old college courses while marooned on a ranch, and that "Tescher" studied more in the West than when at Harvard. At the same time, one need not be divorced from civilization, since the Cheyenne Club lay close at hand. Writing to "Dear Momie" on Sunday, March 6, 1887, from the Club, Trimble assured his family that he had access to leading newspapers—the *Times, World,* and *Tribune,* and to *Harper's* and the *Century* magazine. Teschy personally subscribed to the *Nation,* so he could read that too if he wished. Trimble and his poodle, "Mifouche," thus had no need to feel shut off from the outside world.[14]

Nor was the Club divorced from the life immediately around it. John Clay, who became a member in 1883, spoke of it as a place where business deals were made during the course of a friendly drink. Some, of course, belonged primarily for the social advantages. Nevertheless, according to Clay, the membership included the thinkers and workers who constituted the backbone of the cattle industry in the field of management and finance.[15] When the hard winter of 1886-1887 and declining cattle prices bankrupted many members, ownership of the Club passed to a local group that paid its bondholders twenty cents on the dollar. That catastrophe undoubtedly lessened exclusiveness of membership without destroying the intention of maintaining high social aims. To the extent that they had never experienced club life, visitors to the Cheyenne Club became aware of how gentlemen could spend their money in the interest of prestige and comfort.

When the Helena, Montana, *Weekly Herald* described the local Montana Club in 1885, it commented that every city of any note possessed one or more such organizations and that they exerted a wide and beneficial influence. The Montana Club was incorporated in 1885 for "literary, mutual improvement, and social purposes." The constitution, by-laws, and rules of conduct were strikingly similar to those of the Cheyenne Club, but the great importance of mining in Montana meant that cattlemen, mining operators, and businessmen mingled much more freely there than at Cheyenne, where ranching interests dominated. Conrad Kohrs, who rose to wealth as cattleman and butcher shop operator, and S. T. Hauser of the ranching fraternity rubbed shoulders at the club with F. A. Heinze of the mining profession.

In 1885 the Montana Club occupied the third story of a building in the Parchen block, its quarters being divided into two large rooms separated by a corridor. The room on the west side was subdivided into two compartments, one the parlor and the other the reading room. Cherry and walnut furniture, magnificent glass chandeliers, Brussels carpets, and marble-topped tables gave them an air of luxury. There one could read files of all the territorial papers, all New York papers, and all the sporting sheets, except for the *Police News* and the *Gazette,* which were banned from the Club. The bar, billiard, and card rooms were across the corridor. The billiard room measured twenty-seven by thirty feet and contained three handsome tables, one for pool and two for billiards.

Club members watched games from comfortable chairs, but no gambling or treating was permitted.[16]

Some clubs maintained fairly extensive libraries for the use of their members. At the Denver, Colorado, Club mine owners constituted a large percentage of the membership, but ranchers and businessmen also belonged, thus providing a varied group of patrons. Its library, now a part of the University of Wyoming collection, contained the works of Hubert Howe Bancroft, the American Nation Series, the works of Francis Parkman, the writings of Thomas Jefferson and Woodrow Wilson, numerous biographies of prominent historical figures, considerable English literature, and some travel books.[17] Because of its heavy content, the library perhaps grew as much through purchase of books offered on a subscription basis as from the reading preferences of club members.

Of course, such clubs could develop only at urban points or at times when a great many wealthy outsiders poured into a region. For the rank-and-file rancher, and even for the prosperous on many frontiers, masculine pleasures were simpler and less costly. Around 1860, for instance, Granville and James Stuart participated in the placer mining and open-range ranching activities on the Montana frontier. Organized local government lay in the future, white women were a novelty, and men rushed from one mining prospect to another or drove their herds of cattle from winter pasture to mining camps and immigrant routes with the change of seasons. As a consequence, they seemed no less migratory than the Indians whom they were beginning to displace. Drunkenness was universal, although Granville Stuart and a minority of others deplored its contributions to violence. Surfeited with visits from drunken individuals, Stuart commented: "Oh! for a lodge in some vast wilderness where drunks could never come . . . ,"[18] a strange wish for a man already living well beyond the bounds of organized society. Poker surpassed reading in popularity for most, but Stuart rode one hundred and fifty miles to obtain books abandoned by a former owner. They covered a wide range of material: a volume of Shakespeare, Byron's poems, a history of Napoleon and his generals, a French Bible, and Adam Smith's *Wealth of Nations*. While others gambled and caroused, Stuart read.

He was no recluse, however, and enjoyed dancing most of all. Two violins furnished the music on such occasions. Indian and half-breed women served as partners, but there were never enough to go round. To balance the discrepancy between the sexes, some of the men tied handkerchiefs around their arms and took the part of a woman. The women came dressed in Indian finery—bright calicoes, scarlet leggings, handsomely beaded moccasins, gay plaid blankets, and ornaments of feathers, shells, silver money, and beads. The men wore flannel shirts, highly ornamented buckskin suits, and moccasins. Squaw men were the norm in such a society. The Stuarts held off from marrying among the Indians for a time but both finally did. James married an Indian woman who had been ransomed by him and two other white men from a tribe that had stolen her. James felt obligated to look after her until she could find her own people. Within a short time, however, he was commenting: "I might do worse. She is neat and rather good look-ing and seems to be of a good disposition. So I find myself a mar-ried man."[19] In 1862 Granville married a Snake Indian girl, a sister of the wife of another white man in whose family she was living. James sized her up as a fairly good cook, an amiable person, and devoid of very many relatives who would look to Granville for support.

Such marriages did little to change the nature of society on the ranching frontier. Although often loyal to their Indian wives, men continued to set the social standards. Squaw men and patrons of the Cheyenne Club alike emphasized masculine values. Despite its cosmopolitan nature, the ranching frontier remained largely a man's world.

Perhaps the most remarkable thing of all about the cattleman's frontier was the contemporary feeling that ranchers and cow-boys did play a common role, a concept ordinarily arising out of much longer periods of time and from more stable conditions. Rapid changes militate against men falling into common roles, and change certainly characterized the frontier. Nevertheless, one who ponders Joseph G. McCoy's *Historic Sketches of the Cattle Trade*, written near the beginning rather than at the close of the cattle kingdom, must recognize the existence of a role concept very early.

Of course, McCoy stressed variations in personalities. He distinguished between drovers and cowboys, and between drovers and ranchers. In his opinion, ranchers "were not adapted by nature" to face the financial and personal hazards associated with the long drives, preferring instead the more commonplace and routine duties of the home ranch. By nature, too, cowboys generally were unsuited to fill the duties of a drover. Even within these groupings he noted variations. Among the drovers, J. L. Driskill impressed him as versatile in business—a "quiet operator," courteous and dignified, a friendly man. H. M. Childress, on the other hand, was a heavy plunger, a convivial fellow, full of fun and frolic, big-hearted, chivalrous, and devoted to making his friends happy. Still another drover, Captain E. B. Millett, loved to spend his leisure hours reading.[20] Seemingly, it would be difficult to establish a common role for three men as diverse in personality and personal interests as Driskill, Childress, and Millett.

Nevertheless, McCoy stated a "few reflections" on Texas ranchmen and drovers as a whole, generalizations colored by his own experiences and prejudices but definitely suggesting a somewhat common role for the entire group. According to McCoy, they lacked any public spirit in matters pertaining to the common good, being selfish and indifferent to the public welfare. They spent money freely only to gratify their appetites and passions, measured the motives of other men by their own rules of selfishness, but had a reputation for keeping their word. Their love of firearms, ability to shoot, and tendency to settle disputes with revolvers gave them a reputation for great bravery. They were almost invariably convivial in habit, taking their liquor straight, but not sots. They universally loved the ladies, would have been a discouraging field for Quaker missionaries, but gave ready obedience to the command to multiply and replenish the earth. They were sanguine, speculative, warm and cordial, hot and hasty in anger, posessed a strong innate sense of right and wrong, and were hardy, self-reliant, free and independent, acknowledging no superior or master in the whole wide universe.[21] Although McCoy thought their reputation wholly undeserved in some of the above respects, he recognized a fairly well-developed image of the rancher by the early 1870's.

In 1916 George W. Saunders and others founded the "Old Time Trail Drivers Association," made up largely of Texans but including any who had been associated with the history of the early drives. In 1925 the organization published biographies of a considerable number of early cattlemen, many written by survivors. In these accounts old-timers spoke at length of hardships, such as storms, floods, stampedes, Indian troubles, and desperate undertakings. But they also mentioned common patterns of behavior. Trail drivers were whole-souled and big-hearted. Every cowboy was the champion of womanhood. Hospitality abounded. Courage, self-reliance, willingness to take responsibility, and longheadedness marked the successful man. Although often "diamonds in the rough," trail drivers were charitable and chivalrous. A killing in a fair fight went unpunished. Hard work was the lot of most, but those who faced it had a real chance to make good. Far more interested in recording colorful episodes than in considering common characteristics, given to action rather than to ideas, such men analyzed their contemporaries less thoroughly than had McCoy long before, but, like him, they obviously felt that a common role prevailed in the early days.[22]

Although ranchers modified that role in their efforts to establish an orderly, settled society, they continued to cherish many of its traits. Marriage and companionship with respectable white women proved more satisfying than dalliances with prostitutes and squaws; fenced pastures possessed advantages over open range; and formal agencies of government afforded greater protection to life and property than had been possible before their establishment. Nevertheless, ranchers joined with their cowboys in wails of "Don't fence me in" that reflected more than nostalgic allegiance to the past. In the prosperity of later life they sometimes sought to recapture the sense of freedom that once had prevailed in a man's

world, gaining thereby relief from the conformity of their surroundings and also renewed assurance that they had chosen well
after all. Such were the rewards of a pleasure trip to the Isthmus
of Panama by four prosperous residents of Roswell, New Mexico,
in 1909.

In January of that year J. F. Hinkle and E. A. Cahoon, local bankers with cattle-ranching connections, J. P. Church, who
owned a saloon, and J. P. White, Sr., New Mexico's leading
rancher, decided to carry out a long-planned journey to the Isthmus. As old cronies of twenty years' standing who devoted serious
attention to business affairs, they felt entitled to a pleasure trip
and vacation "leaving all care behind and expecting no business
letters or telegrams except in case of sickness of our families." They
traveled by train to and from New Orleans and by boat on the
United Fruit Company Line out of New Orleans.

They organized their "outfit" at the start of the journey, with
Hinkle as "general manager," Cahoon as "paymaster," Church as
"commissary," and White as "horse wrangler." Practical jokes on
one another enlivened their whole trip. They tricked Hinkle into
shaving with a dull razor, compelled Church to pay for a group
portrait as the ugliest member of the party, and bribed a steward
to put cheap cigars in Cahoon's reach so they could tease him for
his inability to distinguish good tobacco from bad. While on board
the boat they made friends with everyone and became known as
"the four cattlemen from Mexico." Impromptu evening entertainment staged by a young traveling man from New Orleans was much
to their liking. When White, who was outwardly shy and reserved,
found himself called upon for a speech at the end of such an evening, he met the occasion by remarking to the passengers that
"from the looks of things around here it would be a fine place to
water a herd of cattle." White's friends accused him of setting a
bad example for the group by going to bed early, of arousing them
at four or five in the morning, and of droning innumerable verses
of the cowboy song "Sam Bass." Although they affectionately
ribbed their 223-pound ranching companion for inability to throw

off habits acquired on the open range, they shared his preferences, even to a meat diet. Financial success had not blunted their interest in people and places. They argued the merits of the Canal project and of the country through which they passed. At their stops in New Orleans they rode a rubberneck bus, ate at Antoine's famous restaurant, and attended the theatre. On their return home, the diarist of the trip summarized it as "THE" incident of a lifetime for all of them.

Their argosy was surprisingly mild, however, for cattlemen seeking to recapture a feeling of the freedom they had known in the early days of the cattle kingdom. At the start of the trip, White boasted so much of the recent birth of twin sons in his family that the others outlawed further reference to the matter, in part it seems because they enjoyed their temporary freedom from family associations less than they cared to admit. Although they drank moderately on the trip, they also attended church and wrote home to assure their families of their safety and health.[23] They were contented men, happy to be fenced in by a code of manners which they and other ranchers had done so much to create. Restrictions tugged all the more gently at them because they were self-imposed.

From the days of the dime novel and Buffalo Bill's Wild West Show, however, the public has assumed that ranchers lived in a far more exciting if not more satisfying manner. Had J. P. White and his cronies preferred, they could have visited the 101 Wild West Show rather than the Isthmus of Panama, for that stellar attraction got under way in 1907. As a family enterprise, the show exemplified the personalities of "Colonel" George W. Miller and his three flamboyant sons. Born in Kentucky in 1841, Miller became a successful rancher in what is now Oklahoma, but throughout his life he played the role of a Kentucky colonel, even in its more ironic aspects. In 1866 he married Mary Anne (Molly) Carson, who, according to the official family biography, was reared in the plantation tradition. As soon as finances permitted, Miller began to erect "The White House," a white-columned mansion, on his 101 Ranch. Although this was incomplete at the time of his death in 1903, his wife and sons finished the project.[24] Sensitive to their environment and essentially actors by nature, the Millers also became enamored of the code of the West, which afforded them as much or more attention than they received from playing the role of a Southern planter. In some respects they found the two roles highly compatible, planters and Westerners alike supposedly being addicted to hospitality. As members of a local Rotary Club who applied the principles of Rotary to their own employees on the 101 Ranch, and as Colonels on the staff of the governor of Oklahoma, the Miller boys drew on traditions of Rotary, Southern planters, and Western ranchers to justify an openhanded hospitality. Any one of those traditions justified them in inviting famous people to visit their ranch. Even the less well known were welcomed to short daytime tours.

The official biographers of the Ranch speak of the many prominent names entered in the guest book kept at the White House. "Colonel Joe," the greatest showman among the three brothers, obviously enjoyed stepping out on the porch of the White House, with arms extended in a dramatic gesture, to welcome famous and obscure alike, and to utter in a "southern drawling voice" his well-known phrase "Come on in, children," for to him all visitors fitted that category. Architectural setting and voice may have been sired directly out of the plantation tradition, but the Colonel preferred to wear Western costume, and his title was only as sound as that of the average "Colonel" on any governor's staff. Nevertheless, the Millers all looked the part of Western pioneers. Their official biographers describe them as bronzed, sturdy, steel-eyed men, typical of the plains. They wore Stetson hats, chaps, and high-heeled, decoratively tooled cowboy boots, and gaily colored handkerchiefs knotted about their necks. Few Americans have ever played the role of so many different stereotypes as did Colonel Joe in welcoming the hordes of "children" to his empire.

The Millers thrived on publicity. On two occasions, they invited the National Editorial Association to hold its annual meeting at their ranch, the first of which resulted in several thousand newspaper columns extolling their achievements. When Colonel Joe died, five thousand people crowded the front lawn of the White House for the service. A reporter for the New York *Sun* described the occasion as reminiscent of another age, when adherents of a clan or a feudal barony gathered to mourn a departed chieftain.[25] No one seems to have troubled himself with trying to square such obvious emphasis on paternalism with the individualism supposedly characteristic of the code of the West. Nor did it bother the Millers.

Seeking still more notoriety over the years, the Millers put too much of their income from ranching and oil wells into their Wild West Show and other gigantic enterprises to be able to escape the bankruptcy which overtook them during the Great Depression of the early 1930's. Before Colonel Joe died in 1927, however, he knew the satisfaction of providing a ranch home on which such famous actors as Tom Mix and Buck Jones acquired the rudimentary skills necessary to portray cowboys on the movie screen. Tom Mix, who claimed to have spent ten years on the 101 Ranch, said that he learned far more than that. He praised "Colonel Joe's horse sense" and his "keen understanding of men" and from him claimed to have gained faith in humanity and squareness of purpose in dealing with others.

The Millers developed their Wild West Show over a period of years. At first they staged rodeos and similar entertainment for conventions and gatherings at their ranch. In 1907 they gave a display at the Jamestown Exposition as "the most famous representative of the cattle raising business." For years Colonel Joe had wanted to preserve frontier customs and traditions, and had been moving in the direction of putting together the only show that would portray "ranch and frontier life as it actually existed in the days of the Old West." By 1908 his show was on the road. Naturally, the Colonel was one of its chief attractions, mounted as he was on a favorite horse whose saddle and equipment cost several thousand dollars. According to "oldtime cowboys," he had never used a six-shooter in the old days except when necessary, thus making him a reliable representative of that bygone era. Moreover, his supporting cast of cowboys traced their antecedents to that same era when:

Accustomed to roam and range upon their wiry, fleet-footed cow ponies, for days and nights over miles of unclaimed country, the cowboy became, perforce, the pilot of the would-be pioneers, the scout of military expeditions, the leader of colonies and boomers, the nemesis and prosecutor of ferocious Indians bent on devastation and ravage.[26]

At least, it seemed that way to participants in the circus performance and to their audience.

The truth was less exciting. Although Colonel Joe began life as a rancher, he participated primarily in its tamer aspects. His direct connection with the era of the long drives was limited to one episode late in its history. On that occasion he drove a herd of cattle to his father's ranch on his way home to make peace with his family after having failed to establish his financial independence. Moreover, it seems doubtful if he ever engaged in any gunfights. Perhaps he did refuse an offer of twenty-five thousand dollars for his performing horse, and perhaps that did exemplify a cowboy's affection for a favorite mount. Audiences did not know that the Millers sold old horses to Kansas farmers after they had passed their usefulness and that many other ranchers disposed of aging horses to cotton farmers for use in ignominious tasks unsuited to former "fleet-footed cow ponies." But realism did not stand in the way of a good show.

On the contrary, the 101 Wild West Show convinced audiences that ranchers engaged in a continuous round of danger, excitement, and thrilling escapes. It depicted savage Indians massacring helpless whites, being driven off by rescue parties, and staging weird, primitive dances. Trick riding and shooting, bucking broncos, Texas longhorn cattle, buffaloes, the Pony Express, Mexican bandits robbing the Deadwood stage, and vigilantes all passed in review. Undoubtedly, oldtimers goggled at display No. 9 in which the "chief of the cowboys" demonstrated his skill with the Australian boomerang in hunt, chase, and battle. Even more astounding were the feats of the "cowgirls" during a six months' run of the show at Shepherd's Bush, London, in 1914, a part of the Anglo-American Exposition celebrating one hundred years of peace. Ranch girls often liked to ride, and on small ranches they helped at busy seasons in handling livestock, but as a species "cowgirls" simply did not exist. They lived only in the West of commercial entertainment. Nevertheless, the English found them fascinating, dressed, as they were, in divided skirts, top boots, and wide, gray felt Stetson hats. According to newspaper reports, they, like the men with the show, disliked large cities, and so they camped directly on the showgrounds near London so they could be in the open. Before bankruptcy closed the show in 1931, it added a troop of Russian Cossacks to compete with the cowboys, exotic animals such as elephants and camels, and an opening spectacle, "Arabia," featuring dancing girls. Even ballet came in for attention.[27] By then the Millers had expanded their roles beyond Kentucky colonels, Southern planters, Western cowboy-ranchers, and Rotarians to encompass stereotypes from all corners of the earth. In so doing, they reduced the code of the West to an absurdity never before achieved.

With the passing of the Wild West Shows, the American public turned its attention to rodeos, which today rank near the top of commercial entertainment in attendance. Professional cowboys still compete in riding and roping contests, and the public at large considers this the major form of entertainment in ranch country. Although ranchers enjoy rodeos along with the rest of the American public, they attend stock shows much more faithfully. Their sons belong to 4-H Clubs and compete ardently with one another for prizes awarded to exhibitors of blooded stock. In doing so, they carry on the more accurate and more important traditions of the ranching frontier. Even in the days of open range, ranchers hired professional bronc busters to break in horses needed for their work. Then as now, they considered it good business to leave the dramatic in the hands of those who preferred that form of exhibitionism. For them, profits were more important.

FIVE

The Moderating Hand of Woman

WOMEN contributed to the speed and thoroughness with which civilization conquered the ranching frontier. Shortly after James and Granville Stuart married Indian wives on the Montana frontier, a white family with two handsome daughters, a blonde and a brunette, arrived in their community. As a result, manners and dress immediately improved: "Every man in camp has shaved and changed his shirt. . . . We are all trying to appear like civilized men." Blue flannel shirts and black neckties began to replace buckskin shirts, and moccasins gave way to shoes. Men even selected some other day than Sunday to do their washing. Before long the Granville Stuarts purchased a violin so they could invite a neighboring white couple over for dancing. The neighbor obligingly played the violin on such occasions while Stuart danced with his wife, a girl of seventeen. Stuart confided to his diary that he enjoyed "the society of an intellectual white woman and good music," an indication of his preference for his own race.[1]

Other evidences of transition to an orderly society rapidly appeared. In 1858 Stuart had seen a drunken wagon master shoot down a teamster who dared talk back to him, and no one apparently thought of punishing the murderer. Within a few years, however, regular agencies for dealing with crime focused more sharply on the local scene. On July 14, 1862, the citizens of Missoula

County, then in Washington Territory, elected a representative to the territorial legislature. Granville Stuart became one of the three county commissioners, and his brother James shortly thereafter was elected sheriff. In 1863 Idaho Territory was carved out of parts of the territories of Dakota and Washington, and in 1864 Montana Territory was separated from the Idaho jurisdiction. From 1865 to 1870 the region prospered economically. Placer mines produced over twenty million dollars in gold dust and the valleys filled with prosperous ranchers. The town of Deer Lodge became a center of education and refinement for the territory, many beautiful homes being constructed there because of its superior educational advantages for children. The first newspaper in the territory, the *Montana Post,* appeared on August 27, 1864.

Such agencies of civilization did not immediately eliminate all lawlessness or guarantee a steady upsurge of economic developments. Granville Stuart and others employed vigilante action at times to hasten the process of change. Moreover, during the 1870's considerable pessimism existed concerning the future of the territory. Placer mines decreased in output. Cheyenne, Arapahoe, and Sioux Indians, driven north and west from Kansas and Minnesota, united under Red Cloud to harass river transportation, emigrant trains, and ranchers. There, as elsewhere on the frontier, improvements seemed excruciatingly slow at times to those most directly involved.

Nevertheless, they came within the normal life span of pioneer settlers. Granville Stuart witnessed and participated in the changes from open-range ranching, itinerant merchandising, and placer mining to modern-day scientific ranching, specialized retailing, and deep-rock mining. He saw the Indians brought under control, courts of law established, and Montana rise to statehood. His own life reflected the changes that took place. He who had danced with half-wild Indian women, witnessed unredressed murders, and claimed the honor of first discovering gold in the region, by 1891 was acting as state agent to select the six hundred thousand acres of federal land given to Montana for school purposes. After serving as American minister to Uruguay and

Paraguay for a time, he became librarian of the Butte, Montana, public library in 1904 and began to prepare his reminiscences for publication. In 1916 the state commissioned him to write its history, a project on which he continued until his death in 1918.[2] Many others could say with him that they had participated in all the stages of transformation from raw frontier to civilization.

Young, healthy, and adventurous, the argonauts of the ranching frontier were inclined to prize female companionship and to associate with prostitutes if respectable women were unavailable. Those who have read Owen Wister's great cowboy novel, *The Virginian,* know that the hero idolized the New England schoolmarm. Before meeting her, however, he was not immune to the charms of less reputable females. Wister recorded this weakness of the Virginian with the delicacy typical of Westerns, thus enabling readers to interpret his actions as they wished. As Wister told the story, an uncouth traveling salesman failed to impress the waitress in an eating place in a small frontier town, but she considered the Virginian a most attractive customer. When the Virginian later galloped off to more serious business elsewhere, he brushed from his coat a hair that looked surprisingly like one of hers. Of course, no one could prove him guilty of wrongdoing on the basis of such flimsy evidence, but his fellow cowboys would have drawn conclusions nevertheless.[3] In the end, the Virginian married the educated, refined schoolmarm and gladly assumed the heavy responsibility of managing a ranch. To him, there were good women and bad, and no responsible member of ranching society could hesitate in making a choice between them.

All observers agreed that women ranked exceptionally high in the cattle kingdom, and a wealth of evidence confirms their conclusions. Superficially, of course, this attitude could be attributed to the scarcity of women, for men continued to outnumber them in the ranch country. Imbalance between the sexes, however, contributed more to the exaggerated courtesy generally shown to women than it did to the basically high regard in which they were held. A Texan who started life as a cowboy recalled years later his embarrassment as a youngster when given the duty of escorting a young lady on a sight-seeing tour of a ranch. Accustomed to the rough and easy association of his outfit, he dreaded the ordeal of conversing with a girl. The manager had assigned her a gentle horse, which the cowboys called "Old Guts" because of the constant rumbling of its digestive organs. Truthful and yet discreet, the cowboy was thrown into considerable confusion when his companion asked the name of her mount. Lamely, he replied that he thought it was called "Old Bowels."[4] Such niceties of language were reserved for one's mother and other good women.

More fundamental explanations account for the high degree of marriage stability in the cattle kingdom. Like farming, ranching was a family enterprise for those fortunate enough to find wives. With them, family life became the focal point of social and economic activities. John C. Jacobs' comment that in fifty years on the cattle range he had never known a cowboy to insult a woman or "to attempt the unpardonable crime" reflected both the strait-laced code and the actuality that prevailed as a rule on the cattleman's frontier.[5] In contrast, white women were non-existent on the fur-trading frontier, and there the white man more often than not displayed little interest in offspring resulting from "marriage" to Indian mates. Although respectable white women could be found in mining camps and towns, they failed often to arouse an enduring loyalty from the masculine element. "Haw" Tabor, one of Colorado's silver kings, abandoned his wife to marry the more exciting "Baby Doe" and to lavish wealth on her. F. Augustus Heinze of Montana did not even bother to marry a series of mistresses. Still others maintained their families in luxury abroad but continued to live in the United States, immersed in business affairs. Indeed, fur traders and many of the western mining magnates must have considered ranchers rather provincial in their attitude.

Women played a prominent role in the cattle kingdom so long as they respected the prevailing code of live and let live. Mrs. Gregor Lang adjusted readily to the Bad Lands environment, although she was well along in her forties when she left the well-to-do, British middle-class society of her family and friends to start a new life on the frontier. Her arrival at the Lang ranch resulted in stoppage of family work on Sunday, less cursing, better grooming, and a more diversified diet of milk, butter, and vegetables in season. Mrs. Lang extended her own high social standards beyond the family circle only by example. She entertained easily and well, and guests responded readily to her code of manners because it never smacked of superiority to the ways of others. Ranchers, cowboys, hunters, trappers, and Indians ate at the Lang ranch without embarrassment. The Lang piano became the talk of the country. One evening twenty-five cowboys appeared to ask the Lang's daughter to play and sing for them, and before the evening ended all participated in group singing.[6]

In contrast, "Deacon" (D. King) Wade and his wife found life most unpleasant at their ranch home some four miles from Roosevelt's Maltese Cross outfit. As his nickname indicated, the Deacon and his Eastern wife irritated other people by trying to force their standards on others. An accomplished woman, Mrs. Wade expected upper-class people to observe the social proprieties to which she was accustomed, even when she invited guests from diverse backgrounds. On one occasion, when Gregor Lang, Roosevelt, and some others ate dinner at her home, Mrs. Wade produced one of her husband's coats for Roosevelt to wear, remarking that she knew he would be uncomfortable dining in shirt sleeves. In doing so, she irritated Roosevelt to the point where he avoided her thereafter. Understandably, the Wades found the West not to their liking and returned to more pleasant surroundings.[7]

Marriages of early-day ranchers to Indian women naturally suffered considerable strain when civilization took over. Cattlemen who made money or achieved prominence could easily come to feel that their Indian mates handicapped them in white society. A few considered such alliances as mere conveniences and terminated them when it seemed socially or materially advantageous. Nevertheless, as one commentator concluded in regard to Wyoming Territory, "a rather numerous company of others" thought of themselves as "married 'for keeps' and were faithful to their wives of tribal blood to the end of their days."[8] Unlike business leaders on the fur-trading frontier, they tended to remain in the region where they made their money. Many of their associates understood the conditions that had fostered inter-marriages only a few years in the past and honored them for fidelity to family obligations in spite of rapidly changing environ-mental conditions. Perhaps, too, the code of live and let live eased the strain on those who refused to desert their Indian wives.

Whatever the explanation, intermarriage between races on the ranching frontier seems not to have involved the same degree of heartache for husbands and wives or so much necessity for adjustment on the part of their children as on the fur-trading frontier. Both Granville and James Stuart remained loyal to their Indian wives. Granville's wife, Aubony (or Ellen), lived until 1887, bore him nine children, and raised two of James' children after his death.[9] John W. Prowers, famous Colorado cattleman, married the daughter of a Cheyenne chief in 1861. She wore her hair in braids throughout her life, learned to speak English only after many years of marriage, and even then spoke her tribal tongue in the home. Prowers remained friendly with her people and presented them with gifts whenever they visited him. At the same time, he educated his children, prospered in ranching, became president of the local bank, and held a number of public offices.[10] E. W. Whitcomb, one of Wyoming's earliest ranchers, built a home on "cattleman's row" in Cheyenne for his half-breed wife and children, and they were highly respected in that com-munity.[11] Quite obviously, no stigma of "squaw man" applied to ranchers married to Indian wives, whether they lived on a ranch or in some cowtown.

Nevertheless, even in the early days, ranchers generally married white women. As a rule, their wives came from the same social strata in which they had been reared, another factor which con-tributed to the stability of marriages in the cattle kingdom. Some brought their wives when they migrated to cattle country; others first obtained a foothold in ranching and then returned home to marry childhood acquaintances. As years passed, it became progressively easier to find wives in the ranching country. Since brides knew the cattleman's frontier either by direct experience or through hearsay, and willingly faced hardships and dangers with their husbands, perhaps those least suited to such a life refused to marry ranchers. At least, ranch wives adjusted to their new environment remarkably well.

Numerous marriages illustrate the pattern. Edward Swan, for instance, was born in Ohio in 1830 in moderate circumstances and moved on at an early age to farming virgin land in Iowa and Indiana. While teaching a rural school in Iowa, he met Catherine Ann Bales, whom he married in 1855. Although her father gave Catherine a pair of hand-made club shoes and a calico dress for her trousseau, Swan considered them unworthy of his bride, and furnished her with store-bought items for the occasion. A justice of the peace married them at her father's modest home. They set out at once on a migratory career which ultimately brought prosperity to them through ranching and investments in real estate. Swan's early consideration for his bride's attire was prophetic of the attention that he lavished on her and their children over the years. Like other ranchers, he shielded his wife as much as possible, more as a matter of fact than wives often thought necessary. In 1882 Swan purchased a home in Salt Lake City which permitted the family to spend winters in town and summers on their ranch, a common pattern among successful cattlemen.[12]

Many Europeans also brought their wives when they came to the ranching frontier. The Marquis de Mores and James Adair both had beautiful wives who matched their own zest for adventure. Pierre Wibaux and his English wife worked well together in managing their Dakota ranch. When he found it necessary to spend a winter in France on business, she proved thoroughly capable of overseeing their American holdings. Although her hired girl committed suicide during that winter, she continued to meet her responsibilities. Gregor Lang's wife proved equally

adaptable and a fitting mistress of his household. Murdo Mackenzie married his childhood sweetheart, Isabella MacBain, and
started a family before coming to America to assume management of ranch property purchased by Scottish investors. His wife
remained at their Trinidad, Colorado, home with the children
during his frequent trips on ranch business, and there she maintained much the same way of life that the family had known in
Scotland.[13] In all these cases, of course, the husbands could afford
to provide good living conditions for their wives, and thus perhaps
felt less compunction about taking them to frontier communities.
Undoubtedly, however, they knew that their mates possessed
adequate strength of character to meet new and sometimes unpleasant challenges. Moreover, the sharing of so many common
values between husband and wife resulted in a high degree of
companionship.

Even less prosperous foreigners dared to bring their wives
directly to the ranching frontier. Marlin Murphy, Jr., was born in
Ireland in 1807, from where he migrated to Quebec. In 1831,
he married Mary Bulger, of Irish Catholic background, and they
settled in Missouri, only to find it uncongenial to their way of
life. The whole Murphy clan moved on to ranch life in California,
where they lived pleasantly with one another and their neighbors
and saw their fortune grow through constantly rising land
values.[14]

Still another group of ranchers established their holdings before
returning to older settlements to claim a wife. Charles Goodnight
blazed his famous trails and laid out a ranch in Colorado before
going to Kentucky to marry his first wife in 1870. At the time,
he was thirty-four and she thirty-one. Goodnight apparently first
met her in Texas and the courtship continued for several years.
Mrs. Goodnight found Colorado ranch life sufficiently adventure-
some to satisfy her, but she faced a much greater test when the
Panic of 1873 virtually bankrupted her husband. He took her
to California to stay while he settled his Colorado losses, and
wanted her to remain there until he could provide comfortable
surroundings in some new location. When Goodnight planned

his new ranching venture in the Texas Panhandle, he urged his wife not to accompany him because of the rough life that lay ahead. To this she would not listen. Consequently, she became a member of the party of eight that set out from Trinidad, Colorado, to establish the new ranch, driving one of the wagon teams all the way. Goodnight's partner, James Adair, and his wife also went along, Mrs. Adair riding horseback. While Goodnight scouted ahead for water at one point on the trip, the rest of the party suffered from what they mistakenly thought was evidence of an impending Indian attack, a possibility real enough to justify apprehension.

When they reached the mesa overlooking the canyon which became the center of their ranch, they gazed down on a herd of grazing buffalo. That night Mrs. Goodnight experienced real terror. Rain fell in torrents; lightning blazed everywhere, with thousands of flashes shimmering on the wagon sheet; and rutting buffalo stampeded madly in the storm. Within a few days, the Adairs returned to civilization, leaving Mrs. Goodnight the only woman for miles around. During the second winter another woman arrived, the wife of a rancher just eighty miles from the Goodnight home. Mrs. Goodnight saw no other woman for six months, and the wind and solitude became a trial to her. She kept busy, however, by patching the clothing of the cowhands and looking after the small building that she called home. A cowboy brought her a sack of three chickens, which soon learned to follow her and to which she talked in moments of loneliness.[15] As elsewhere in the cattle kingdom, the Panhandle rapidly filled with ranches, and the Goodnights prospered in the years ahead. Nevertheless, Goodnight must have chafed at his temporary inability to surround his wife with comforts and the associations of friends. His concern for her welfare and his deference to her wishes in matters of philanthropy demonstrated the close bonds of affection and respect that united them.

Some ranchers, of course, never succeeded sufficiently well to ease the burdens of their families. In early Panhandle days:

Women had only a round of monotonous drudgery. The wives of a few of the big ranchers had men to do the work for them, but most of them endured the same hardships as did the wives of small ranchers and nesters. So little could be hauled in at a time, so much had to be brought in, that they got along with as little as possible and made no protests. They did the family washing though they had but one tub, ironed with but one iron, dried the clothes on the grass because there were no clothes lines, yet kept the family clean. Everybody washed, even women who had never previously rinsed a handkerchief. Scarcity of water and lack of skill gave their clothes a dingy hue until wells were drilled and windmills made their appearance on the plains and water was more abundant. . . . The lives of women were associated with dirt floors, dirt walls, dirt roofs, a pallet or homemade bunk for a bed, homemade furniture of all kinds, a few dishes, insufficient cooking utensils, every inconvenience of living.[16]

They came in hope—and endured with thoughts of better times ahead. Only when one bears in mind the many failures to achieve prosperity does the courage of women like Mrs. Goodnight stand in proper perspective. There was no assurance that discomfort for a few years would lead to wealth and leisure.

Like Goodnight, John W. Iliff wanted to wait until he was established before bringing a wife to the new country, and he was additionally fortunate in escaping the ill effects of the Panic of 1873. Iliff came west in 1856 to Princeton, Kansas, where he spent three years as a merchant before moving to Denver in 1859 to engage in merchandising and cattle trading. Late in 1863 he returned to Princeton for a visit, and on January 11, 1864, married Sarah Elizabeth Smith, who lived with her parents on a homestead near that town. Like Iliff, she was born in Ohio, but the two became acquainted during his residence in Princeton. At the time of their marriage she was twenty-nine and he thirty-three.[17]

Goodnight and Iliff were not unusual in delaying marriage for a considerable period of years, but only a statistical study could determine whether a majority of ranchers conformed to that pattern. Though devoted to his family, Iliff immersed himself in managing his rapidly expanding business empire. Possibly, like Dennis Sheedy, another rancher-entrepreneur, he wanted to delay marriage until it exerted no strain on his finances; but, unlike Sheedy, who waited until age thirty-six to risk part of his bankroll on a helpmate, he never gloated over his financial triumphs.[18] Knowing the hazards of frontier ranching and the burdens that it imposed on women, Iliff and Goodnight very probably thought it unfair to marry any woman until they could hope to shield her from its rougher aspects.

Even the foreign-born cattlemen who remained bachelors during their early years on the ranching frontier were inclined to turn to childhood acquaintances when ready to marry. Conrad Kohrs, Montana rancher and businessman, was born to a middle-class German family in 1835. At age fifteen, dislike for a new stepfather caused him to sign on as cabin boy on a vessel bound for South America and Africa. Adventure, illness, and a variety of jobs came his way in the next few years, and by 1854 he and most of his family were living in the United States. Kohrs tried his hand in the California gold fields and in other mining rushes but soon recognized that a knowledge of sausage-making and butchering afforded greater opportunities than the hit-and-miss life of a placer miner. Through the wholesaling and retailing of meat to mining camps he naturally became interested in ranching on his own.

As soon as Kohrs achieved some prosperity he went east to visit his mother and to marry Augusta Kruse, whom he had known as a child in Europe. Since Augusta grew up in cities, she found the ranching frontier rather forbidding at first. Still, as a German girl, she took pride in her wifely duties, insisted on discharging the male ranch cook, and assumed all the household tasks. She gave birth to her first child without benefit of professional medical attention. When the second child came along, Kohrs was able to pay a doctor one thousand dollars to come to the ranch and stay for a week to supervise the delivery.

Kohrs and his wife had no trouble finding a common scale

Mrs. Conrad Kohrs. (Historical Society of Montana)

Conrad Kohrs. (Historical Society of Montana)

Cattle on Conrad Kohrs' range near Missouri River. (L. A. Huffman photo)

Mrs. John H. Slaughter. (Arizona
Pioneers' Historical Society)

John H. Slaughter. (Arizona Pioneers' Historical Society)

Mrs. John W. Prowers. (State Historical Society of Colorado)

John W. Prowers. (State Historical
Society of Colorado)

Mrs. John B. Kendrick. (University
of Wyoming Library)

John B. Kendrick. (University of
Wyoming Library)

of values for they liked the same things. They indulged a mutual love of travel by visiting the Chicago World's Fair, Mardi Gras in New Orleans, and their old home in Germany. On their return from Europe they purchased their first silverware in New York City and obtained carpets and furniture in Chicago. In 1898 they toured the continent of Europe and made a trip up the Nile River. Mrs. Kohrs also spent a year in their German homeland with the children so they could benefit from the cultural advantages there. In 1899 the Kohrs purchased a home in Helena, Montana, where they spent the rest of their lives. Increasing prosperity enabled Mrs. Kohrs to indulge her love for music, and for many years she went to New York City annually for the Metropolitan Opera season.[19]

A good many ranchers found wives locally in spite of the relative scarcity of white women. Of these, perhaps none attracted more attention than John B. Kendrick and his wife, the former Eula Wulfjen. Their rags-to-riches story thrilled an America devoted to the cult of the self-made man, and all the more so because they came from the frontier where such triumphs supposedly were best achieved. Orphaned at an early age and without financial resources, Kendrick started life as a cowpuncher, rose to prosperity as a rancher, and became Governor and United States Senator from Wyoming. Eula's father, Charles Wulfjen, also began life as a penniless orphan and acquired a ranch of his own. As a child, Eula climbed on the knee of the young cowboy, Kendrick, when he came to her father's ranch looking for work. At seventeen she married him, and they spent two months on a honeymoon trip to Chicago, Niagara Falls, New York, and Washington.

On their return, they settled down on a ranch fifty miles from Sheridan, Wyoming, so isolated that they lacked even a regular mail delivery. Like Mrs. Kohrs, Eula conserved her husband's property. She kept the ranch records and handled much of the business correspondence. She and her husband neglected no opportunity to improve their education. Eula studied German with her cook, who spoke that tongue, and history and science on her own. She heard the lessons of her children in the absence of a school. If necessary, she cooked for the roundup crew at the ranch. When her husband's ranching interests began to prosper, she accompanied him on business trips to distant cities, but his rise to the governorship of their state came so rapidly that she thought it advisable to consult with a Denver merchant concerning the proper clothes to wear to the inaugural ball. Then as always, however, she proved equal to any occasion in her husband's rapidly expanding political and social life.[20] The Kendricks started out from the same backgrounds, possessed the same ambitions, and experienced the same mutual enjoyment of political life that they had known in ranching.

Except possibly for those who stemmed directly from the Old South plantation tradition, ranchers liked women of an independent turn of mind and faith in their ability to take care of themselves. They admired educated women, as did the Virginian in Owen Wister's novel. Efforts to shield their families from unnecessary hardships resulted from pride in their own abilities, not from admiration for helpless females. Luke Brite of the Texas ranching family, for instance, married Miss Eddie Anderson, a schoolteacher from Missouri.[21] J. P. White, Sr., George W. Littlefield's nephew and chief business lieutenant, married Miss Lou Tomlinson of Roswell, New Mexico, in 1903, a young woman who had earned her way as an employee of a local business firm.[22] Similarly, John W. Iliff liked the "spunk" of a young lady with whom he offered to share his buggy seat one day in 1868 while driving in open country. She was Elizabeth Sarah Frasier of Chicago, formerly of Canada, and had come to Denver to open a retail agency for Singer sewing machines. Iliff had to assure Miss Frasier of his gentlemanly intentions before she accepted the proffered ride, even though walking handicapped her efforts to locate prospective customers. She demonstrated her business ability by becoming cashier of the Singer Sewing Machine office in Chicago before Iliff finally persuaded her to marry him in 1870.[23] This was his second marriage, and by now he owned considerable property. As a man who found business a fascinating game, he obviously saw a kindred spirit in a virtuous, business-minded young woman.

Richard King's marriage to Henrietta Chamberlain in 1854 deviated somewhat from the tendency for ranchers to marry women of similar interests. King led a rough life previous to their marriage: as cabin boy; steamboat captain; owner, operator, and chief bouncer of a combination flophouse and saloon; businessman and rancher. He loved a rough-and-tumble life, swore frequently, and found solace in his favorite brand of "Rose Bud" whiskey to the end of his days. Henrietta's father was the Reverend Hiram Chamberlain, a Presbyterian missionary, a graduate of Middlebury College and Princeton and Andover theological seminaries. Imbued with a strong sense of religious duty, Chamberlain left his native Vermont to preach the gospel in frontier regions. King first saw Henrietta in 1850 on her father's houseboat at the Brownsville, Texas, landing, where her family established the first Protestant church on the Rio Grande. Supposedly, King cursed the houseboat for obstructing the landing of his steamboat, and Henrietta rebuked him for his profanity. True or not, the story fitted the character of the two at the time and throughout their lives. Thoroughly committed to her father's ethical and religious standards, Henrietta practiced them on all occasions. Two years of sheltered life in the Female Institute at Holly Springs, Mississippi, where her studies ranged from music to painting flowers on cloth backgrounds, did nothing to weaken Henrietta's independent spirit. At seventeen, she was singing in the choir of her father's church, the First Presbyterian at Brownsville, and had no patience with unregenerate young men.

Perhaps Henrietta's defense of her convictions explains King's immediate infatuation. At least, he attended his first prayer meeting as a means of gaining an introduction. Four years later, Henrietta stepped down from the choir at the close of the service to become his bride. They remained a devoted couple for the rest of his life without either surrendering the personalities they brought to their marriage. To a considerable degree they exemplified the role that marriage played in the cattle kingdom. Like most ranchers, King admired his wife's independence of mind and, like others, he wanted the best for her and their children. She in turn conserved her husband's resources and remained "boss" in her home. King called her Etta, sometimes Pet, and showered her with gifts. When he presented her with a set of expensive diamond earrings, her Presbyterian conscience rebelled against such worldly display, but appreciation of the gift let her compromise sufficiently to have the jewels covered over with enamel and to wear them so disguised. Except for personal handouts to cronies, King left matters of religion and philanthropy in her hands.[24] He took great pride in her background and moral standards, although it proved difficult for him to tone down his language at times when in her presence.

Ranch women in more moderate circumstances needed a large measure of Henrietta King's independence of spirit when they lost a husband. In his account of ranch life in the Dakota Bad Lands, Lincoln Lang recalled having taken Teddy Roosevelt to the Maddox Ranch, which lay twenty-five miles away, so that Teddy could hire "Old Lady Maddox" to make him a suit of buckskin clothes. She had married a buffalo hunter of unsavory reputation but ran him off when she discovered his true nature. About forty years old when the Langs knew her, muscular and heavy set, she showed no fear of the disreputable local elements. She was a dead shot, an excellent cook, hunted her own meat, and made her living by sewing and from the returns of her road ranch.[25]

In the same region, Lloyd Roberts managed a ranch owned by the Eaton brothers of Meadville, Pennsylvania. His wife Margaret had attractive curly hair, with a shimmer of gold, and a jovial, garrulous personality that made her a favorite with all. Of a fearless disposition, she looked after their five little girls and their own small ranch when her husband was absent on business for his employers. During such a trip he disappeared from sight, murdered perhaps by a desperado in Cheyenne, Wyoming. Nevertheless, Mrs. Roberts kept the home ranch and reared and educated their five children.[26]

Even the prosperous could not avoid a measure of loneliness in ranch country. The Spur Ranch of Texas has been described as having neighbors in all directions, but the nearest, the huge Matador spread, lay thirty-five miles to the north. The word "neighbor" thus had a meaning all its own in ranch country. In that region, four large ranches operating under corporate charters dominated the picture, the Spur, the Matador, the Kentucky Land and Cattle Company, and the Llano Land and Cattle Company, but smaller ranches and nesters were also present. The early managers of the four large ranches shared a community of interests, and all were men of broad outlook. Although they maintained harmony with the self-made cattlemen in their region, they were lonely for people of their own kind. They looked forward to entertaining guests from the outside world and wrote letters urging them to come for a visit or for the hunting season. In the spring of 1898 the Spur Ranch enlarged its living quarters for the convenience of visitors. A buggy stood ready to transport guests to and from the railroad station, although it was a two-day trip each way. When H. H. Campbell, manager of the Matador, and his wife stopped overnight on their way to the town of Colorado, they received a warm welcome.[27]

Hospitality did characterize the ranching frontier, and for very good reasons. One could love the open spaces and still feel the need for human companionship. Moreover, in a sparsely settled country without commercial accommodations travelers had to depend upon ranch homes for food and lodging or sleep in the open. By participating universally in the entertainment of travelers, ranchers lessened their own likelihood of being stranded without food or lodging. When R. T. Millard recorded his early experiences in Texas, he headed his sketch with the phrase "The Latch String is Out" in appreciation of early-day hospitality. Still another Texan recalled the "unwritten law" that a woman cheerfully baked bread day or night for any party of cow hunters who rode up to her door with such a request. His own mother willingly baked bread from flour brought to her by cowboys, and they in turn left either a half sack of flour or a money donation.[28] Wandering cowboys and strangers received a free meal and forage for their horses, and knew that no payment was expected. If no one was at home, the traveler supplied his immediate needs from the family larder.

Prosperous ranchers mitigated their loneliness by maintaining homes in town, where they found companionship during slack seasons of ranch work. In the early 1870's, according to Joseph G. McCoy, not one Texas cattleman in ten lived directly on his ranch, preferring instead to reside in some nearby village with a post office or even in a city. On the range they selected a well-watered spot, centrally located in relation to their grazing land, and there they built a rude house and corrals of logs along with a small chute for branding.[29] Such rude accommodations limited family visits to the ranch to short periods of time. Even those who built more elaborate ranch homes were inclined to maintain town houses as well. Many successful cattlemen traveled a great deal to study market conditions, trade in livestock, and dispose of their annual cattle crop. Littlefield and Iliff, for instance, frequently were away from home on business trips, and a town residence served their occupational needs quite as adequately or even better than living directly on their ranches. Town life was thus both pleasant and convenient.

Those who built or bought homes in town seem to have had no particular preference as to architectural styles. George W. Littlefield's red-turreted home on the edge of the University of Texas campus would have fitted nicely among the residences of prosperous businessmen in many Eastern cities. John W. Iliff and his second wife lived at Cheyenne for a time because of its proximity to many of his business interests, but in 1874 they bought the "Shaffenburg Place" in Denver, a two-story brick Victorian house surrounded by an iron fence.[30] The Littlefield and Iliff homes reflected no yearning on the part of their owners for some distinct "ranch style" of architecture; they did advertise the solid financial standing of their occupants, for only a wealthy man could afford them.

Ranchers were only human in wanting to occupy fine homes.

Sam Isaac worked his way up from cowhand and trail boss to owner of a Texas ranch. Following his marriage late in life, he moved to Canadian, Texas, and built the red-brick home of which he had long dreamed. There he continued his habit of rising at an early hour and of thinking in terms of horses and cattle.[31] Like many another rancher, he found in his city home and his connections with the local bank proof of his success, not a new way of life.

Ownership of thousands of acres of land and herds of cattle could well cause a man to want to build for the ages. Perhaps his empire could pass from generation to generation, with his initial success buttressing a dynasty of ranchers bearing the family name. To achieve that, one must put family roots down on the ranch itself, not in a town home. George Miller had such a dream when he built the White House on his 101 Ranch near Ponca City, Oklahoma. It replaced the dugout quarters that he occupied while laying the basis for his empire. Although Miller died before the mansion reached completion, his wife and sons finished that project and added auxiliary buildings until the layout resembled the capital city of a small empire. When the White House burned in 1909, the family naturally built another of similar design, in keeping with their intention of defying fate to terminate their dynastic reign.

Richard King had the same urge to build for the ages in carving out his huge Texas ranch. When Henrietta Chamberlain went there as a bride of twenty-two, ranch headquarters consisted of a cluster of earth-brown wattled huts occupied by King's Mexican vaqueros and their families, a gray tangle of shaggy mesquite corrals, and a gaunt-faced blockhouse and stockade garnished with a brass cannon glinting in the sun, as the biographer of the ranch described it. Henrietta loved the ranch from the first. King let her ride out on the prairies with him, and, when she became tired, he spread a Mexican blanket in the shade of a mesquite tree for her siesta. Religious humility on her part curbed any feeling that she was helping build an eternal earthly empire, but she joined her husband in conserving the material blessings with which God had endowed them. To King, it was enough to build solidly for the future of his family and his descendants.

Within two decades the King ranch quarters became an impressive sight. Visitors marveled at the distance still to be covered in reaching the living quarters after they arrived at the entrance to King's property. The large and commodious home and its many auxiliary buildings nestled in a parklike setting, floored with Bermuda grass and shaded by magnificent trees, a neat and substantial picket fence surrounding the whole. Visitors could see for twenty miles in all directions from a tower or lookout on top of a large brick warehouse. The regular labor force on the "hacienda" exceeded one hundred men. King operated a virtually self-sufficient empire, his employees being equal to any task from forging a horseshoe nail to erecting a fine home.[33] When the original home burned a quarter of a century after King's death, his son-in-law replaced it with a mansion costing $350,000. According to the biographer of the ranch, this structure incorporated Mexican, Moorish, California Mission, Long Island, and Wild Horse Desert architectural designs, but attained a curious grandeur that mellowed to become attractive with the passage of time. Its towers contained stained-glass windows from Tiffany's, but the interior furnishings were utilitarian, plain, and, for the most part, uncomfortable.[34] For many years King also maintained a cottage in Brownsville for family use, but both he and Henrietta considered the ranch their home. Until her death at the age of ninety-two in 1935, she presided over the household and the dinner table at the King Ranch, dominating its daily life to the end.

Since the labor force on most ranches consisted almost wholly of unmarried men, the wives of resident owners or of resident managers largely determined the extent of organized social activities. As a consequence, this varied according to the personalities and interests of the women concerned. Spottswood Lomax, the first resident manager of the Spur Ranch, was born in Virginia, spent two years in Spain as a young man, and lived in St. Louis before migrating to Texas. His men respected him greatly throughout his tenure as manager from 1884 to 1889 because of his many fine qualities. Nevertheless, this tall, slender, sociable, soft-spoken, polished, educated, and widely traveled manager made people around him feel somewhat inferior. Moreover, his wife disliked the isolation and privations of ranch life, and spent very little time at the Spur, preferring to move in Fort Worth society, where Lomax maintained a home for his family. Quite obviously, hands on the Spur Ranch could expect little formal social attention from the Lomaxes, and such was the case.[35]

On the other hand, Mrs. H. H. Campbell, wife of the resident manager of the neighboring Matador, took an active interest in the social life of its cowboys, an interest which extended to hands from nearby ranches as well. From actual experience she and her husband knew how lonely ranch life could be. Starting out with virtually nothing and with little formal education, Campbell advanced rapidly in the cattle business. His wife, the former Lizzie Bundy, married him in 1871 and was a "neighbor" of Mrs. Goodnight when their husbands pioneered in the Texas Panhandle. Mrs. Campbell opened the Panhandle social whirl by giving a Christmas dance in 1882, and continued it as an annual event until her husband severed connections with owners of the Matador in 1890.[36] In addition, she sponsored religious services for those who cared to attend.

Owen Wister's description of the pleasure derived from community dances in the cattle kingdom is substantiated in surviving accounts of Christmas dances on the Matador. Mrs. Campbell has been remembered as beautiful, capable, and dignified, with the accent of an aristocrat and a real fondness for the ranch hands. Whether she literally possessed all of those admirable traits or not, ranch hands obviously thought she did because of their appreciation for her kindnesses. At the first Matador Christmas dance in 1882, the six women present gathered from a distance of fifty miles in all directions. Over fifty men attended from the same region. Ben Brock, headquarters cook, and Bud Browning furnished the music, the latter being too religious to dance but not to fiddle for the better part of the two nights and a day that the gathering lasted. Annually, Mrs. Campbell prepared food to serve from fifty to one hundred people for a three-day period. After the first meal on the first night of the dance, people ate buffet style when they pleased for the remainder of their stay. Dancing went on almost constantly. When exhaustion compelled celebrants to drop out for an hour or two of sleep, women bedded down on the floor of the ranch house and men looked out for themselves. Quadrilles, waltzes, and schottisches were all popular. Mrs. Campbell forbade drinking and quarreling on such occassions, and her wishes were generally respected. Everyone was welcome to come and many looked forward to the dance from one year to another.[37]

Whether living in town or directly on a ranch, cattlemen and their families gravitated most of all to informal social life or to organized community-wide activities involving family participation. Husbands belonged to restricted organizations like the Cheyenne and Helena Clubs but most of them spent little time there. Although Conrad Kohrs belonged to the Helena Club, the obituary sketch of his wife spoke of the family preference for home life, church activities, YMCA work, and travel.[38] Similarly, when the King family occupied their Brownsville cottage, they visited informally with their friends, the Kenedys, next door and took little interest in "the Brick House Crowd," the term applied to local residents of fine homes who mingled freely with army people stationed on the border. Mrs. King preferred homemaking duties and her church; her husband liked best of all a cup or a frolic with male companions in less formal surroundings.[39] When Dennis Sheedy penned his autobiography, his pomposity and self-esteem caused him to list memberships in the Denver Club, the Denver Country Club, and the Denver Athletic Club, but he seems to have been quite sincere and accurate in saying that he took little active part in such organizations, his home being his club and his intimate friends his chief source of pleasure.[40]

Many prosperous cattlemen lacked time and opportunity for formal social activity during their early years. In maturity, they felt no need for it. They did appreciate comfortable homes and leisure to visit with those who had shared the pattern of their early lives.

They also liked to travel with their wives and children. As soon as he could afford it, George W. Littlefield took his wife with him on combined business and pleasure trips until her health no longer permitted. In 1869 the Littlefields could buy only the bare necessities out of a total income of one hundred and fifty dollars for the year. By 1873 Mrs. Littlefield could write home of her hopes that she and the Major would come "whirling" home to Gonzales, Texas, on the new railroad from Council Bluffs, Iowa, where she had accompanied him on business. Because of her Southern plantation background, she preferred Negro serv-ants, but on trips north with her husband she learned to accept the services of whites without feeling uncomfortable. During her stay in Council Bluffs she enjoyed release from the sweltering summer heat of their Gonzales home and thought how hard it was to live there without "a single iced soda or plate of ice cream." During another stay in Omaha with the Major she indulged in as many as three glasses of "soda" a day, an indica-tion of how much she relished the simple pleasures that family prosperity afforded after the lean post-Civil War years.[41] Sim-ilarly, Captain Richard King's family traveled frequently, ac-companying him on business trips or meeting him in Galveston, San Antonio, New Orleans, St. Louis, and other cities as he shuttled back and forth on cattle deals.[42] Both King and Littlefield liked to indulge their families on such occasions and to travel in the finest available style. Scenic spots like Niagara Falls and major expositions like the Chicago World's Fair also attracted many a ranch family bent on having a holiday.

Those with European backgrounds naturally desired to visit their homeland and for their children to become acquainted with its culture. Murdo Mackenzie and his family returned to their native Scotland on several occasions. Although Mackenzie, like

Conrad Kohrs, became a naturalized American citizen and loved his adopted country, he was more nearly a world citizen. In 1911 Mackenzie moved his family to Brazil for eight years, where he managed an enormous ranching venture involving twenty-five million dollars in capital assets. Wherever he lived, Mackenzie dressed well, loved to play the fiddle, and indulged his interest in hunting and fishing.[43] His family adjusted equally as well.

Of all ranchers who visited foreign countries, Shanghai Pierce could be expected to react most volubly, and he ran true to form. Born and reared in Rhode Island, he became a prosperous Texas rancher before getting the itch to visit Europe. In 1891 this transplanted Yankee took his wife and the daughters of a friend on a European tour. Unfortunately, pursuit of culture frayed the women's nerves to the point of quarreling, which dampened Shang's normally bouncy spirits. As for himself, he tried to see important people and cows at all stops. He came home with a new crop of stories to entertain his friends at San Antonio. According to one, when Shang's party reached Rome they decided to visit the Pope. As Shang and the ladies marched down a long hall at the Vatican, they found a guard blocking the way. Shang offered him fifty cents to let them through and, on refusal, raised the bribe to seventy-five cents. When the guard still refused to cooperate, Shang gave up, knowing from his understanding of foreigners that if one could not bribe an Italian for seventy-five cents it was useless to offer more. Still, he saw the Vatican and the Quirinal, and gazed out upon the Seven Hills. At that point in his narrative, fat old Dillard Fant interrupted to inquire if he saw any of the Papal Bulls at the Vatican. "Nary a damn critter. Nary a critter," replied Shang, "but I did see some fine old cows out there, just out of town."[44]

Shang's Yankee shrewdness had not deserted him simply because he had turned to cattle ranching in Texas as a career. The necessity of looking at so much statuary with the women of his party gave him an idea of how to perpetuate his own fame as a most unusual person. After his return to America, he paid a San Antonio sculptor to make a "fair likeness" of him, bigger than the statue of any Confederate general, and erected this as his future monument in a Texas cemetery. To make his act all the more impressive, Shang boasted that the statue cost him twenty thousand dollars. Such was his contribution of European culture to the Texas cattle kingdom.[45]

Self-made and self-satisfied, Shanghai Pierce could scarcely be expected to pay tribute to women's importance in the cattle kingdom. In his constant self-esteem, however, he did manifest the rugged individualism that characterized his fellow ranchers.

The Cult of the Self-Made Man

THE cattle kingdom neither created nor monopo-
lized the cult of the self-made man. Well before
the Civil War William Holmes McGuffey's *Readers* indoctrinated
Midwestern farm boys with its precepts, and industrialists in the
urban East explained and justified their success in terms of its
gospel. Ranchers could and did, however, contribute to its popularity. As dedicated and vocal apostles of the cult, they extended
its message both geographically and in point of time. Indeed, their
fervent devotion to it became a major characteristic of their role
in Western society.

The gospel of self-help flourished in range country partially
because so many different agencies emphasized the opportunities available there. Eastern and European promoters, state
and local governments, railroads and chambers of commerce all
urged prospective settlers to become wealthy by raising cattle
on free public lands. According to them, a minimum of initiative
and ability was sufficient to assure success under the circumstances. Superior opportunities also lessened any need for government help, thus paving the way for individual achievement. So
ran the advertising.

Moreover, the cattle kingdom furnished much evidence to
confirm the self-help philosophy. A considerable number of poor
boys did become wealthy ranchers. A sizable number of them

also started out on frontiers devoid of law enforcement agencies and could justly claim that society furnished them little aid in their early struggles. Everywhere, cattlemen witnessed enormous improvements in livestock through selective breeding. Did not the same principle apply to humans? Was not good blood sufficient to assure success? Murdo Mackenzie and Teddy Roosevelt were inclined to think so. Their early associations quickly ripened into a "mutual admiration society," each considering the other a superior breed of man. Supposedly, Mackenzie said that one of the bulls on the Matador Ranch looked like Roosevelt, having the same squareness of face and rugged appearance. Mackenzie wanted to buy and use still more bulls of that type on the Matador.[1] Similarly, Dan Dillon Casement, a widely known cattle breeder, concluded that every man's nature was determined by the sources of his blood stream, and that environment could not alter fundamentals.[2] Since Casement came from a prosperous family, he could scarcely call himself self-made, but he obviously emphasized innate abilities most heavily in explaining success. Men like him and Charles Goodnight recognized the extent to which nature handicapped or eliminated the weakling. They did not expect all men to rise in the world, and they could not help but feel that blood would tell.

This cult of the self-made man found expression in the early 1870's in Joseph G. McCoy's account of the cattle trade. For instance, after describing W. H. Kingsberry's hard struggles, self-denial, and economy in his early years, McCoy concluded:

Men who in their youth receive a thorough drilling in adversity, and thus not only learn the intrinsic value of a dollar but how to make and take care of one, invariably make earth's most successful business men. . . .[3]

McCoy praised Charles Goodnight in much the same way, calling him a fine example of the many energetic young men in the West. Goodnight's early life as a poor farm boy had fitted him for privations and labors; nature gave him the superior talents and moral character necessary for command. His success was as deserved as it was great. McCoy had often heard people say that in ninety-nine cases out of a hundred inherited wealth was only a curse. Although unwilling to go so far in his own convictions, he knew one thing for certain—999 of every 1,000 successful men in the West began life extremely poor in cash assets. They were rich only in energy and manly determination. The best inheritance consisted of a clear, well-developed, and educated mind; good, fixed moral principles; energy and honorable ambition; and the necessity for self-exertion. One did not inherit business principles; he must learn them, and the best time for that was in one's youth.[4]

McCoy also praised Dennis Sheedy, a paragon of virtue who took delight throughout his life in extolling his own thrift, hard work, and high moral character. McCoy traced Sheedy's career from age twelve in Massachusetts, when he found himself on his own following his father's death from a broken heart occasioned by loss of the family fortune. McCoy told of Sheedy's fainting while doing hard work in his early Western days and of others laughing at him for his weakness. But he persevered and became a rich man. After acquiring a fortune, he sought to adorn his mind so he could walk in life upon a higher plane than mere love of money. McCoy pictured him as impulsive and warm in manner, kind and courteous, but reticent and reserved among strangers. Moreover, he was free from the ordinary vices.[5]

Sheedy's own autobiography reveals him as an ambitious, cautious, and highly successful trader who took full credit for his own success. He claimed to have led a very eventful life and that he helped to "make the West." In spite of early misfortunes and later challenges, such as Indian raids, cattle thieves, and even plots by desperadoes to kill him, he had gained success. He urged those tempted to conclude that small boys could more easily fight their way to success in early days to recognize that growth of population and business offered even greater opportunities in the modern world. One needed only to look around to see the boys who would become the captains of industry in the future. Sheedy's career furnished them a blueprint to follow.

As a boy, he raised rabbits, an evidence of his early business precocity; later he read Blackstone and the classics as a means of self-improvement. Sheedy boasted of a common saying throughout the cattle country: "Dennis Sheedy always finds the cheapest market when he buys, and the highest market when he sells."[6] Other businessmen may have thought well of him, but cowboy employees considered him stingy and inclined to skimp on food. Apparently, one of the cowboy songs used to quiet animals at night in Sheedy's part of the country elaborated on the less savory aspects of his rise to wealth.[7]

Jerome Churchill of California surpassed even Sheedy in praising himself as self-made. Sheedy granted that he came from good stock, but Churchill frankly said: "I never inherited anything from my parents, I helped to support them before I was of age, and I supported them for years before they died." Even a penniless orphan surpassed Churchill's start in life because he had to support a family from the very first. But he overcame that handicap, as well as many a loss by fire and flood, his energy and thrift carrying him on to fortune. He assured an interviewer engaged in writing him up for a price in one of the "mug" books of the period that he had never had what one might call luck: his gains had always come through economy and perseverance in the school of hard knocks. Churchill considered himself "entirely" self-made.[8]

Although Sheedy and Churchill boasted far more than most business men involved in ranching, others were equally sure that their success came from their own abilities and efforts. A number of biographies in the *Trail Drivers of Texas* emphasize the rags-to-riches theme, and still more speak of achieving comfortable prosperity. J. B. Pumphrey, for instance, boasted of having worked eighteen hours a day for seventeen dollars a month at age seventeen in 1869. Looking back as a wealthy man, he remembered when individuals worked for their living, and without thought of short hours and big pay.[9] Still other ranchers made their point by understatement. Samuel R. Gwin, a self-made Wyoming cattleman, was far less wordy than Jerome Churchill when interviewed for inclusion in a "mug" book. Gwin was downright laconic. Nevertheless, pride in his foresight and achievements shone through his answer to a request for information concerning his hardships and privations in pioneer days: "None at all. Went well prepared."[10] Thus, the self-made rancher listed his early troubles as proof of his capacity to rise above them or claimed that foresight had enabled him to escape the difficulties that tripped the less successful.

Everywhere in the cattle kingdom examples existed of the self-made rancher. Without doubt, a commentator in a Fort Worth, Texas, livestock paper in 1882 could have cited many specific names to buttress his comment that most of the Texas cattle kings had been cowboys only a few years in the past.[11] Kendrick, Kohrs, Goodnight, Littlefield, Pierce, King, Iliff, Swan, Kenedy, and many others built their fortunes from scratch. Owen Wister's novel, *The Virginian,* thus had a solid basis in fact for its story of the rise of the cowboy financially to ranch management and socially to marriage with the schoolmarm in whose veins flowed the blood of Revolutionary War ancestors. One commentator has even suggested that Wister illustrated Spencer's and Sumner's theme of the survival of the fittest in *The Virginian,* and that George Horace Lorimer welcomed cowboy and ranch stories to the pages of the *Saturday Evening Post* because they so aptly bulwarked the philosophy of self-help and rugged individualism.[12]

Only a statistical study, however, would reveal the degree to which ranching surpassed other occupations in percentage of self-made men, if in actuality it did. Many of those who contributed sketches to the *Trail Drivers of Texas* recognized the highly speculative nature of the ranching industry, and that a man could achieve prosperity and then lose everything through accident or a surprising turn in market conditions. J. F. Ellison, for instance, prospered for several years by driving cattle to distant markets but suffered financial reverses in 1880 which he never fully overcame.[13] C. S. Brodbent's sketch quite properly bore the title "Lost Many Thousands of Dollars." According to him, trail driving did not automatically produce halcyon days of easy

Captain Richard King. (King Ranch, Inc.)

D. H. Snyder. (Barker Texas History Library)

Major George W. Littlefield. (Barker Texas History Library)

Captain Burton C. Mossman, 1936. (Arizona Pioneers' Society)

Left, A. H. (Shanghai) Pierce, 1874. (From McCoy, *Historic Sketches*)

Below, John W. Iliff. (State Historical Society of Colorado)

Three Block trail outfit of New Mexico en route to Kansas in 1898. (Barker Texas History Library)

money. Many a prosperous Texan went broke; many a Kansas farmer who bought cattle dirt cheap found himself financially embarrassed when drouth sharply reduced his supply of livestock forage. Still, Brodbent insisted that the man counted for more than the occupation in determining success or failure.[14] Recognition of the highly speculative nature of ranching tempered the self-made man theme but did not eradicate it from the volume.

George W. Saunders, a prominent member of the Trail Drivers Association, estimated that some 35,000 men accompanied herds up the trail. Quite obviously, biographies of only a limited number of them could be included in the *Trail Drivers of Texas*. Although some of those honored achieved only a moderate degree of success, and a few not even that, those who failed completely served only as a shadowy backdrop for the more successful. Only about a third of those involved participated in more than one drive. According to Saunders, a third of the whole group consisted of Mexicans and Negroes, racial minorities that seldom shared in the rewards of the self-made man. Moreover, Saunders estimated that about one hundred of the men included in the volume and their connections handled fully 75 per cent of all the cattle and horses driven to the North from Texas.[15] Such evidence indicates very definitely that the lesser fry and the rank-and-file cowhands failed to achieve sufficient prosperity to convince them of the immutable workings of the law of the self-made man.

Nor did the average American cowboy care particularly about financial success. He disliked the stinginess of a Dennis Sheedy and disagreed with Jerome Churchill's dictum that it was more fun to make money than to spend it. Since possession of money gave Churchill a sense of independence, he refused to squander it. To many a cowboy, however, money had one purpose: to be spent on a good time. John Clay had ample opportunity to observe cowboys while supervising ranches for a period of years. He thought that Easterners tended to invest them with an air of romance, an attitude intensified by the influence of Wister's novel, *The Virginian*. Occasionally Clay came across such personalities in range country, men who were simple-minded, generous, and with just enough of the cavalier about them to fascinate women. They took life more seriously as they grew older, becoming good citizens on the range and elsewhere, and generally did well financially. The ordinary cowboy, however, degenerated, drifted, disappeared, or worse still became a saloonkeeper. Clay never saw an old cowpuncher; where they disappeared to remained a mystery.[16] Having no interest in becoming self-made men financially, cowboys in general felt little urge to apotheosize the philosophy underlying that urge.

Ranchers and cowboys alike, however, expressed allegiance to individualism from the earliest days of the cattle kingdom. In describing ranchers and drovers, Joseph G. McCoy used word after word that correlated nicely with that concept. Such men were hardy, self-reliant, free, and independent, and acknowledged no superior or master in the whole wide universe. Possessed as they were with a strong innate sense of right and wrong, they quickly resented any infringement on their freedoms.[17] In a highly cosmopolitan society committed to a live-and-let-live philosophy, cowboy and cattleman could expect to find toleration for their individual points of view. Nor did government itself exert heavy pressure in favor of conformity.

Nevertheless, some varieties of individualism failed to flourish on the ranching frontier. There seems, for instance, to have been little urge to move on beyond the bounds of organized society simply to escape its limitations. Ranchers favored an orderly existence conducive to raising and marketing cattle, not a philosophical anarchism that would remove all of society's restraints. Since there was seldom a labor shortage in range country, cattlemen could select employees who agreed with their views. Moreover, cattleman and cowboy alike displayed little addiction to unique ways of living or to distinct sets of values contrary to those accepted by the common run of people. Even in matters of dress they were conformists. Granted that they found their common uniform well suited to their occupational needs, it still demonstrated a preference for utility over individualism.

The principles underlying "rugged individualism" proved far more to their liking. Involved here was the concept of the rights of private property, which could be acquired by prescription quite as much as by outright purchase or gift. Included, too, was the idea that government should promote the economic fortunes of the individual and should restrict him only when he transgressed on the property rights of others. Moreover, the government should punish crimes such as murder and theft, but could not hope by its very nature to succeed so well in the field of economic enterprise as individuals dominated by the profit motive. Only in terms of "rugged individualism" can one make a strong case for individualism on the ranching frontier. In that sense a somewhat common role did exist, although it was not unique to the cattle kingdom.

As rugged individualists who opposed governmental paternalism, ranchers cooperated freely with one another. They agreed as to the number of bulls each cattleman must maintain on open range where herds intermingled. They returned strays to their rightful owners without charging for that service. Ranches provided shelter and aid to all travelers and help to neighboring outfits in case of accident, illness, or other need. Everywhere, community roundups developed at an early date, and associations of stockmen to handle common problems met with widespread approval. Convenience, economy, and necessity all played a part in fostering such cooperation. As in any joint effort, individual ranchers occasionally objected to decisions that did not exactly fit their needs, but they approved the over-all principles which lay behind these. They cooperated in determining dates for roundups, the number of hands to be furnished from each ranch, the method for handling mavericks, and in a multitude of other common procedures. As a matter of fact, they proudly assumed leadership in forming cooperative undertakings. In 1885, James E. Temple of New Mexico Territory told an interviewer that he had promoted the recently formed cattleman's association in his community, a move occasioned by a need for a greater number of bulls on the common range and other problems. The expected improvement took precedence in Temple's mind over any curbing of individual freedom.[18]

Since necessity often compelled early-day cattlemen to rely upon their own resources, their actions created a superficial impression that individual effort constituted the preferred way of life. In dangerous situations, however, even such able men as Charles Goodnight cooperated with other drovers in moving cattle to markets. In doing so, they surrendered the possibility of obtaining very high prices by arriving at their destination ahead of competitors, but safety through cooperation weighed more heavily with them. In the fall of 1868 Goodnight met with other stockmen in his community in southern Colorado to create "local regulations as to the grazing of stock." In November, 1871, he and others formed a stock raisers' association to plan roundups, record brands, condemn the driving of cattle except by their owners, terminate the releasing of scrub bulls on open range, and to warn sheepmen to stay off the range occupied by cattlemen.[19] Throughout his life Goodnight acted alone when necessary and welcomed cooperation when available. He obviously was no doctrinaire individualist.

Cattlemen's associations proved flexible enough to care for a wide variety of needs. Richard King and other ranchers on the northern bank of the Rio Grande formed an association to curb cattle rustling and to exert pressure on both the United States government and Texas to compel Mexico to cooperate in protecting American ranch property from raids across the border.[20] As a rugged individualist, King saw nothing wrong with government aid to private enterprise in this case. Colonel George W. Miller and other ranchers who grazed cattle on the Cherokee Outlet formed an association in 1883 to lease all unoccupied government land locally for five years at an annual rental of one hundred thousand dollars. The association then subleased the land to its members at a rate sufficient to cover the annual payment.[21] Ranchers' associations were so numerous that one can scarcely pick up a book or article on the subject of ranching without finding one or more examples. This spirit of cooperation must be given full recognition in any definition of individualism on the ranching frontier. Ranchers definitely preferred cooperation to competition when the latter would lead to chaos or seriously affect common interests.

Moreover, ranching involved a considerable measure of paternalism, especially on the part of those who owned or managed spreads of considerable size. Richard King's biographer describes him as a blend of steamboat captain and hacienda patriarch in his attitude toward his Mexican vaqueros and other employees. He looked after them when they were sick or injured and reduced the work load for elderly employees with many years of service to their credit. Profit sharing and specific programs for social security still lay in the future. As a product of his time, King handled his business as he saw fit, and would have considered it a reflection on his own innate sense of rightness if anyone had questioned his fairness in dealing individually with employees. Similarly, Colonel Joe Miller displayed his paternalistic outlook in his famous phrase "Come in, children" when he welcomed guests to his ranch, for it also reflected his attitude toward employees. He loved the role of benevolent father to guest, Indian tribesman, and employee alike. In playing that role, it is doubtful if he realized the extent to which it lessened opportunity for others to express their own individuality. Although Charles Goodnight and other ranchers in his section acted in the interest of efficiency when they instituted rules governing the personal lives of cowboy employees, they were at the same time insisting upon their right to set any standard of conduct that appealed to them. In doing so, they exemplified the same rugged individualism that characterized American business leaders everywhere in the United States.

The ramifications of the concept of rugged individualism are revealed even more fully in problems connected with the use of public lands for grazing purposes. John W. Iliff's holdings illustrate how such problems could arise. The inventory of his estate following his death in 1878 listed ownership of 105 parcels of range land totaling 15,558 acres in 54 different locations. Of these, 44 consisted of 40-acre tracts; 27 of 80 acres each; 15 of 160-acre size; and others as small as 14 acres in extent. He had acquired the land to obtain control of water and as sites for ranch headquarters and line camps, the latter consisting of lesser improvements for occupation by cowboys assigned to care for herds of cattle on the open range. One company used the term "range pirates" to designate those who turned cattle loose without owning water rights and prescriptive possession of range in sufficient quantity to maintain them. Iliff's pattern of land ownership freed him from the likelihood of ever having such an accusation made against him. Nevertheless, by owning only a very small amount of land he exerted a considerable measure of control on a range extending one hundred miles from the eastern boundary of Colorado and for sixty miles north and south.[22] A few ranchers, like Richard King, bought at an early date most of the land upon which they grazed their herds but others delayed until pressure of population made it impossible to round out their holdings. Virtually everywhere this problem was sure to lead to trouble. Homesteaders complicated matters by laying out farms directly on range lands that ranchers had come to consider their own bailiwick through prescriptive use. Solutions ranged all the way from outright murder of those who dared to trespass, as ranchers saw it, to a graceful giving away to the inevitable spread of population.

To the extent that ranchers defied government policies in efforts to maintain their hold on public lands they qualified as rugged individualists of the most extreme sort. In the famous Johnson County War of the early 1890's, ranchers overstepped the bounds of propriety to the point where even the newspapers that relied on them for advertising criticized their arrogant disregard for the rights of others. When an editorial against the so-called highhanded methods employed by the ranchers appeared in the Cheyenne *Sun,* published in the "Holy City of the Cow," the rancher's association demanded that the editor appear before it to explain his action. Newspapers stood firm in that crisis, however, leaving blank pages in their editions where ranch advertisements normally appeared. The Cheyenne *Leader,* backed by the *Sun,* deplored the un-American spirit of dominance that would force "the weaker elements to immigrate or crawl, cowed and subdued, to the feet of the fierce and implacable oligarchy."[23]

Whether wealthy or not, ranchers were easily subject to attack as big businessmen intent upon eliminating the little fellow. Even the smaller ranchers needed a considerable acreage to sustain their pastoral occupation, and, to the uninformed, that marked them as plutocrats. In their battles, legal and otherwise, to hold the line against a rising tide of settlers they thus became known as "cattle-raising monopolists." When Henry Moore Teller, Secretary of the Interior, visited Denver in 1883, a local reporter interviewed him concerning frequent complaints made by "small herders, who, like the little fish in the sea, are fast being gobbled by the bigger ones." Teller assured the reporter that the government understood the need for action and would take steps to eliminate injustices. When asked how the large rancher carried out his attack against the little fellow, Teller replied:

One process is by fencing the plains, and the other is by covering the ranges with great herds of cattle, to the exclusion of the herds of the humble ranchman. The man with many completely absorbs the lesser number, so that when the round-up takes place it is almost impossible for the little fellow to get out his herd, especially if the big fellow is tricky or bears a grudge.[24]

In spite of being castigated as a united group bent upon monopolizing the public lands, ranchers differed markedly among themselves as to land policy. Charles Goodnight said that if the Plains proved suitable for farming, it would be foolish for ranchers to oppose the inevitable drift to that economy. Others refused to be so philosophical. Moreover, Goodnight found himself in opposition to several different points of view. In 1880 Panhandle ranchers agreed that it would be best to try to lease the state land on which they were located, if it could not be purchased outright. When Goodnight and an attorney lobbied for that policy in the Texas legislative session of 1881, free-grassers in West Texas succeeded in defeating his program. Instead, the legislature passed the Land Board Act of 1883, which provided for ten-year leases at a minimum of four cents an acre annually and competitive sale of as many as seven sections per individual. Since ranchers already had the range divided by established practice, they all bid the minimum lease fee for the land that they occupied, an action that led to charges of collusion on their part. At least, by tacit agreement they defeated the intention of the act to enforce competitive bidding for use of range lands. When the Land Board took matters into its own hands and set higher lease rates, a legal battle resulted, with newspapers, cattlemen, and citizens alike very much excited.

To charges that large cattlemen like himself wanted to graze their cattle free of charge on public lands and to erect illegal fencing, Goodnight replied that he opposed the free-grass idea because it meant that land would go to the strongest, the six-shooter and free grass being essential parts of one and the same system. Goodnight argued that reasonable range rents and permission to fence land would make for a prosperous economy, for only in that way could cattlemen hope to breed up their stock and stabilize their operations. Lacking direct experience with ranching, East Texans thought the lease law favored large ranchers; Goodnight and his group insisted on their right to occupy the range by submitting the minimum legal bids; and West Texans wanted free grass and open range. When the latter fostered a legislative bill to remove all fences on government land, Goodnight's group paid a lobbyist five thousand dollars to defeat the measure. In carrying out his assignment, the lobbyist purposely misinformed the legislature as to Goodnight's real views, saying that he really favored free grass but took the opposite position in public because he knew that people would want to vote against the expressed wishes of the large ranchers.[25] In such fights, rugged individualism alone can define the stands taken, insofar as individualism had anything at all to do with matters so patently swayed by self-interest of competing groups. In every case, such groups wanted the hand of government to promote but not to curb their own individual enterprises. Moreover, ranchers proved quite as adept as the East Texans in cooperating for common ends.

Ranchers also understood the advantages of a monopolistic position, as witnessed by their acquisition of water rights on range lands, and they applied the principle in other ways as well. Richard King and his associates long held a virtual monopoly of steamboat transportation on the Rio Grande, buying out competitors when they could not be eliminated in other ways. When railroad competition threatened, they obtained a railroad charter from the Texas legislature and then refused to build the line. This led to revocation of their charter by the legislature and the granting of a new one to a group of "antimonopolists." When obstructive suits initiated by King's group to block the construction of a railroad failed of their purpose, he and his partners sold out their steamboat interests.[26] King's philosophy found continued expression in the career of his grandson, Richard Kleberg, who served in the United States Congress from 1932 to 1944. An admirer of John Nance Garner, another conservative Texan, Kleberg believed that the New Deal was violating "Old-Time Principles" and so voted against much of its program.[27] Like the descendants of Charles Schreiner, early-day Texas merchant and rancher, he stood for a free enterprise system that found its antecedents in the rugged individualism of the cattle kingdom.

Edna Ferber's novel, *Giant,* and the motion picture based on it present ranchers as arrogant people inclined to think only of their own tastes and desires. Although that type of individualism was less prevalent in the cattle kingdom than the more fundamental convictions previously mentioned, it did exist to some degree. Again, Richard King perhaps constitutes the outstanding example. Even his best friends considered him "violently opinionated" on all matters, and his sense of right reached its peak of intensity in affairs concerning his wife and children. Sometimes, when he had indulged his fondness for Rose Bud whiskey, he embarrassed them by his protective impulses. On one occasion, his wife was entertaining a lady friend at dinner in a Galveston hotel when King arrived from New Orleans somewhat inebriated. Noticing that his wife's guest was having trouble cutting her meat, King ordered the waiter to replace it with a better piece. Failing to obtain immediate compliance, King marched across the street, ordered a complete meal, had waiters bring it over, and demanded that the table be cleared. When the local waiter again hesitated to comply, King jerked away the tablecloth, spilling dishes and food alike upon the floor, smoothed out a new cloth upon the table, and, riveting the waiters with his pale eyes, said to them "now, serve *that* one." When the family visited San Antonio they always occupied the same rooms at the Menger Hotel. Arriving there on one occasion hot and tired from a long trip, King asked that a pitcher of water be sent at once to his wife's room. Because of a short delay in meeting his request, King took the empty pitcher from his wife's stand to the balcony overlooking the lobby and dropped it on the marble floor below, where it smashed into many pieces. To the startled staff and onlookers King remarked that if he couldn't get any water for the family rooms, they had no need for an empty pitcher.[28]

Shanghai Pierce supposedly even bought a hotel in order to have his way. On a trip to Hot Springs, Arkansas, to try the waters of that health resort, he could not obtain reservations at the hotel where he wished to stay. Suspecting that the clerk considered him undesirable, Shang bellowed, "Then, by God, Sir. Is this hotel for sale?" Being informed that it was, Shang purchased a half interest, thus restoring his self-esteem.[29] Men accustomed to having their own way on enormous ranches could easily find the inconveniences of travel irksome, but few seem to have gone to the lengths that Captain King and Colonel Pierce occasionally thought necessary.

Addicted as they were to the cult of the self-made man and rugged individualism, they did feel that private enterprise surpassed government activity in economic efficiency. When J. P. White, Sr., and his cronies visited the Panama Canal Zone, they speculated as to the wisdom, difficulties, and cost of that project. They agreed that the government should have maintained three eight-hour shifts to speed up construction, but generously admitted that labor's monopolistic position made that impossible. But they also agreed that gross mismanagement and enormous waste accompanied construction of the canal, the inevitable result of government red tape in their opinion.[30]

As rugged individualists, ranchers saw nothing wrong with bigness, even to the point of monopoly, so long as all sections of the business community behaved properly in relations with others. Like Teddy Roosevelt, whose economic philosophy was influenced by the ranching frontier, they differentiated between good and bad business, and not according to size. Government intervention was anathema to them except as it curbed the excesses of "bad" business or promoted the welfare of the private business world.

These principles governed the cattleman's relations with the railroads. Since the trans-Mississippi lines often extended rails in advance of settlement, they found it imperative to develop the countryside in order to have sufficient traffic to survive. Consequently, they eagerly sought the cattleman's business, gave him free passes, cooperated in establishing convenient loading points, and reduced shipping rates for those who marketed large numbers of livestock. When John Clay attended his first meeting of the Wyoming Stock Growers Association in 1884, he heard no criticism of railroads, stockyards, or packers, all of which came under attack within a few years. Instead, many railroad men, mostly from the traffic departments, and representatives of Chicago commission houses mingled freely and amiably with the ranchers in efforts to promote business.[31] As late as 1887, when Theodore Roosevelt attended the annual meeting of the Montana Stock Growers Association, he had trouble in defeating a report blaming part of the stockman's troubles on the passage of the Interstate Commerce Act. Some ranchers felt that the act prevented them from obtaining rate reductions that would have eased their problems in that troublous period.[32]

In the long run, however, ranchers became convinced that federal regulation of railroad rates would benefit their economy, and they actively supported such legislation. Even the large cattle corporations found it increasingly difficult to obtain acceptable agreements from the railroads. As early as 1896, Murdo Mackenzie, manager of the great Matador spread, began to agitate for enlargement of the powers of the Interstate Commerce Commission. As president or as an active member of several cattlemen's organizations, Mackenzie urged governmental agencies and the railroads to give serious consideration to the advisability of closer regulation. Since he earned several thousand dollars yearly through his entrepreneurial skill, Mackenzie acted through no hostility toward the structure and methods of big business as a whole. When a committee representing the National Live Stock Association failed to obtain satisfactory agreements with the railroads on the rate problem in 1907, Mackenzie reluctantly assumed a major role in agitation for strengthening the powers of the Interstate Commerce Commission. He appeared several times before that agency and provided statistical data for use in its hearings. Perhaps his greatest contribution lay in his ability to harmonize conflicting suggestions on the part of the cattlemen whom he represented. When the Hepburn Act passed in 1906, Mackenzie thanked Roosevelt for supporting the measure, and the President in turn acknowledged Mackenzie's great influence in making the triumph possible.[33]

Ranchers also began to talk of a packer's monopoly in Chicago that set livestock prices much as it pleased. An article in the Santa Fe, New Mexico, paper in 1886, headed "Cast off the Yoke," criticized the power of men like Philip D. Armour, who was said to handle the slaughtering and marketing of three-fourths of all Western beef. The paper accused him and the "Chicago syndicate" of taking advantage of disorganization in the range country to push cattle prices down to disastrous levels for ranchers without lowering prices to consumers of meat.[34] Such reports contributed to the growing demand for remedial legislation by the federal government.

Scottish stockholders in the Matador Company also became

alarmed about the "Beef Ring's" manipulations, but Mackenzie was inclined to discount the ability of men like Armour and Swift to control market prices. By 1904, however, he had changed his mind and was furnishing information to the government. That year he visited Washington to interview the secretary of the campaign committee of the Democratic party and also the Department of Commerce and Labor concerning its investigations. He warned the home office in Dundee, Scotland, not to publicize his activities lest the packers take vengeance on shipments of cattle from the Matador Ranch. In turn, the packers seem to have appreciated Mackenzie's hesitancy to castigate them publicly,[35] an indication perhaps that his company received preferential treatment at their hands. Although Mackenzie failed to act as openly and as aggressively in this matter as on the railroad problem, he obviously considered federal action necessary.

Thus large and small rancher alike came to endorse federal supervision of railroad rates, meat packing, and stockyards. They also welcomed research by state and federal agencies on problems common to their occupations. They supported creation of the Bureau of Animal Industry in the Department of Agriculture in 1884, and a greatly expanded program for it in later years. In doing so, they exemplified the tenets of American rugged individualism, a national rather than a regional or sectional concept.

The rancher's live-and-let-live philosophy, his addiction to the self-made man concept, and his rugged individualism shaped his views on class structure and the problem of human equality. He expected some people to *achieve* greater status than others and was somewhat impatient with inherited status. Still, he tolerated foreign titles so long as their owners did not insist that he adopt their scale of value for rating people and granting privileges. His observations and his own success convinced him of the great inequality among men in native ability, but he favored equality of opportunity so long as it did not hamper his enjoyment of his own property, prescriptive in origin or otherwise. In a new region such as the cattle kingdom, prescriptive rights generally had been acquired originally by those still in possession, and thus seemed less incongruous with equality of opportunity than in older societies.

Unless one acted according to these principles, he failed to gain widespread approval in the cattle kingdom. John McNab, an important stockholder and director in the Spur Ranch corporation, visited its holdings in 1889 on an inspection tour. Suspicious of his employees, ignorant of ranching procedure, proud of his family wealth but scared that he might lose it, bigoted, and obviously unwilling and unable to fit in or enjoy ranch life, McNab made himself conspicuous by insisting on being driven around the ranch in a buggy, with an umbrella held aloft to shield him from the sun. As a result, the resident manager had to issue strict orders to ranch hands to leave McNab alone. Otherwise, they would have shot holes in his hat and umbrella to express their disdain.[36] John George Adair, Goodnight's partner in the Panhandle, aroused similar feelings there by his arrogance, and Goodnight had to shield him from the fists of touchy Westerners.[37]

Although unpleasant individuals arouse hostility in any society, McNab and Adair got along well in older sections of the country. Their difficulties in the cattle kingdom went deeper than problems of personality. Basically, they failed to understand that in ranch country status must be achieved. Had they been willing to respect the skills and accomplishments essential to standing in the ranching outfits with which they came in contact, they would at least have been tolerated if not wholly accepted. In Owen Wister's novel, *The Virginian,* classes not only existed side by side, they got along well. "Judge Henry," owner of the ranch, represented wealth and education, and he preferred to associate with Eastern visitors who shared his scale of values. At the same time, he recognized the special skills of the Virginian and turned over to him active management of the ranch. Quite obviously that heroic character was on his way to owning a ranch of his own and of moving in the same social circles as the Judge, for classes were fluid in nature. But he and the Judge alike had the good sense not to *assume* a status to which their achievements did not entitle them.

Similarly, Emerson Hough in writing about cowboy society spoke of it as curiously democratic: each man knew his own place but considered himself as good as any other individual.

In such a society, ranch owners had difficulty in finding efficient and reliable wagon, ranch, and trail bosses in spite of a plentiful over-all labor supply capable of performing the ordinary duties of a cowboy. Such foremen needed a remarkable combination of aggressiveness and restraint, of leadership and initiative, if they were to keep employees steadily at work without antagonizing them.[39] Their basic power rested not on any mandate given them by their employers but on positive evidence of their knowledge of the job at hand and ability to win the confidence and respect of the cowhands. Such a subtle relationship might be achieved in various ways, and force was the least of these. Nevertheless, Richard King's fight with an employee when well along in years illustrates the *achieved* status on which authority rested. On that occasion, an angry hand suggested to King that if he were not rich and a captain he would not be able to get away with the profane remarks that he had just addressed to the man. Whereupon, the Captain supposedly replied, "Damn you, forget the riches and the captain title and let's fight."[40] The ensuing fisticuffs restored a sense of harmony and good will, as well as increased respect on both sides.

Owners and operators of large ranches were careful to show proper respect for small neighboring cattlemen. The Spur Ranch of Texas and its three incorporated neighbors boarded line riders and other employees doing outside work free of charge, but hesitated to ask similar favors of small ranchers who had fewer employees to be fed free in return. In 1888, Spottswood Lomax, manager of the Spur, sent forty dollars to the owner of a small, neighboring ranch to compensate him for boarding a line rider during the past season. But Lomax knew better than to present the pay bluntly. Consequently, he disclaimed any intention of trying to square the account in terms of the money sent but suggested that it be accepted as an indication of the Spur's unwillingness to impose on the good nature of a neighbor. If the rancher could not take the money in that light, Lomax hoped he would accept it as a token of good will and buy himself a suit or a saddle. Lomax said that he had thought of sending such a gift but, not knowing the rancher's preference in size or make, did not want to give something undesirable. He concluded his comments with an expression of hope that the Spur would have an opportunity in the future to return its neighbor's many favors.[41] Although Lomax could be very blunt in dealing with small ranchers and nesters who encroached on Spur property, he took infinite pains to soothe the sensibilities of those who proudly bore the name of rancher, however small their capital assets.

In turn, rank-and-file members of the cattle kingdom honored their more successful associates with titles commensurate with their achievements. Ranch owners, resident managers, bosses, and common hands had status according to their duties, and even more so because of their understanding. Teddy Roosevelt and Lomax of the Spur Ranch were addressed as "Mr." by their hands out of real respect. W. F. Friend, who remembers with pride his service under the great trail driver John Blocker, recalls that employees might address their manager as Mr. John or Mr. Ab, or as Uncle Blue or Mr. Blue, using the given name in such instances. Friend gave little thought to democratic or class issues when addressing another; he judged a man worthy of a title if he had proved his right to it. To Friend, John Blocker was such a man.[42]

Military titles also flourished in the cattle kingdom. Many of them traced back to Civil War service, Major Littlefield and Captain John T. Lytle, for instance, having held commissions during that conflict. Here again, however, the popularity of titles stemmed from something deeper than literal evidence of military service. Colonel Ike T. Pryor's title rested on respect for him as a man. The Miller brothers of Oklahoma were colonels by courtesy of the governor of their state. Captain Burton C. Mossman won his title as head of the Arizona Rangers, a state law enforcement agency, and Captain Richard King had been a steamboat captain before turning to ranching. Such titles seemed appropriate for ranchers who controlled large quantities of land and set the rules for numerous employees. Moreover, ranchers liked to be addressed by their titles, viewing them as thoroughly compatible with their achieved status in society.

A considerable part of the cattle kingdom even applied a caste system to segments of its population, and that in spite of its vaunted emphasis on social democracy and individualism. Although Negroes and Mexicans constituted a sizable part of the labor force in the Southwest, and could be found virtually everywhere in ranch country, they were subject to considerable discrimination. The caste system which handicapped them in the land of the self-made men traced back to the section where they were most heavily concentrated and to an earlier day, an evidence that methods of handling humans as well as cattle owed much to the influence of the Southwest. Other parts of the range country furnished apt students, however. Although Lincoln Lang treated a Negro as an equal in his outfit in the Dakota Bad Lands, he was severely criticized by others in his community for doing so.[43] In commenting on Mexican hands in the same region and for the same period, Teddy Roosevelt said that they were distrusted and that Southern-born whites refused to work with them and all half-caste races.[44] Thus, although the degree of feeling against Mexicans and Negroes varied, they could expect to find elements of the caste system present wherever they sought employment.

Writing in the early 1870's, Joseph G. McCoy spoke of the Mexicans in New Mexico as lazy, lascivious, and unprogressive, although he excepted those of "pure Castilian blood" from his remarks.[45] New Mexico produced a number of ranchers of Mexican background, but in most parts of the cattle kingdom they found it difficult to rise above the status of common hands. Some of them became bosses on the King Ranch, but there and elsewhere they felt the pressure of the caste system. Mifflin Kenedy married a woman of Spanish descent, and she and her children moved in the circle of mutual friends that King and Kenedy knew. For the Mexican, however, the relationship was one of patron and worker, with a strict line of demarcation drawn between the two socially.

As for the Negro, the line could be even more sharply maintained on color, which served to advertise his lack of the qualities
essential for becoming a self-made man. Therefore, it seemed
perfectly natural to insist that he keep his "place." If he complied,
he could achieve a fair measure of distinction, but always as an
adjunct of some white man's ego. Under the heading "A Faithful
Negro Servant," he might even be included among the biographies
in the *Trail Drivers of Texas*. A Negro, George Glenn, received
that honor for bringing home from Abilene, Kansas, the em-
balmed body of his employer on a long trip of forty-two days and
nights, during which he slept in the wagon bed with the corpse.[46]

Similarly, "Old Nath," Major Littlefield's body servant, became
his faithful shadow over the years. After Littlefield settled in Austin to devote his time to banking and management of his ranching
enterprises, Old Nath strolled behind him each morning as the
two made their way to the bank, Nath dressed in the Major's cast-
off clothing and unconsciously imitated many of his mannerisms.
In his will, Littlefield specified that Nath was to receive two dollars every Saturday night and a home as long as he lived. At death,
he was buried on one side of the Major's grave, the opposite spot
being reserved for Littlefield's wife.[47] Such conspicuous display of
prestige impressed even those ranchers with non-Southern backgrounds. A transplanted Yankee, Shanghai Pierce, always anxious
concerning his social standing, acquired a Negro servant, "Old
Nep," who for thirty-five years carried his moneybags, always at
a respectful distance behind his master.[48]

Negroes could even win fame as cowboys, if they kept their
"place" otherwise. "Nigger Add" of the LFD Ranch in New Mexico became famous for his great strength and superb horsemanship, and his employers enjoyed showing him off to visitors.[49]
Later on, the Miller Wild West Show featured Bill Pickett, a Negro cowboy from the 101 Ranch, who was billed as the first "bull-
dogger." Pickett would slide off his horse, hook a steer on the
horns with both hands, twist its neck, and sink his teeth in its nos-
trils to bring it down.[50] Charles Goodnight paid tribute to Bose
Ikard on many occasions, saying "I have trusted him farther than

any living man." Ikard served Goodnight as detective, banker (in transmitting money), and in many other ways during his early hazardous days in Colorado and New Mexico. When Goodnight settled in Colorado for a time, he advised Ikard to return to a Texas farm because there were so few Negroes in Colorado with whom to associate. In later years, Goodnight sent Ikard money from time to time and erected a monument to his memory when he died.[51] Such were the usual rewards for outstanding service by Negroes in the cattle kingdom.

As a race, Indians too felt the heavy hand of the caste system. In early times they depended upon the buffalo for food and for hides, from which they made many items essential to their economy. When cattle replaced the buffalo, Indians naturally preyed on them, in part because they represented a continuing meat supply in a region that tribesmen considered their own. Often, however, hunger drove them to such depredations, government policy being so inefficient as to leave them no other choice. Plains Indians also counted wealth in terms of horses owned, and had long played at a game of "counting coup," a system of keeping track of a brave's prowess through adventurous action ranging from killing an enemy to stealing his horses. Necessity and cultural conditioning thus combined to make the Indian an inveterate thief of cow ponies and livestock. Nevertheless, ranchers plunged deeper and deeper into Indian country, thus exerting pressure on the Federal government to remove tribes standing in their way.

Unlike the Negro, an occasional Indian became an accepted member of ranch society, particularly Indian women who had married ranchers in early days. As a race, however, they constituted a problem to the rancher, and he saw no way of incorporating them into the society which he wished to create. When Granville Stuart laid out a ranch in northern Montana in the early 1880's, he took an active part in demanding removal of Indians from his vicinity. During the first winter he estimated that roving bands stole five per cent of his cattle. To him, federal Indian policy was stupid, foolish, sentimental, hypocritical, and venal in execution. Although married to an Indian wife, he had to protect his property from the Indians, whom he labeled "dirty, poverty-stricken thieves."[52]

Ranchers varied in their manner of dealing with the Indian problem. Gregor Lang's family in the Dakota Bad Lands felt a warm sympathy for the scattered bands of hungry Indians who visited their ranch. Mrs. Lang fed them when hungry and, according to Lincoln Lang, they did not molest the family's property. To him, Sitting Bull was one of nature's great noblemen and a Bismarck of his people. Lang quoted with evident approval his exhortation to his braves preceding the battle with Custer's troops: "Be brave, my children, your wives and little ones are like birds without a nest."[53] The Langs simply refused to apply a caste system to Negroes and Indians.

Charles Goodnight, on the other hand, knew the cruelties that Indians could inflict on helpless captives. Human though they were, their culture was that of a stone-age savage. Any white man who dared penetrate their country with the idea of establishing a ranch had to recognize that fact as well as the inevitable conflict sure to follow. Goodnight had fought Indians during the Civil War, and one of his early partners, Oliver Loving, died from a wound received in an Indian attack while driving cattle north from Texas. Although Goodnight was determined to push his ranching enterprises into frontier regions in spite of Indian claims, his sense of justice enabled him to see the Indian's problem. In the fall of 1878, for instance, several small bands of Kiowas and Comanches left their reservation to hunt buffalo. By then the buffalo had virtually disappeared in Goodnight's region, with the result that the hungry Indians began to kill his cattle. Goodnight met with their chief, Quanah Parker, to discuss the matter. He assured Parker that he was not responsible for killing off the buffalo since he had cattle upon which to feed. As to the land, Goodnight suggested that Parker settle the matter of ownership with the state of Texas, after which Goodnight would pay rent to the lawful owner. In the meantime, he would give Parker's band two beeves daily until they could locate the buffalo. When troops arrived to return the Indians to their reservation, Goodnight's mediation prevented bloodshed, and they left peacefully. He and Parker remained friends to death.[54]

Some ranchers took direct and more violent action to protect their herds. John S. Chisum, early New Mexico cattle king, lost many cattle from Indian raids in the 1870's. In the fall of 1877 Chisum sent a band of armed men north to the Mescalero Indian reservation, where they got the government agents sufficiently drunk to put them out of action and then murdered a large number of Indians within a mile of the central post.[55] Thereafter the Indians hesitated to molest Chisum's cattle. Whatever the degree of kindness or forbearance displayed in particular episodes, the inevitable result was the displacement of the Indian by the rancher. The white man's values prevailed and, in doing so, they placed the Indian in a caste system scarcely less rigid than that applied to the Negro.

Jerome Churchill, California businessman and rancher, who spoke so positively concerning the doctrine of the self-made man, believed it wise to exclude all "inferior classes" from the country, including Negroes, Chinese, and the inferior classes of Europe.[56] In ranching as in mining the Chinese held the more menial jobs, while the cattle kings drew their membership from the white race.

For the white man, the cattle kingdom was a land of promise. Coming to it with youth and hope, he found its live-and-let-live philosophy attractive in his dreams of wealth or self-expression. He could cite examples close at hand of self-made men, if any dared to doubt his own chances to rise in the world. The concept of rugged individualism seemed wholly appropriate to the young and vigorous, and thoroughly compatible with the other precepts. In time, the rancher would speak of courage, self-reliance, daring, and fortitude as having been essential traits of an earlier, simpler, and more manly day, and would cite the wisdom of that age in justifying his stand on modern issues. In placing a premium upon such concepts, he marked out for himself a role of a distinct, if not unique, nature.

SEVEN

God's Elect

THE cattle kingdom applied its live-and-let-live philosophy in religion as in other fields. There one found Bible-reading, practicing Christians as well as those devoid of any organized religious affiliations or professions. Religious attitudes ranged from a mild kind of deism to a fundamentalist theology involving strict moral precepts. In discussing frontier types, Teddy Roosevelt recalled meeting two Bible-reading, strait-laced Methodist cowboys at a roundup, both of whom were first-class workers. Since they did not inflict their opinions on others, they got along well in the group, which also contained "two or three blear-eyed, slit-mouthed ruffians," who were as loose of tongue as of life.[1] Only the atheist seems to have been absent from the scene.

Many ranchers and cowboys spent their formative years in older parts of the country which emphasized the importance of religious worship. As adults in a male society on the ranching frontier they never quite freed themselves from that early indoctrination, pastoral duties and starry nights reminding them of Biblical stories of the shepherds of old that they had heard as children. Their cowboy songs recognized God's existence and also occasionally touched on matters of salvation. Highly symbolic, such songs pictured the hereafter in terms of the last roundup or the last trail drive, and hell as riding herd on a wild stampede for eternity. Mournful ballads of tragic death included reference to the forgiveness of sin and the need for Christian burial.[2]

Proximity to nature and the hazards of their occupation also reminded ranchers and cowboys of man's short duration on earth. Cowboys riding herd on restless cattle during an electrical storm knew that a stampede could occur at any moment. If it did, they must lead and direct the charging mass in such a way as to prevent the animals from drifting off. They needed tremendous courage to perform that duty since they could easily be trampled to death if their horses stumbled. At such times God seemed very real to a cowboy.[3] He could indeed vouch for the truth of the song:

> My books are the brooks, my sermons the stones,
> My parson a wolf on his pulpit of bones. . . .

Nevertheless, formal religious activities flourished less on the ranching frontier than in older communities. Young men on the make lacked time and inclination for religious exercises, an attitude more easily sustained because so few wives and mothers were present to counteract it. An early-day Texas rancher, C. H. Rust, and his associates lived in conditions that prevented them from being bound by the conventions of an established society. As an old man and a good Methodist, Rust regretted the excesses of his youth, which at the time had seemed completely in harmony with his surroundings.[4]

Nor did conditions favorable to organized religious worship develop rapidly. Sunday was seldom observed as a day of rest, and still less often as a day of worship. On the Spur Ranch in Texas the hands worked on Sundays, preferring to find rest and relaxation in ways other than Sabbath observance. When the XIT Ranch in western Texas drew up its twenty-three rules governing the conduct of employees, the manager decided that all work should cease on Sundays. Nevertheless, for seven to eight months of the year work continued without interruption, that being the most convenient pattern for organizing it.[5] During roundup season and on drives men thought it foolish to cease operations for twenty-four hours. When the Miller ranch in Oklahoma began to diversify by combining scientific farming with ranching, the labor force worked twenty-six days and then had four off, but received a bonus for not taking the four-day break during harvest season.[6]

Moreover, some respectable citizens of the cattle kingdom appreciated the release that it provided from an overly strict upbringing elsewhere. As a youth in Iowa, Granville Stuart was forced to attend preaching services regularly and to listen to personal exhortations of circuit riders, his mother serving as hostess to all who came that way. In the West, Stuart lost his fear of the hellfire that had frightened him as a boy. During a leisurely Sunday morning on the Montana frontier Granville recorded in his diary his appreciation for not having to attend a church, sit on a hard bench for two hours, and listen to a preacher describe the horrors of hell.[7]

Nor did the doctrine of the total depravity of man and salvation by grace alone sit well with men who based their recognition of status upon personal achievement. They felt that a man must earn his own salvation, and they found it difficult to square their convictions of God's goodness with the idea of eternal hellfire. W. F. Friend, long-time cowboy and rancher, refused to raise his hand along with other members of the congregation at a twentieth-century revival meeting when the evangelist asked his hearers if they believed themselves "saved." Recognizing his own imperfections and feeling a responsibility for them, Friend doubted the ready answer of another member of the congregation who based his assurance on grace.[8] A code of self-reliance, courage, and individual responsibility, combined with daily observation of nature's way of eliminating the weak or thoughtless, made it hard for him to accept the gift of eternal salvation by grace alone.

Owen Wister had the hero of his cowboy novel express the same point of view. In that story, a missionary of fundamentalist, doctrinaire outlook visited the ranch where the Virginian was working. The ranch owner and his guests endured a long harangue by the preacher on man's depravity, and even the cowboys listened, although unwillingly. As a means of ridiculing so foolish a doctrine, the Virginian expressed interest in salvation and kept the missionary up most of the night praying for him. When the preacher discovered the true state of affairs, he left in wrath. Wister had the Virginian say:

"As for salvation, I have got this far: somebody," he swept an arm at the sunset and the mountains, "must have made all that I know. But I know one more thing I would tell Him to his face: if I can't do nothing long enough and good enough to earn eternal happiness, I can't do nothing long enough and bad enough to be damned. I reckon He plays a square game with us if He plays at all, and I ain't bothering my haid about other worlds."[9]

To the Virginian the doctrine of original sin and the depravity of man simply did not make sense.

Many of the early-day preachers in the cattle kingdom hurt their cause by unwillingness or inability to recognize the nature and outlook of their prospective converts. Itinerant preachers held services in a depot, a local store, or in a dance hall above some saloon during the early days of ranching in the Dakota Bad Lands, but attendance was invariably small. Anything or anyone associated with religion was likely to be shunned in that period, religion being looked upon as an institution for old women and weaklings. To the preachers, that attitude was nothing short of blasphemy, and they condemned it roundly, without, however, giving thought to more appealing ways of reaching hardened sinners. Ranchers and cowboys treated them with respect, but left the church-going to nesters and homesteaders. In explaining why, one contemporary observer suggested that missionaries were less honest fundamentally than the gay-hearted cowboy argonauts. The latter had no illusions about their piety. Moreover, the preachers were less than human. Addicted to very long sermons, thick-skinned and impervious to hints, they let their self-righteousness stand in the way of seeking a common meeting ground. On one occasion when a long and dry sermon drove the listeners to looking at their watches, the parson retaliated with "See here, you don't want to be lookin' at your watches. You don't hear a sermon often."[10] Still another minister, whom some of the respectable element were trying to help, fled precipitately after committing a violent murder. There was considerable truth in the comment "Them preachers broke us fellows from going to church."[11]

Rancher and cowboy alike, however, respected associates who participated in organized religion so long as they demonstrated in their actions its beneficent influences. Church attendance meant little to them, preaching by example a great deal. Owen Wister recognized this in his cowboy novel by including the "Bishop of Wyoming" in his cast of religious characters. Since the Bishop took a decidedly humanistic view of religion and understood the cowboy's simple faith in a divine being, he had no trouble in obtaining a hearing when he visited a ranch. Ministerial ordination per se meant no more than did the title of some European nobleman unless those claiming such distinction proved their right to it. Moreover, creedal self-righteousness had a sour taste in a society committed to a rule of live and let live.

Many of the best-known ranchers saw no essential connection between a faith in God and formal church membership. John Wesley Iliff, for instance, carried the name of Methodism's founder, an indication of the deeply religious family background of his people. Nevertheless, he joined no church before his death at age forty-six. During his last illness his wife and her ministerial friends urged him to repent and to confess his religious faith. Obituaries following his death mentioned that he had told his wife in his dying moments that he had made peace with God and that he had urged servants in the household to do the same. One of the officiating ministers at his funeral, a cousin, stressed Iliff's devotion to religious ideals in his business dealings. According to the minister, Iliff's respect for real Christians was as great as his intolerance for "pretended" Christians, and he had excused himself for not joining the church on grounds of "the inexcusable inconsistencies of so many professed Christians betrayed in their business transactions."[12] Similarly, Charles Goodnight apparently felt no need for formal religious participation, although his wife persuaded him to join a church just before his death. One suspects that both he and Iliff conformed as much as they did to please their wives. At least, when one of Goodnight's friends asked him which church he had joined, the old man replied, "I don't know, but it's a damned good one."[13]

Thus, the ranching fraternity squared its religious convictions with its observations. A few, like Nelson Story, prided themselves on an analytical turn of mind which rejected "theologies." Story read and reread the old family Bible, making comments in the margins as he went along. At the side of a passage saying that the streets of heaven would be paved with gold, he wrote, "Fools, don't they know that if gold is that plentiful it will be cheaper than horse manure?"[14] The great majority, however, simply looked to the life around them for lessons in religion and morality.

In doing so, they saw no harm in profanity. Again, Owen Wister stuck to the facts when he endowed his cowboy hero with a penchant for profanity and off-color songs. Teddy Roosevelt admired cowboys above all others who labored at menial tasks, but of their conversation he could only say that it was no worse than that among any group composed wholly of males.[15] Others commented that profanity was an art among the cowboys,[16] or that it lost its shock from constant overuse. Goodnight's biographer said that he cursed heavily but without offense, his language being the vernacular of his time, full of saltiness rather than sheer profanity.[17] Such men found it difficult not to swear in the presence of ladies. Shanghai Pierce's rough and profane stories made him a favorite among his associates but he fared less well in court. While on the witness stand testifying as to the reputation of his enemy, George W. Miller, Shang bellowed: "He is not only the biggest liar, but the biggest thief and a son of a bitch."[18] Court immediately recessed to give the judge time to determine a proper penalty for Shang's misbehavior. When it reconvened, Shang apologized, and suggested that the judge simply raise a hand in warning whenever his language began to threaten the bounds of propriety.

Drinking and smoking also were universal. At the Cheyenne Club and other places where cattlemen gathered, the management maintained elaborate bars that served the finest of whiskey. Most cattlemen drank moderately, however, and some not at all. Of the latter, some refrained for religious reasons, some disliked the taste of liquor, and still more found it a handicap in business negotiations. Few ranchers among the top echelon indulged excessively but moral scruples made fewer still teetotalers.

Perhaps the cattleman's proudest claim in the field of moral principles was that he always kept his word. George N. Steen, for instance, headed his biographical sketch in the *Trail Drivers of Texas* with the title "When a man's word was as good as a gilt-edged note."[19] Among ranchers who knew one another this was undoubtedly true in most cases, and constant harping upon the reliability of an oral promise naturally brought down a greater measure of contempt upon the head of anyone violating the rule. The basic reason for the sanctity of an oral pledge lay, however, in the fact that ranchers were dependent upon their neighbors in so many ways.[20] A man who refused to honor an oral agreement found himself seriously handicapped in the future conduct of his business affairs quite apart from any feeling of guilt that might attach to his action.

The emphasis on the sacredness of a man's word naturally developed quite early in the cattle kingdom, for that was the very time when personal relationships held greatest meaning. Charles Goodnight's promise to his early partner, Oliver Loving, to perform certain financial obligations for the dying man, and the scrupulous manner in which he carried out his pledge,[21] resulted in considerable part from the fact that they were personal friends and neighboring families. Perhaps, too, Goodnight continued to keep his word with all parties, friends or not, because he learned to do so at a time when economic and personal necessity made it advisable.

In the early days of the long drives, Texas longhorns went up the trail at times under oral agreements between drovers and owners that accounts would be settled after marketing was completed. Joseph G. McCoy said that the early drovers kept their words individually and as a group. When one slipped away from Abilene without settling local obligations, other cattlemen sent out men to bring him back to pay his just debts. Nevertheless, in summarizing his reflections on ranchmen and drovers as a whole, McCoy concluded that their over-all record for keeping verbal contracts was no better than that of people from any other section of the country.[22] While Charles Goodnight was building a reputation as a man of his word, another rancher, John Chisum, engaged in a series of questionable business deals. During the troubled Reconstruction period Chisum obtained power of attorney to market various Texas brands, the cattle ostensibly to be paid for on his return to Texas. According to one account, he even gave notes for them. In spite of rapidly increasing wealth on the New Mexico frontier, Chisum apparently failed to settle his obligations to many of the Texans. Although some writers have defended Chisum against charges of failure to honor his moral obligations, the necessity for doing so indicates that among contemporaries his word was not considered as good as his bond.[23]

Moreover, sanctity of the spoken word did little or nothing to reduce sharp trading practices. As good businessmen, ranchers like King, Iliff, and Littlefield used their considerable ability as judges of cattle and men to achieve the best possible terms in dealing with others. They quickly disillusioned any greenhorn who assumed that a reputation for keeping one's word also extended to protecting the uninitiated from bad business judgments. Buying and selling with an eye to profit, ranchers expected others to recognize that a man did not necessarily tell the whole truth when negotiating a business deal.

Some ranchers went even further. Since Shanghai Pierce, for instance, had little confidence in man's fundamental goodness, he loved nothing better than to outsmart others in business deals. On one occasion he agreed to let George Miller of the 101 Ranch "top" a herd of cattle at a set price, that is, select the best animals from the group. Immediately, however, he ordered his local manager to ship out the best stock from that particular herd before Miller could arrive to make his selection. Moreover, the manager was to show the remainder of the cattle to Miller very early in the morning or near dusk in hopes of confusing his judgment.[24] After several years as manager of cattle corporations, John Clay had no trouble recalling incidents that in his opinion proved a rancher's word much less reliable than his bond.[25] Certainly, many a rancher limited his responsibilities to the letter rather than the spirit of the principle.

Nor did the cowboy come off any better where money matters were concerned. Records of the Spur Ranch in Texas show that the managers occasionally advanced money to needy cowboys, loaned horses to them for long trips, paid their medical bills, and staked them to sufficient money at times to last through the slack winter season. As acts of kindness, these favors merited prompt repayment, but some of the cowhands completely ignored their obligations.[26]

Of course, the Spur was a soulless corporation, owned by outsiders, a sufficient excuse for many native Westerners to take advantage. Eastern and European investors in early days quite often purchased herds by "book count," that is, an estimated number of cattle belonging to the vendor. In time, many of them discovered that they had been seriously swindled. As a result, later deals were more often based on actual counts, but even then investors occasionally suffered because of dishonesty on the part of those engaged to do the checking. Charles Goodnight made some of his neighbors angry by agreeing to check the actual number of cattle involved in such a transaction. When still another corporation requested the same favor, he declined because of the time required and the hostility that acceptance would engender locally. Only after a representative of the stockholders visited Goodnight's ranch to make a personal appeal would he consent to serve, saying that it would be disgraceful for the cattle country to lack sufficient justice and honesty to provide an honest cattle count for strangers.[27]

Individuals as well as corporations suffered at the hands of local sharpsters. Among his other grandiose schemes in the Dakota Bad Lands, the Marquis de Mores included sheep ranching on a grand scale. Local cattlemen, of course, disliked the idea. Partially to allay such hostility, he hired twenty-four experienced herders locally and supplied them with flocks, buildings, and funds to operate for seven years, after which the profits were to be divided. The Marquis had no trouble in finding the twenty-four men but they turned the sheep loose without supervision. One of the men, proving more honest than the rest, told the Marquis's manager that many of the wethers and ewes purchased by the herders were too old to survive on the open range. The project had no chance of succeeding because of the dishonesty of the very men that the Marquis had staked as partners.[28]

In truth, then, the sacredness of a man's word in the code of the West rested upon personalized relationships. The concept flourished at an early day when men were highly dependent upon one another, and it continued to find favor in the rancher's code because of its ethical appeal. It seems to have handicapped people's consciences very little, if any, in strictly business dealings, however, and it did not prevent outsiders from being fleeced unmercifully. Perhaps it even contributed to that end by lulling them into a conviction that they need not go behind the word of a Westerner to check the truth of his statements.

While the great majority of ranchers drank, swore, smoked, and found deistic concepts adequate to their religious needs, their wives displayed considerably greater interest in revealed religion. J. P. White, Sr., for instance, followed a very common pattern in seldom attending church, although his mother and his wife were strong Presbyterians. Also, like many another rancher, White contributed to the building and upkeep of churches.[29] Most ranchers willingly left formal religious matters in the hands of their wives and mothers, whose influence in family affairs enabled them to donate financially to religious causes. As "good" women, they disliked whiskey, tobacco, and profanity. Some, like Goodnight's wife, won their husbands over to token church membership in later life, and a still smaller number had the pleasure of working side by side with their husbands in organized religious activities throughout their married years.

The religious and moral environment of the ranching frontier naturally pushed those ranchers who became active church members in the direction of puritanical codes of personal conduct and fundamentalist convictions. Otherwise, they could easily be satisfied with the prevailing deistic sentiments of their contemporaries. As churchmen, they had a role to play, and they played it openly and consistently. Otherwise, their fellow ranchers branded them as hypocrites. Every denomination could boast of men like H. S. Boice, last manager of the great XIT spread in Texas, who did not smoke, drink, or swear and prayed openly every night, no matter where. A skilled cattleman of long experience, a forceful individual, and a devout Christian, he was highly respected by cowboy and rancher alike.[30]

The Baptists pointed to the Slaughter family as outstanding members of their denomination. George W. Slaughter moved to Texas in 1830, where he worked equally hard at ranching and at preaching the gospel for miles around. His son, Colonel C. C. (Lum) Slaughter, became even more widely known in the cattle kingdom for his religious convictions. Colonel Lum supposedly was the first child born in the Republic of Texas, and his family played an honored role in its fight for independence from Mexico. At age twelve Lum participated in his first long drive; by age eighteen he had become a full-fledged cattleman. Service in the famous Texas Rangers, a successful career in ranching and banking, and the presidency of cattle associations placed him in the top echelon of the cattle kings. For years he served as chairman of the Baptist General Convention of Texas. While president of a West Texas cattleman's association in 1886, he opened its meetings with prayer, an innovation, since praying cattlemen were the exception rather than the rule in Texas at the time.[31] Like Boice, he lived his religion openly and devoutly.

The Snyder family played an equally prominent role in Methodism. Like the Slaughters, they were highly skilled ranchers, expected their hands to observe moral principles, and took an active part in church work. Colonel D. H. Snyder rested his trail herds on Sunday and practiced his religious precepts everywhere. For fifty-five years, beginning in 1866, he continuously held an office in his local church. Between 1869 and 1886 he served almost yearly as a delegate to the Northwest Texas Conference, and also attended general conferences at Nashville and Richmond. Snyder found great satisfaction in his religion. Writing to his wife at Georgetown, Texas, from Mexico in 1903, he recalled their grief at the death of a daughter two years before. At the same time, he mentioned the joy of a Christian life, which prepared one to die and to look up in confidence to God, knowing that all was well. In his daily prayers he asked God to sustain him and his family in Christian living so that all might see Him and their loved ones in heaven. To him, Christianity guaranteed an unbroken family in the presence of a great and merciful God.[32]

Whatever the denomination, such families displayed a common pattern of devotion in time and money, their contributions being unique only to the extent that variations in personality came into play. The Brites of Texas, for instance, were highly aggressive and extroverted members of the Christian Church. Naturally, they were among the ranch families which pitched their tents at the famous Bloys Camp Meeting in 1897, an annual event since that date. There, in the Davis Mountains of Texas, cattlemen meet with their families for revival services lasting several days. Some have built cabins on the grounds; others camp in tents. In "true cattleman's style" nobody pays for anything, a free-will offering underwriting the annual expenses.[33] Although the Marlin Murphys of California were as devoted to the Catholic Church as the Brites were to the Christian, and were equally as effective in promoting its welfare, they expressed their faith somewhat more placidly in keeping with their personalities.[34]

Such dedicated ranch families through financial contributions and personal service extended their influence beyond what mere numbers alone might have achieved. Added to them were the many families in which wives and daughters took a lead in church work and philanthropy. Certainly the role of religion in the cattle kingdom involved two groups: those committed to a somewhat vague deistic faith, and those who believed and worked devoutly in the field of organized religion.

Somewhat the same division existed when it came to philan-

thropy, with those of deistic outlook inclined to make their contributions out of pocket and the others giving more often to
organized institutions, like churches and schools. As a whole, of
course, all philanthropy on the ranching frontier was highly personalized. Organized philanthropic giving had not as yet developed fully anywhere in America, and self-made men naturally
were not inclined to surrender control to some agency that stood
between them and the recipient of their favors. Nevertheless, there
was a correlation between religious convictions and the degree of
support of church and educational institutions.

Unlike his wife, for instance, Richard King was not a faithful
church member, and so was more inclined than she to give to individuals rather than to institutions. King enjoyed presenting handouts directly to those who asked for help. On visits to Brownsville
he generally stopped by the saloon of Celestin Jagou, where a
crowd gathered as soon as his presence became known. Almost
invariably he was good for a drink or two, and usually for a touch.
On such occasions he kept his money loose in a side pocket, from
which he handed out five, ten, and even twenty dollar bills if he
heard a case of sufficient woe. At the end of the day, he carefully
counted the money remaining in his side pocket and entered in
his memorandum book a record of any appreciable handout.
When he died, some of his "jug" acquaintances presented small
claims to his lawyer, who, by reference to King's records, quickly
demonstrated that any unpaid obligations lay in the other direction.[35]

George W. Miller, founder of the 101 Ranch, naturally assumed a personalized and paternalistic philanthropic role in his
efforts to exemplify plantation traditions of the Old South. While
the family lived at Winfield, Kansas, Miller attended Sunday services in formal dress, his silk hat and gold-headed cane demon-
strating that he was indeed the squire of Winfield. Miller instructed the local Provident Association to send the poor directly
to his meat market for food to relieve their hunger. On national
holidays, such as Thanksgiving, Miller slaughtered a beef for distribution to the poor.[36] Unlike those ranch families already men-

tioned as typifying the religious group within the cattle kingdom, the Millers took little part in church work. Social rather than theological motivations brought them into contact with the church, and their philanthropies were more highly personalized for that reason.

Even a cynic like Shanghai Pierce could indulge his ego by personalized philanthropy. Pierce leased Texas convicts to work his rich, bottom ranchlands, fed them according to his New England concepts of thrift, and boasted of this and other evidences of his sharp trading practices. Possession of money gave him power to repel limitations which society otherwise might have imposed upon expressions of his flamboyant personality. Quite naturally he built and equipped a church on his own land when people requested it, and quite naturally when asked whether he belonged to the church, he replied, "Hell, no! The church belongs to me."[37] A direct contribution of eighty thousand dollars for relief of people affected by the great Galveston storm assured him of more than local recognition.

More sedate ranchers like John W. Prowers contributed liberally to the support of resident pastors of all denominations in their communities but never joined a church.[38] In such giving they knew exactly to whom their money went and for what purposes. No intervening agency determined policies of which they might not approve, or, if it did, they ceased donating to the cause. Moreover, ranchers whose families took a personal interest in religious activities while they themselves remained more or less inactive certainly offered a less promising source of funds than did active churchmen. The famous Texas rancher, William T. Waggoner, was a case in point. When a church committee in Decatur, Texas, called on him for a subscription to help build a new church, he suggested that they put him down for a hundred dollars. Disappointed, the spokesman for the committee mentioned that Waggoner's son had already subscribed one thousand dollars, to which the old gentleman dryly replied, "Yes, I know; but the boy has a rich daddy."[39]

A society devoted to rugged individualism and the cult of the

self-made man sympathized more with the temporarily unfortunate than with the chronically handicapped. It seemed fitting
and proper to concentrate on helping individuals eliminate ob-
stacles that otherwise would prevent them from achieving the
place in life to which their talents and energies would normally
entitle them. Religious convictions also helped shape philanthropic giving. As a result, churches, church schools, and hospitals became favorite charities, with orphan asylums somewhat less
prominent. In the latter case, children perhaps found homes more
easily in ranch country than in urban centers, thus lessening the
need for institutional care. Nevertheless, Henry Sieben, a German
immigrant who arrived in Montana in 1864 with little property
to become a leading rancher and banker, was widely known as
president and financial backer of the Montana Home Society, an
organization devoted to the care and placement of homeless
babies in good families.[40]

Successful ranchers recognized the value of education in the
conduct of business affairs, and some attended college before
turning to ranching. John W. Iliff studied for three years at Ohio
Wesleyan College and George W. Littlefield attended Baylor for a
short time. Others, like Charles Goodnight, regretted their lack of
formal education. Moreover, as they rose in the world, ranchers
wanted their children to have all possible advantages. The Miller
and the King families maintained private tutors in their homes to
train the younger children. King issued instructions that "Papa's
pets," as he called his children, should want for nothing that
money could buy.[41] His wife's religious austerity kept his indul-
gence of the children within bounds, but both agreed that the
girls should attend fashionable boarding schools and the boys college for as long as they liked. Similarly, Shanghai Pierce sent his
only daughter to the Virginia Female Institute for the type of
training expected of a young lady in polite society. Like George
W. Littlefield, Shang also agreed to underwrite the education of
a nephew so long as he did well in school.[44]

As a whole, however, large ranchers seem not to have taken
the lead in establishing a common school system. Nonresident

owners of incorporated ranches staffed largely by unmarried men had no incentive to subsidize institutions that would attract small farmers and their families. Even the large independent ranchers felt much the same way. When they did establish schools for the children of nesters, they seem to have acted through personal kindliness toward children or possibly because they considered education a bulwark of their own code of values.

On the other hand, promoters of denominational colleges obtained much financial support from ranchers within their own churches, so much as a matter of fact as to make religion and higher education handmaidens in a common cause in the cattle kingdom. For instance, according to Dr. Rupert N. Richardson, President Emeritus of Hardin Simmons College of Abilene, Texas, his school could not have survived its infancy without financial aid from ranchers. Gifts from the Cowden family made possible the erection of the first men's dormitory. The Partamore family also contributed frequently, perhaps never more than five thousand dollars at one time, but vital gifts nevertheless because of the general scarcity of money.[45]

Since many ranchers left matters of philanthropy and religion to their wives, women naturally played a major role in such activities. As previously seen, John Wesley Iliff devoted little attention to such things during his short but intensively active business career. As her second husband, Mrs. Iliff married Bishop Henry White Warren of the Methodist Church, who probably strengthened her intention of doing something to commemorate Iliff's memory. In 1884 she gave one hundred thousand dollars to aid in establishing a seminary for the training of Methodist ministers west of the Mississippi River, the school to be called the Iliff School of Theology. Additional gifts by her and the Iliff children contributed greatly to the growth of that institution.[46]

When Richard King died, his will specified that all his property should pass to his wife, and he made no specific contributions to philanthropy. As in life, he expected his wife to handle such matters. During her long widowhood Mrs. King contributed to various activities. In 1901 she gave money in memory of her husband for a new Presbyterian Church in Corpus Christi. Her daughter, Alice Kleberg, wishing to show her gratitude to their family doctor in Corpus Christi, solicited contributions to build him a hospital. Mrs. King contributed the building site and twenty-five thousand dollars. When the town of Kleberg was laid out on King Ranch land, Mrs. King financed the new Presbyterian Church and donated building lots to all other donominations. She provided a meeting place for the local Masonic lodge, which bore her own father's name, and donated the ground and money for a two-story brick school building. In addition, she gave seven hundred acres of land near Kingsville to the Texas-Mexican Industrial Institute, a vocational training school for Mexican boys sponsored by the Presbyterian Synod of Texas.[47]

Like Captain Richard King, Charles Goodnight deferred to his wife in matters of organized philanthropy. His appreciation of a disciplined, well-trained mind and his own lack of schooling beyond the age of nine undoubtedly influenced him in doing something for the education of others, but both his first and second wives played major roles in urging him to carry through his wishes. In 1898 he and the first Mrs. Goodnight founded Goodnight College at Goodnight Station on the Fort Worth and Denver Railroad, some three hundred miles northwest of Fort Worth, with the help of the Reverend Marshall McIlhaney, its first president. Over the years, the Goodnights contributed land and some seventy-five to eighty thousand dollars to the school. Goodnight thought that its purposes could best be attained by vesting ownership and operation in a religious denomination. Apparently, however, he failed to reach such agreement with the Methodist Church because of his reluctance to surrender full control over policy, a problem that also plagued other colleges fostered by individualistic ranchers. For a time, the Baptists supervised the school. Financial difficulties finally reduced it to the status of a junior college before Goodnight finally surrendered control to the local town. The building served as an orphanage for a time and then became a part of the local public school system. By 1910 it ceased to exist as a separate entity.

Nevertheless, Goodnight College promised well for a time. In the early days some forty to fifty young women from Texas, Arkansas, and the Territories attended the school, along with a number of young men, since it was coeducational. A visitor during this period reported everything new, and stressed the rich promise of success which pervaded the institution. She commented on the broad fields, the spacious campus, and the pastures which spread out from the central building. The president and his wife were ably assisted by some four or five faculty members. Although music and other cultural subjects were taught, the curriculum emphasized skills of utilitarian value for the Great Plains region. The president hoped to introduce industrial training along the lines of domestic work. The young ladies were to be taught plain sewing, dressmaking, cutting and fitting garments, cooking and buttermaking. The young men were to concentrate on agriculture, horticulture, and dairying. During its brief career the college held the first summer school and the first summer normal session for the training of teachers in the Texas Panhandle.[48] Goodnight undoubtedly stamped his ideas of education upon the college but records are too scanty to judge the extent to which his personal interest in its affairs may have contributed to its later troubles. Certainly, he did not want to see this "child of his dreams" depart radically from his hopes for it.

When both husband and wife took an active interest in religious affairs they were also more likely to contribute to philanthropy. Colonel C. C. Slaughter's family sponsored various activities, notably the building to the Baptist Memorial Hospital in Dallas, Texas.[49] Historians of Southwestern University in Georgetown, Texas, credit D. H. Snyder and his brothers with making it possible for Texas Methodism to have that institution. When President F. A. Mood found that a promised subsidy of $154,000 at a critical period actually amounted to much less, he poured out his heart to D. H. Snyder, his financial adviser. Having assured Methodist officials that the subsidy would be realized in full and that the school would involve the church in no debts, the president thought that unless he could solve the financial problem it would be necessary for him to resign or admit to willful lying. He felt that he and Snyder would be considered liars and imposters, fools, and idiots, an indication of how seriously he took his predicament. Then and later, Snyder's financial advice and direct gifts by his family helped Southwestern reach a stable condition. Colonel and Mrs. Snyder also maintained open house for students and visitors at their home on the edge of the campus.

Although Snyder obviously deserved President Mood's high regard, faculty members must have felt that the president's frequent statements to them about his obligations to Snyder promised them little leeway in shaping educational policies. It must have galled them to hear the president say:

Gentlemen, should all of you advise and agree upon a certain policy and D. H. Snyder advise contrary to it such are my obligations to him and my confidence in him, I would feel compelled to follow his instructions rather than yours.[50]

Texas Christian University at Fort Worth was less successful in concealing stresses created by conflicts between leading donors and other interested parties. Lucas Charles Brite and his wife became interested in the University during a revival meeting conducted at their home town of Marfa, Texas, in 1897 by Addison Clark, who had demonstrated the vitality of the small church-supported school. The Brites made a number of financial donations over the years, including funds for Brite College of the Bible, the theological seminary of Texas Christian University. In return, Brite expected to take an active part in shaping university policies and to be recognized for his work. In the spring of 1914 he asked to give the commencement address following completion of the Bible College building. According to a history of the Brite family published by Texas Christian University Press, any apprehensions arising from use of a West Texas rancher as commencement speaker soon evaporated as Brite's speech was clear, simple, and probably one of the shortest on record.

As president of the board of trustees of the Bible College, Brite exerted influence in various directions. In the early 1920's he remarked that any professor in the Bible College drawing a salary of two thousand dollars a year had an income equal to that derived from a ranch or farm investment of forty thousand dollars. Furthermore, he thought professors should be interested in knowing how few donors to the school possessed that much money, a hint that the staff failed to appreciate the generous financial support accorded it. Moreover, he insisted that funds must be used strictly for the exact purposes for which originally given, a reaction on his part against the idea that changing conditions justified modifications in stated purposes of bequests. As an ardent fundamentalist, he feuded with the editor of a religious paper, who accused Brite of injuring the cause of religion by insisting upon a literal interpretation of the Bible. A man of strong convictions, Brite stood by his rule that "Bible College trustees who do not exact of the faculty the duty of teaching principles of Christianity by agreement verbal or written are to my mind derelict of their duties."[51] His religious convictions had a strong moral slant, as in his opposition to the sale of liquor. Although he disliked the idea of women voting, he was pleased to have his wife engage actively in club work. She, like her husband, enjoyed the honors which came her way, such as the honorary LL.D. given her by Texas Christian University in 1948 and membership in the Daughters of the American Revolution in 1949. Her husband served as president of the 31st and 32nd conventions of the American National Live Stock Association.[52] As rugged individualists, fundamentalists, and moralists the Brites typified the religious pattern of most ranchers who gloried in being churchmen.

After oil discoveries added to the wealth of the Waggoner family of Texas, they contributed to schools and churches alike. Included in their gifts was money for enlarging and refurnishing the First Methodist Church at Fort Worth and the construction of three buildings on the campus of Texas Women's College.[53] In California the Murphy family gave land, money, and personal support to the development of Santa Clara College and to the Convent of Notre Dame.[54] Many religiously inclined ranchers gave sparingly of their resources, it is true, but religious convictions did incline them in the direction of philanthropy, and especially toward those projects in which religion and education were combined.

Those of a somewhat more deistic turn of mind, or whose activities beyond the strictly business field could not easily be encompassed within the term "churchmen," seem to have been as ruggedly individualistic as the group previously discussed, but their philanthropy displayed greater secular emphasis. Captain Charles Schreiner has been called the "Father of the Texas Hill Country" because his benefactions in Kerr, Kimble, and Real Counties exceeded $1,300,000. He gave $550,000 and 140 acres of land to the Presbyterian Church in 1916 for the construction of Schreiner Institute, a boy's school. In addition he contributed: $300,000 for building public roads in ranch country; 600 acres of land and $40,000 for a United States Veterans' Hospital; $40,000 to the Kerrville General Hospital for treatment of the poor; $150,000 for railroad construction beneficial to the region; and $50,000 to a local high school. Born in Alsace-Lorraine in 1838, he came to Texas with his parents in 1852, where through service in the Texas Rangers, merchandising, ranching, and a multitude of other activities he exemplified the same code of values as his American-born associates.[55] An account of the family's mercantile career published by the Texas State Historical Association is redolent with the virtues of rugged individualism.[56] Quite naturally, his son Gus would serve on the advisory board of an organization in the 1940's called the "Fight for Free Enterprise."[57]

Nelson Story and George W. Littlefield took little personal interest in organized religion, and so their contributions went to secular schools. Story gave most of the sixty acres of land for the campus of the State College at Bozeman, Montana,[58] and Littlefield contributed generously to the University of Texas. He provided money to purchase the John Henry Wrenn Library of rare and beautiful literary volumes for the university and funds for construction of buildings. Like his more religiously inclined contemporaries, however, Littlefield created problems as well as opportunities through his gifts. In establishing the Littlefield Fund in Southern History he hoped to glorify the Old South, but his own intense loyalty to the past was highly provincial. Fortunately, those in charge of the fund have spent it more wisely. A magnificent newspaper collection and a scholarly multi-volume history of the South have been only part of the fruits resulting from his gift.

As a member of the board of regents and a supporter of James E. Ferguson's gubernatorial campaign, Littlefield became involved in the latter's fight for control of the university. Of stronger personal than institutional loyalties, Littlefield supported a considerable part of Ferguson's program. Impatient with principles of academic tenure, Littlefield voted with other Board members to dismiss professors for improper opinions. When Littlefield favored retention of a president or a professor, he did so on grounds of the man's soundness according to his conception of the term, or because Ferguson or others were transgressing on the authority of the board of regents. In academic freedom as such he took little stock.[59]

Thus, in the field of philanthropy, cattlemen displayed characteristics similar to those of businessmen elsewhere in the United States. Addicted to rugged individualism and the cult of the self-made man, they believed that a rancher should handle his property as he alone thought best. If he chose not to share it with the less fortunate, that was his own business, and many felt no call to do so. If they chose to help others, they looked for ways to aid worthy individuals to overcome temporary handicaps. Churches, schools, and hospitals met that test. For the chronically ineffective, however, they had little sympathy. They disliked the idea of surrendering complete control of gifts, and so insisted upon sharing in policy making and administrative decisions of institutions aided by them. Many ranchers also helped individuals in their own communities without making their benefactions known, but in giving to institutions they generally wanted their names attached to their gifts.

But religion and philanthropy in the cattle kingdom differed in degree if not in substance from patterns prevailing elsewhere in America. The relative newness and rural nature of ranch society accentuated the personalized link between giver and recipient. There were probably fewer church members relative to total population, but those who belonged to organized churches felt a special need to demonstrate God's guidance in their daily living. Rank-and-file citizens of the cattle kingdom respected only achieved status, and they expected works to demonstrate the soundness of any assumption of grace. God's elect therefore bore an especially heavy burden of proof in the cattle kingdom.

Changing Tides of Fortune

G LAMOR, romance, and legend tend to obscure business aspects of the ranching industry. Although raising and marketing cattle constituted the very core of the business, modern TV-Westerns seldom display a herd of cattle, even as an adjunct of their plots. Supposedly, success rested on a combination of great opportunities, good luck, and outstanding bravery, not on constant and dogged attention to details. Accident rather than business judgment has been used to explain why some ranchers failed and others succeeded. Ranching supposedly got started simply because a freighter's team of oxen survived the winter when their driver had to abandon them in a snow storm, thereby proving the suitability of the region for cattle raising. Around Roswell, New Mexico, today one hears a story of the origin of the LFD brand, which contributed so much to the wealth of George W. Littlefield and his nephew J. P. White, Sr. According to this story, drovers on their way to distant markets through that semi-arid region "Left For Dead" the animals that could not withstand the rigors of the trip. By nursing them back to health, White established the nucleus of his herd and the basis for his wealth, a windfall that encouraged him to commemorate his good fortune in the LFD brand. Actually, the brand was selected from letters in the surname of George W. LittleFielD when the partners disposed of another brand, the LIT, originally chosen in the same manner, along with the sale of the herd bearing it, to one of the syndicates of the period. The popular story of the brand's origin completely ignores the fact that its owners displayed remarkably astute business practices in building their ranching kingdom.

There were indeed sharp reverses and new opportunities occasioned by the rapidly and constantly changing nature of the ranching industry. Men could not afford to stand pat on business practices over a considerable period of time for new conditions demanded new approaches. After a lifetime of coping with this shifting pattern Charles Goodnight could be excused for speaking of his career in terms of luck in spite of his high average of success. As an old man, he wryly observed that "If all the good luck and all the bad luck I've had were put together, I reckon it'd make the biggest damned pile of luck in the world."[1] And yet Goodnight planned carefully in all that he did, recognizing that ranchers needed something more than opportunity, luck, and bravery to sustain their business enterprises.

But contemporary promoters discounted that necessity in their constant emphasis on opportunity. They spoke of men who purchased cattle cheaply in Texas, grazed them free on government land, and marketed them at huge profits. A few cowboys sufficed to care for sizable herds and taxes were low or nonexistent. In older regions one had to reckon with costs of land, labor, and taxes, but on the frontier one could concentrate investments in herds of cattle, the direct source of returns. Interest rates alone among the factors of production seemed unusually high, but the uninitiated could easily assume that high profits naturally led to high interest rates on borrowed capital. Such promotional pictures glossed over the need for business judgment.

Most effective of all, however, in obscuring the story of ranching as a business enterprise has been the tendency to emphasize the episodic and romantic rather than the enduring and the commonplace in Western history. When a WPA interviewer for the state of Utah visited William Cooley, an old farmer at Moab, on March 25, 1937, and asked him about his experiences dating back to 1874, he used the episodic, romantic approach in narrating the important things in his life. As a mine worker and small farmer he seems to have led a rather humdrum life. Nevertheless, according to his memory, he met over the years fifteen famous Westerners, including Jesse James, Billy the Kid, Buffalo Bill, Sitting Bull, and General Custer. When it came to the cattle industry, he naturally remembered the famous Johnson County, Wyoming, War and that, according to his account, John Clay and other large ranchers imported Texas gunmen to dispel or kill the squatters. But the squatters won and thereby took possession of the region.[2] Although more serious students have in some cases agreed with Cooley's version of Clay's part in that most famous of all conflicts between ranchers and nesters, to Cooley the Johnson County War highlighted the history of ranching. In it he saw a conflict of good and evil but nothing of the complex problems and the shifting social and economic patterns of which it was only a manifestation.

In establishing the cattle kingdom, ranchers faced a multitude of problems that tested their business judgment to the fullest. Early-day opportunities were balanced by early-day difficulties. Texas drovers who headed for Abilene, Kansas, in 1867 ran into all kinds of difficulty, such as Indian troubles, excessive rainstorms, flooded rivers that hampered their progress, and cholera. Heavy rains created an immense growth of grass along the trail but also made it too "coarse and washy" to provide proper nutriment for cattle. As a result, much of the stock arrived in unsuitable condition for market. Trail conditions improved later on, but Joseph G. McCoy commented in 1874 that few of the adventurous drovers of 1867 still continued in that business. Some had retired, others had changed occupations, and several had become bankrupt through "some adverse turn of fortune's wheel." According to McCoy, every Western cattle market annually ruined a full score of young, ambitious, and energetic cattle shippers who lacked necessary funds to tide them over unexpected losses.[3]

Ranchers and drovers alike suffered from the vicissitudes of nature. Although the hard winter of 1886-1887 has been credited with proving once and for all that open-range ranching would not work on the Great Plains, blizzards had seriously injured ranchers in previous years. John W. Iliff lost cattle by that means, and Claib Merchant, a Texas rancher, suffered heavily in the same manner. While holding a considerable herd of cattle in Colorado for spring delivery to a purchaser, Merchant lost over 75 per cent of his stock.[4] Colonel Ike T. Pryor suffered a similar disaster in 1885. Pryor sold a herd on the Colorado range for spring delivery to a Cleveland syndicate at one-half million dollars, receiving one hundred thousand dollars, in advance. A blizzard reduced his herd before delivery to the point where it was worth only sixty-five thousand dollars, thus leaving him thirty-five thousand dollars in debt when he had expected to receive a half million.[5]

Drouths lacked the sudden dramatic qualities of blizzards but could punish cattlemen even more effectively in their slow and agonizing way of destroying hopes. They decimated herds in New Mexico in the 1880's, challenged the ingenuity of the manager of the King Ranch during the years from 1886 to 1893, and threatened to bankrupt the XIT in the early 1890's. At times, they broke the courage of even the most experienced ranchers. Sam Doss, for instance, started running cattle in Texas as early as 1845, and operated ranches at various frontier locations during his long career. When illness combined with the hard times and long drouth of the early nineties broke his spirit, he committed suicide by throwing himself in front of a train at the station in Trinidad, Colorado. An inventory of his cattle showed later that he had underestimated his holdings, but the wear and tear of management proved more than the old man could bear.[6]

In his account of the XIT Ranch of Texas, J. Evetts Haley devotes a chapter to bog camps, lobos, and prairie fires, problems that plagued ranchers in many parts of the West.[7] In seasons of drouth, cattle bogged down in the mud that ringed water holes and soon died if cowboys did not rescue them. Prairie fires seldom took human lives but destroyed cattle and seriously reduced the forage necessary for their survival. Wolves preyed on cattle to such an extent that ranchers had to fight back or see their herds decimated. During his first winter as manager and part owner of a ranch in Montana in the early eighties, Granville Stuart estimated that losses of stock to predatory animals ran five per cent. Cattlemen began to hire former trappers to poison the creatures. By the middle 1880's people learned that wolf skins were valuable, and thus wolfing became an important Montana industry. Indians disliked the wolfers because their dogs ate the poisoned meat, and so took revenge whenever possible. Nevertheless, wolfers could not resist the possibility of making two to three thousand dollars during a good season. This they spent in drink and carousing, then turned to chopping wood for steamboats on the rivers or to working for freighters until winter arrived again, when they returned to their old life of hardship and peril as wolfers.[8] Farther south, ranchers assigned the task to some hand or let the work out to professional wolfers under contract.

Cattle diseases also plagued ranchers. Fear of the Texas tick fever, to which Texas cattle were immune but which spread among herds farther north, caused states and territories to the north and east to enact legislation against the importation of Texas cattle until their immunity had been established. Such action naturally hampered the long drives and the marketing of Texas cattle. Pleuropneumonia among herds on the Great Plains led to restrictions of shipments abroad and regulations within the United States. Even heel flies constituted a problem in parts of the cattle kingdom at certain seasons of the year. To escape their sting, cattle tended to bunch up and cease to graze, thereby failing to increase normally in weight. Such were some of the difficulties that kept the ranching frontier from being as glamorous as many have pictured it.

Moreover, problems seldom came singly. In the years immediately following its establishment in 1882, the Matador Ranch of Texas struggled against a drouth cycle, overstocking of the range, and a growing number of settlers on what shortly before had been open range.[9] The latter two problems generally developed some-

what late in range country and served to remind ranchers that solution of old difficulties only made way for a new crop. Granville
Stuart and his partners lost only three per cent of their stock because of storms during their first year on the Montana range.
Stuart attributed this low figure to the scarcity of cattle and the
resulting abundance of forage. Brush and tall rye grass furnished
dry beds and shelter equal to that of a good stable.[10] In time, the
countryside ceased to furnish abundant food and shelter because
of overgrazing, and cattle entered the winter season too weak to
withstand the Northern cold. Lincoln Lang commented on how
rapidly this change took place in the Dakota Bad Lands. When he
went there as a boy, streams often contained water the year
round, the result of beaver dams that retained the moisture from
torrential rains and seepage from springs. Soon the beaver were
trapped out and the streams began to go dry; cattle paths in the
easily eroded land became washouts; springs that had once furnished pure water became trampled mudholes; and many varieties
of migratory birds ceased to appear locally. Overstocking ruined
the Bad Lands for cattlemen, but sheepmen next appeared, and
finally dry farmers—all of whom contributed to giving the name
"Bad Lands" a literal as well as a figurative meaning.[11]

    Although less dramatic than the old, the newer problems con-
tinued to demand sound judgment on the part of those responsible
for decisions. For instance, Robert Samuel Dalton and two companions were killed and mutilated by Indians while returning to
Texas from a long drive in 1870. Ironically, the Indians overlooked eleven thousand dollars in an iron-bound trunk and another eleven thousand in large bills that Dalton had concealed in
his shoes.[12] The advent of railroads reduced the necessity for
cattlemen to expose themselves to such dangers but produced a
new problem of equitable rates. Although an advocate of railroad transportation, Joseph G. McCoy attributed his own financial downfall in his Abilene, Kansas, project to the failure of railroad officials to honor their contract, an agreement under which
McCoy was to have profited on all cattle shipped from Abilene.[13]
In the cattlemen's estimation, railroads, packers, and commission

houses became greater menaces than the Indians as the years went by.

Moreover, the cattle industry could never isolate itself from the financial ups and downs of America and the world at large in spite of its seemingly elementary economic nature and its location on the fringe of civilization. Panics and depressions like those of 1873 and 1893 stunned ranchers on the farthest reaches of the frontier along with financial leaders in metropolitan centers. Joseph G. McCoy's description of the drover's plight in 1873, written almost contemporaneously, reveals how deeply they were affected by climatic conditions and by financial problems to the eastward. Then, as generally, the cattlemen were operating to a considerable extent on borrowed money, the result only in part of efforts to expand their business. The length of time between the birth of a calf and his marketing as finished beef made it hard to adjust easily to shifting market conditions and also encouraged men to borrow funds to see them through the interval. According to McCoy, cattle prices had been good in 1872, which caused drovers to start still larger herds to market in 1873. By then, however, the Northern plains no longer bought so much stock for breeding purposes and were, indeed, beginning to compete with Texas producers for the Eastern markets. Moreover, some herds that had been driven north in 1872 to supply Indian reservations had not brought the expected price, and so their owners continued to hold them on the range to fatten for the fall market. That, of course, necessitated borrowing still more money. Some drovers were already in debt for their herds; others did not have enough money left when they reached Kansas in 1873 to pay off surplus hands or buy supplies. Nevertheless, they borrowed still more rather than accept the bids made to them upon arrival. McCoy estimated that Texas drovers present in Kansas on September 1, 1873, owed a million and a half dollars. Quite obviously, they were vulnerable to any restrictions on credit or a drop in prices.

About the middle of September the Panic of 1873 disrupted things locally, with many of the drovers obligated to pay off their loans the following month. Banks could make no further extensions, thus forcing drovers to sell. A short corn crop had reduced the number of buyers by 50 per cent as compared with the previous year. Moreover, the previous season in the West had been rainy, resulting in coarse, soft, and washy grass upon which the cattle had not fattened well. Stampedes occasioned by stormy weather had been greater than usual, adding to the poor condition of the cattle, of which perhaps 90 per cent were not in shape for sale for immediate slaughter in Eastern markets. To a man who sympathized with the cattlemen, it was like attending daily funerals of friends to watch the distress sales that took place. Many of the cattle shipped east brought no more than enough to cover freight and handling charges. McCoy estimated that the Panic cost Texas drovers two million dollars in losses and bankrupted men by the scores. In his opinion, it constituted the greatest calamity that had ever hit the cattle country.[14]

More accurate information as to supply and demand throughout the country and more rapid means of moving cattle to market would have prevented much of the distress. In September, 1873, a large number of interested ranchers met in Kansas City to consider forming an organization to work on common problems. By then, McCoy was convinced that ranchers should fatten their cattle at home and ship by rail whenever possible. This would lessen the need for borrowing money and would save time in reaching markets. Rail shipments would also decrease the tendency to pour thousands of cattle on the market simultaneously and the necessity of having to sell at the first approach of frosty weather. Moreover, drovers could escape the dangers, hardships, and exposures of the trail and enjoy the comforts of home to a greater extent.[15] Nevertheless, necessity alone extended the period of overland drives for another decade because of lack of sufficient railroads. Nor could cattlemen balance supply and demand sufficiently well to guarantee profitable operations, even with increased market information. It took time to raise a calf to the age of prime beef, and from that point he descended rapidly to canner stock if held off the market for an extended period in hopes of better prices.

Above, Charles Goodnight and his ranch in Colorado, 1874.
Below, Loading cattle at Wichita, Kansas, 1874. (All drawings from McCoy, *Historic Sketches of the Cattle Trade*)

Above, eight of the winter's toll,
1886-87. (L. A. Huffman photo)
At left, C. M. Russell's "Last of the
5,000." (Historical Society of Montana)

Cheyenne, Wyoming, in the early 1880's. (University of Wyoming Library)

Since he was involved in cattle marketing, McCoy probably was overly sensitive to buffetings which drovers and traders suffered from shifting financial conditions in the world at large. He spoke of ranchers as being more cautious and less exposed than drovers to financial ups and downs. Such was true only to a degree, however, since ranchers, too, felt the effects of the Panic of 1873. For instance, when McCoy published his book in 1874 he lacked information as to how Charles Goodnight had fared during the Panic. He spoke of Goodnight's success on his early drives and how profitable they had been for him. He also mentioned that Goodnight had shifted from driving to ranching, and had "settled down" to a life that McCoy considered free of the rough living, dangers, and speculations of the trail.[16] Quite obviously, he approved of Goodnight's decision to concentrate on ranching and assumed that it more or less protected him from happenings such as the Panic of 1873.

In 1869 Goodnight did acquire a fine ranching location on the Arkansas River above Pueblo. Although still mildly involved in trail driving, he brought his bride to the ranch in 1870 and began to develop his lands. He ditched his valley for irrigation, set out the first large orchard in southern Colorado, and began to grow corn. Goodnight invested in farm land and Pueblo real estate, and he and his wife took an active interest in community affairs. In September, 1873, he and other local citizens organized the Stock Growers Bank of Pueblo. Nevertheless, as Goodnight later said, the Panic of 1873 "wiped me off the face of the earth." Nor did cattle driving account for his failure. In addition to loans on local real estate, he owned the Pueblo opera house and other buildings. Rather than pay taxes on property that ceased to make any return, he deeded it over to his creditors.[17] A builder rather than a plunger, Goodnight let the Panic catch him overextended, but his troubles in the 1870's arose from the fact that he was a progressive rancher, not from his activities as a drover. Nor was he unique among ranchers in suffering from the Panic.

During periods of financial stringency loans were unavailable or were made at usurious rates. Charles F. Coffee of Wyoming in

later years vividly recalled his experiences in 1873. On pooled resources of $4,400, he and a partner borrowed an additional
$13,000 to finance a northern drive. The Panic hit before they
could market their herd, thus necessitating additional funds. For
these the partners paid an interest rate of 2 to 3 per cent a month,
24 to 36 per cent a year! For months Coffee was in the saddle
daily, no matter what the weather, and he bought no clothing unless absolutely necessary. By such means he managed to extricate
himself and went on to become a successful rancher.[18] Even more
experienced drovers like the Snyder brothers of Texas could not
escape similarly high interest rates when they were caught north
with a herd of cattle in 1873.[19]

Cattlemen continued to feel the effects of financial stringencies
as the years went by. In 1885 the Snyder brothers refused an
offer of one million dollars for their Wyoming land and cattle
holdings, only to find it necessary to sell everything within a few
months at a great loss to protect their business associates.[20]
George W. Miller experienced an equally quick reversal of fortune. For years he drove Texas cattle to his Oklahoma ranch,
where he fattened them for market. Although he prospered as a
rancher, the Panic of 1893 almost bankrupted him. His agent, a
Kansas City commission house, failed during that crisis, and at a
time when it was holding three hundred thousand dollars of Miller's money, collected for him on cattle shipments. In addition,
Miller had to pay off one hundred thousand dollars in notes to
Eastern banks, an obligation that his commission house had not
met from his deposits before going under. At the time, he had
17,000 beef cattle on his ranch. The bankers' agents took all his
livestock in payment, except for eighty-eight old horses and a few
cows. Miller met the crisis by changing over from straight ranching to diversified agriculture, including wheat farming.[21] Within
a few years he regained his prosperity, but his sons failed to benefit from his experiences, overexpanding in a later period to the
point where the depression of 1929 bankrupted them.

The rapidly changing nature of the ranching industry constituted
perhaps the greatest challenge to cattlemen. Within the lifetime of

men like Charles Goodnight, Conrad Kohrs, and George W. Littlefield, ranching underwent three rather marked changes: an experimental period with nomadic herds on open range; organization of large companies and feverish expansion; and then a contraction—highlighted by great losses of open-range stock in the hard winter of 1886-1887—in which ranchers turned to purchasing and fencing land, winter feeding, emphasis on blooded stock, and a multitude of other changes in the direction of making ranching a science rather than a gamble. It was never a simple operation in which unimaginative men could imitate a course of action that others had successfully pursued and expect to spend a lifetime doing so. Successful ranchers experimented with new methods of operation and changed whenever justified. They needed a high degree of entrepreneurial skill. Although Charles Goodnight and others might speak of the "piles" of good and bad luck that they had experienced during the course of a lifetime, they rode the changing tides of fortune alert to every opportunity. Daring, imaginative, and flexible in policy decisions, they played for and won greater stakes than fell to the professional gamblers who have become stock characters in Western romantic literature. They proved that being a "good businessman" in the cattle kingdom involved more than hard work and attention to details.

Free grazing land, limited access to water, and a sparse population characterized the early, open-range period of ranching. He who controlled the limited number of water holes and streams controlled also the surrounding watershed. Cattle brands identified the rancher's property, no matter where it wandered in the absence of fences. Indeed, the brand mark indicated that cattle rather than land constituted wealth; on them almost alone the rancher put his mark of ownership. He thought it foolish to acquire title to land, other than small amounts for his headquarters and around watering spots, when its use was free to him. Although Texas longhorns and work cattle that pulled the wagons of freighters and travelers on the plains made a stringy beef, they had a greater capacity than blooded stock for survival in the early days. Although they sold for less than corn-fed beef, they could be marketed, and they constituted the foundation herds of many an early rancher.

How soon should a man begin to spend money on wells and windmills and other artificial means of increasing water supply? How soon should he divert part of his operating capital to purchase grazing land that at the moment he could occupy free? How soon should he pay for fencing instead of letting his cattle run at large? How soon should he invest in blooded stock to improve his herds? If done too quickly, he lost the advantages of open-range ranching; if delayed too long, he found others in possession of his range and his markets pre-empted by better beef.

Certainly ranchers could not stand still. The rush of people into ranching and the growing number of farmers who homesteaded or purchased land made that impossible. Cattlemen could of course move on to the edge of the ranching frontier as long as open range remained, and many did so. There they could continue to use many of the methods employed in their old location. Some of them profited by selling herds and range rights to individuals and companies wanting to enter the industry, and moved on after each sale to another advanced outpost, thereby constituting the cutting edge of the cattleman's frontier.

Inclination and profit alike motivated H. B. Kelly in his tendency to move on to new ranch country. He participated in the California gold rush in 1849, but shifted to freighting around Santa Fe, New Mexico, in the early 1850's. For a short time he operated a stage line from Independence, Missouri, to Santa Fe, and in 1858 drove a cargo of freight to Salt Lake City. He tried gold mining at Leadville, Colorado, and then worked for Ben Holladay's stage line. Through such wanderings he gained considerable knowledge of Western opportunities as well as a love for the frontier. By 1864 he was operating a small ranch in the vicinity of Fort Laramie and exchanging cattle with immigrant groups. For a number of years he ranched on the Chugwater, selling cattle to the government forts and Indian tribes. In 1880 he sold his herd to the Swan Land and Cattle Company for several thousand dollars and then put a herd on the North Crazy Woman Creek with the idea of supplying beef to Fort Fetterman. This venture, too, he sold out at a considerable profit. In 1884 he went to England and disposed of his remaining interests on the Chugwater to the Swan Land and Cattle Company for a quarter of a million dollars. After this sale he became interested in herds of cattle on the Belle Fourche and on the Snake River in Idaho. Although not unprogressive as a rancher, Kelly profited most of all by selling out to less adventurous people and starting over again on new frontiers. As a stage driver he suffered frozen feet, at times wandering bands of Indians made him cook a meal for them, and he participated in some of the more exciting gold rushes. All this, however, was only a by-product of a business career characterized, at least until 1885, by remarkable adaptability to opportunity and excellent judgment as to when to sell out and move on.[22]

Lonny Horn and Sam Doss operated much as Kelly did. Both began ranching in Texas before the Civil War but spent their most active years outside their native state. They built up large herds from a shoestring and moved on to new locations as soon as range threatened to become crowded. Doss even thought of going to Argentina in search of new frontiers. In the early 1880's, he found himself squeezed in between the Prairie Cattle Company and the Western Land and Cattle Company, large corporate enterprises so characteristic of the period. Although temporarily reluctant to sell out, Doss found the offer made by the Prairie Company for his range and cattle too tempting to resist. From there he moved on to the Colorado-New Mexico border to start a new outfit. Similarly, Lonny Horn followed the frontier, and in 1886 was operating a breeding range in eastern Utah and western Colorado.[23] In addition to liking the frontier, Doss and Horn found it highly profitable to develop ranches on free land at the edge of settlement and then dispose of these to late-comers.

Joseph G. McCoy, writing in the early 1870's, recorded the advantages and drawbacks of open-range ranching with considerable accuracy. Although convinced that buffalo grass and other natural forage on the Western range would fatten livestock, he warned prospective cattlemen to obtain locations having running water and as much timber and shelter as possible. They should purchase outright a sufficient body of land to control water rights and the tillable soil for miles around. Otherwise, they could expect "agricultural neighbors" to interfere. McCoy recognized few "poetical and sentimental" rewards of the occupation beyond independent freedom. Ranchers could expect to start with a dugout for a home, and to undergo diligent labor, watchfulness, care and risk, and great self-denial. As servants of their herds they would face severe weather and lonely privations. Their food would be of the simplest. If they could meet these challenges, however, "the broad free West" offered great opportunities in cheap land and cheap cattle and in a generally mild climate.[24]

Looking back on such men from the vantage point of his years in the cattle industry, John Clay praised them for building up their herds through economy. They lived in dugouts or log cabins, ate beans and bacon, and used baking powder bread. In contrast, the big cattle corporations, which bought out many of them, employed managers at five thousand dollars a year, maintained offices in Kansas City and London, and burdened themselves with directorates, secretaries, and other extravagances.[25] In spite of his praise, Clay knew that the early open-range cattleman had to give way or adopt better methods of ranching. Although many of the promotional companies of the 1880's operated extravagantly, the solution for all concerned lay in sound administration of progressive policies. Open-range ranching simply had to give way.

Before that became thoroughly evident the industry passed through a second phase in which investment capital poured in from the East and abroad to reap the supposedly great profits from raising cattle on cheap or free land. In reality this period involved speculation, expansion, and changes in business organization more than any fundamental modifications in handling cattle. During the period individual cattlemen, as well as incorporated groups, learned what could and could not be done successfully, a continuation of the trial-and-error process that began with the first days of open-range ranching. Participants discovered the pitfalls and virtues of various policies and managerial methods, tested the advantages of large-scale ranching as versus smaller units, and became more fully aware of the climatic and geographical limitations of the region. In reality, the handling of cattle passed through only two rather well-defined stages, consisting of open-range ranching and the enclosed phase which succeeded it. The hard winter of 1886-1887 and concurrently bad markets only speeded up a transition which had been taking place year by year since the beginning.

The free-grass system of open range collapsed in part through abuses committed by thoughtless or greedy cattlemen. Some ranchers grazed more cattle than the land could reasonably carry and thereby injured their business in the long run. Under such pressure the native grasses disappeared and brush took over. Although ranchers claimed that they respected the range rights of others, early and continued complaints against overstocking resulted to a considerable extent from the growing number of individuals and companies who insisted upon starting new outfits on land that others had already claimed. When the Langs entered the Dakota Bad Lands, for instance, they found only a few scattered ranches under operation by the pioneer outfits. Nevertheless, the region was filling rapidly. They selected their home ranch at the site of a deserted cabin, made preparations to move, and then discovered that someone had started to build a shack and stable less than a mile below them on the river bottom. Inquiry soon established that the builders constituted the vanguard of a large Southern outfit whose trail herd would shortly arrive. A Scotsman accompanying the Lang family threatened open warfare in the hope of dislodging the new outfit but they quickly called his bluff and forced him to retreat. The Langs felt that the Southerners had virtually "jumped" them, since, under the unwritten law of the range, they were supposed to respect the Lang's prior location and to give them ample room. Perhaps they acted honestly, believing that they were not trespassing because of the aban-

doned look of the cabin on the Lang claim. Lang's father was inclined to favor locating eight miles down the river, and for that
reason gave way to the Southerners, but otherwise the incident
could easily have resulted in gun play.[26] Some perhaps overgrazed open-range lands because they realized that they must take
their profits before settlers could purchase or homestead the
region. Certainly, open-range ranching invited land exploitation,
violence, and ruthlessness that could not be endured for any
length of time after population pressure developed.

Moreover, experience convinced progressive ranchers that
they must enclose their ranches if they expected to produce quality
beef to compete in national and international markets. If one's
cattle mingled with those of other ranchers on open range who
used scrub bulls, it did little good to purchase expensive blooded
sires in order to upbreed the stock. Blizzards and drouths provided evidence of the need for supplementary feeding, and many
planned to raise at least part of their feed in fenced enclosures.
Fences also kept cattle from straying unduly and thus becoming
prey to rustlers and predatory animals. Rough handling of cattle
during open-range days became less acceptable when blooded
stock replaced the half-wild animals of an earlier period. Fenced
holdings thus enabled a rancher to institute new policies without
having to consult the wishes of others operating in the same general region.

Long leasing arrangements or outright ownership of land alone
could guarantee a rancher that the costs of fencing would be justified, for otherwise growing population pressure might deprive
him of its use within a short time. Some ranchers took that chance,
feeling that squatters would fear to invade their holdings. By 1884
some of the big companies were starting to fence their range,
much of which they did not own. The cry of "down with the
fences" on the part of those excluded from the public domain
resulted in Congressional legislation ordering the removal of all
illegal fencing. A. S. Mercer expressed the sentiments of many
cattlemen in regard to the act when he remarked at a meeting in
Miles City, Montana, on April 3, 1885:

Every Jim Crow paper from New York to San Francisco is belittling and bemoaning the cattlemen, branding us bulldozers and thieves. . . . they are warped in their ideas. . . . The recent action of the President shows this, and every paper in the East comes to his support, and pats him on the shoulder and cries "Down with the monopolists! Down with the thieves! Down with the bulldozers!" This encourages him and he immediately issues another order, "Down with the fences!"[27]

Although much of the land in question was unsuited to farming, American tradition supported the idea of homesteads of 160 acres upon which sturdy, independent men supposedly would build family lives buttressed in time-honored values. Such ideas developed during the settlement period east of the Mississippi River, where, in reality, 160 acres supported a family nicely. Taking that experience for proof that the same thing was possible in the trans-Mississippi West, many people thought of cattlemen as monopolists, not recognizing that families would starve to death on 160 acres of ranch land. Nor could they understand that hundreds of acres of such land were necessary to maintain even a small ranching outfit. Instead, they correlated wealth with number of acres held—a fair measuring stick east of the Mississippi— instead of recognizing the need to classify land according to its ability to produce. Under such circumstances, cattlemen found it virtually impossible to obtain legislation permitting sensible land usage.

If the public and the government would not listen to them, ranchers were tempted to act beyond the law. If they could not purchase land at a price that would let them graze cattle profitably or lease it for long periods of time, they felt justified in going ahead with their plans for fencing, thereby fencing out those who would defy climate and geography in efforts to live as farmers. As rugged individualists, cattlemen found it all the easier to conclude that sound ranching principles and the nature of the country justified them in acting contrary to the established law. Such was the line of reasoning employed by those who fenced their lands illegally.

Some, of course, still advocated open-range ranching as late as the middle eighties and saw no need to fret about fencing problems or to give serious consideration to farmers. In Wyoming, Thomas Benton Hord, who arrived on the local scene in 1880, took sharp issue with more experienced men who suggested that losses on the open range in severe winters would be excessive without supplementary feeding. Some experienced men, however, like Ora Haley, were inclined to agree with Hord, and remained convinced that the old practice of running cattle in large herds would continue because it was the only profitable way to operate.[28] The Harvard-educated Hubert Engelbrecht Teschemacher still pursued his speculative way, feeling that business would be good for many years. The "Almighty" had intended to create Wyoming as cattle country and the government should recognize such wisdom and lease all land to the cattlemen. Moreover, fences should be removed from all the public domain for they prevented cattle from drifting with the wind during blizzards and thereby caused needless losses.[29]

Others proved more realistic, or at least more prophetic, as to the course which ranchers would take. By the middle 1880's many Wyoming cattlemen felt that fencing and feeding were necessary practices in good ranching. James E. Tuttle thought that the days of the big herds were numbered, that overgrazing had injured the range, and that winter feeding was essential. Fred Hesse, manager of Frewen Brothers Cattle Company, believed that the future lay in feeding cattle and in breeding up herds. He expected ranchers to raise hay as part of their routine. A. R. Converse agreed with him in general. Worden P. Noble even expected settlers to crowd ranchers into more limited holdings, thereby making winter feeding necessary. Arnold A. Mowry thought that winter feeding of cattle in small herds would become the regular practice. Moreover, he favored enforcing the law against illegal fencing and wanted to turn the public domain over to the people. Although this would injure him financially, he insisted that the profit motive should not stand in the way of justice.[30]

The majority of ranchers undoubtedly understood the need for change. A report of the Wyoming Stock Growers Association in 1884 recognized the rapidly changing nature of the industry. According to it, the old days of rule of thumb had passed, days when one needed only to brand calves as they dropped and ship them when fat. In those times the calf tally was notched on a shingle, and the check book was the only additional record kept. By reference to his balance or overdraft at the bank, the rancher judged the degree of his success. Now, one needed system, economy, and judgment. Problems even extended over state lines: control of contagious cattle diseases; creation of a national organization of stock growers; use of government land for grazing; and transportation and marketing of beef. Even problems of a seemingly more localized nature exerted an influence beyond the immediate environment, problems relating to territorial legislation covering cattlemen, the attitude of nonresident members of the Association concerning its actions, and the control of rustling.[31]

Interviewers sent out by the federal government in 1884-1885 reported considerable unanimity of opinion among ranchers. Even the big companies were beginning to accept the idea that fencing was a necessary step in improving the quality of their stock. Land-hungry settlers were pouring in so rapidly that the great majority of cattlemen recognized the necessity for breaking up the large ranches. Most ranchers now accepted the inevitability of smaller herds in fenced pastures on freehold land. They knew that overstocked and overgrazed ranges left them vulnerable to marked variations in climatic conditions. They saw the necessity of improving breeds and winter feeding in order to produce quality beef for urban markets.[32]

Thus the hard winter of 1886-1887 hastened but did not cause the changes in Western ranching in the later 1880's. Their antecedents traced back to earlier decades and they were still being worked out in the 1890's. Nevertheless, one notes a third phase of the ranching industry, a period which witnessed: the breaking up of many of the large companies and a movement toward smaller holdings; ownership by individuals or small companies in place of large corporations; use of the public domain by lease rather than by occupation; control and management by owners rather than by absentees; and marked improvements in methods of handling cattle.[33] Fencing, winter feeding, and improved breeding illustrated but did not begin to exhaust the many changes in the latter category.

During those volatile years many ranchers prospered, but many more fell by the way. Although courage and luck helped lift the successful above their less fortunate contemporaries, no man achieved a stable prosperity on so flimsy a base. Problems were too numerous and too changing in nature for that to happen. It required imagination and business skill to capitalize on the opportunities afforded by the ranching frontier.

Land, Labor, and Capital

ACCESS to free range constituted the greatest advantage to early-day ranchers, an asset that promoters still emphasized as late as the 1880's. In addition to free or cheap land, labor costs supposedly remained low, and there were few capital outlays other than investment in herds of cattle. General James S. Brisbin gave several illustrations of this supposedly ideal combination of the factors of production in his promotional book, *The Beef Bonanza*, in 1881. An investment of $25,000, according to him, would yield a net profit of $51,278 at the end of six years, plus compound interest on the original sum at a rate of 7 per cent. Two hundred dollars would suffice to purchase a headquarters site, the only outlay for land. For two hundred more one could purchase a mower, horse rake, and plow. A few horses and a small reserve to cover wages completed the allocation of funds for everything but cattle, thus leaving the original capital virtually intact to purchase 1750 Texas cows and sufficient Durham bulls to improve the stock. Four men could do the necessary work during the six-year period, thus holding labor costs to a minimum. If one chose to sell out at the end of the period and to take the enormous accumulated profits, he could obtain $450 for his nine horses, $375 for wagons, mules, and harness, and $1,000 for ranch site and "good will of the range," that is, for his prescriptive right to run cattle on public land in his accustomed range. The remainder of the $92,237 realized would come from sale of the cattle. Thus, Brisbin pictured an operation in which only $1,825 represented land and equipment, in which four employees made up the labor force, and from which enormous profits were bound to come because virtually the whole investment went directly into profit-producing cattle.[1] Brisbin might have added that in the absence of organized local government the investor would be wholly tax exempt.

Such a favorable combination of the factors of production actually existed at certain times and in certain places. John W. Iliff benefited tremendously from favorable land, labor, and tax conditions, although a closer look at his methods of operation will also reveal his entrepreneurial skill. Still, the figures indicate that he had great opportunities at hand. In 1874, costs of wintering and herding his cattle for the year totaled only $15,000, yet he had on hand the following year 26,000 cattle valued at $469,000. During 1875 he employed hands ranging in number from 12 to 35 to care for his immense herds, and sold off during that time cattle to the value of $128,000. Obviously, his labor costs were very reasonable. He owned about 160 horses for herding, valued at $35 to $75 a head, again a minor cost in view of the extent of his operations. A newspaper report in 1877 credited him with having over a million dollars worth of cattle and with being the heaviest taxpayer in Weld County, Colorado. The county assessed his personal property at $174,110, including 21,240 cattle and 120 horses. It valued his real estate at only $10,185, an indication of how little he had to tie up in lands to sustain his cattle business. His taxes for the year were only $3,062.60![2]

Virtually all ranchers tried to acquire outright title to their headquarters site and almost as frequently to small plats of land that controlled streams and water holes. When George W. Littlefield and his nephew, Phelps White, established their LFD ranch near Roswell, New Mexico, in the early 1880's, White purchased outright a 160-acre homestead at ten dollars an acre for use as headquarters. John Chisum's old four-room adobe house stood on the land, and to this White added two rooms. In addition, the site provided cottonwood trees for shade and fuel, and a well. From this headquarters on the brackish Pecos River the partners had access to a range some forty by eighty miles in extent.³ There they could run thousands of cattle at a negligible cost, or free, insofar as the land factor was concerned. Ranchers also exercised homestead rights, and encouraged their employees to do likewise with the idea of buying their claims for token sums. Whatever their procedure, they could acquire necessary land reasonably. John Hittson, early Colorado cattle king, controlled all the water for many miles in all directions by owning only one-half section of land. Similarly, J. P. Farmer controlled all the water in the West Bijou River, a tributary of the Platte in Colorado, by owning 640 acres, which assured him ample free range for his 2700 cattle and fifty horses as well as room for expansion.⁴

Although favored by adequate free range in the early years, ranchers were highly vulnerable once settlers arrived in their vicinity. Land suitable for farming yielded a greater net return per acre in crops than if used simply for grazing. Farmers could thus afford to outbid ranchers for such land. Unfortunately, however, many a farmer misjudged the agricultural potential of land, thus homesteading or purchasing tracts suitable only for ranching. Consequently, many ranchers purchased land outright to protect themselves against newcomers if they could buy it at reasonable prices. Moreover, many realized that land would increase in value over the years. Some of the larger cattle companies intended from the first to sell out their holdings in small plats to farmers when population pressure made this profitable.

On the other hand, entrepreneurs like George W. Littlefield learned early in their careers the importance of keeping assets sufficiently liquid to survive crises like that of the Panic of 1873, and in drouth, blizzard, and the other vicissitudes of nature. Investment opportunities of various kinds also came their way. With capital scarce in the West, banking, merchandising, and mining competed with ranching for available funds and might well pay greater dividends. Thus, in spite of marked increase in land values in many regions within a few years, those who seemingly did well in buying land at an early date might have profited still more by other kinds of investments or by concentrating on open-range ranching as long as possible.

Moreover, state and federal land legislation often made it difficult to acquire large holdings of a compact nature. Texas, owning her lands, granted certificates to railroads, corporations, and individuals for millions of acres to be located by the grantee on unclaimed public domain. Firms like Gunter, Munson and Summerfield, surveyors and locators, disposed of such claims for the original grantees and also dealt directly in them. When Charles Goodnight established a ranch in the Texas Panhandle in the late 1870's, Gunter, Munson and Summerfield had already virtually "surveyed" him in—that is, they held the power to dispose of key land by survey and sale in the heart of the range country where he located. Goodnight bought twelve thousand acres from them at seventy-five cents an acre. Knowing the region well, he selected land having access to water and good range, the ownership of which discouraged others from settling nearby. Goodnight also bought additional land through the same firm and others at prices ranging from twenty to thirty-five cents an acre, his selections showing good judgment as to ranching needs and land values.

Nevertheless, by the mid-1880's railroads began to penetrate his region, thus creating an increased flow of settlers. Goodnight expected them to come by the hundreds, to occupy sections reserved for sale for school revenue, and to make it more difficult for him and other ranchers to lease land that they had been unable to purchase outright. Consequently, he terminated his ranching partnership, taking for his share the Quitaque Ranch of 140,000 acres. Even that failed to solve his problems since he owned outright only alternate sections. Farmers began to occupy the remaining sections, vexing him with their wandering stock, their branding of mavericks, burning off the range, butchering strays, and destroying fences.[5] Although Goodnight had selected his holdings as wisely as possible, and they rose in value with increasing population pressure, they did not constitute a sufficiently integrated unit to let him decide freely whether to sell out at a profit or continue to operate.

When a Scottish syndicate bought the Espuela Cattle Company of Texas in 1883, they found it immediately advisable to purchase outright ownership of the range involved. From the New York and Texas Land Company, Ltd., a holding company for railroad lands, the Espuela bought $514,440 worth of land located in alternate sections on the Texas public domain for the Spur Ranch. Since the remaining land within the purchase area could be leased from the state, the Spur was able to fence some 500,000 acres. Only outright ownership of all the land, however, would have saved the Spur from trouble with nesters, who had public opinion in their favor. They entered the fenced Spur pastures to obtain firewood without consideration for the corporation's wishes. Although the Spur gave wood freely to churches and schools, and even to hard-pressed nesters, it never succeeded in getting them to comply with its wishes as to types and location of firewood to be removed.[6] Thus, it was not simply a matter of whether one should buy land, but of whether sufficiently integrated holdings could be obtained.

Successful ranchers differed greatly in their judgment as to the wisdom of buying land at the earliest possible moment. Captain Richard King began to lay the basis of his land empire as early as 1852. Family tradition says that Robert E. Lee, while serving a tour of duty in Texas, visited the King family and advised them to follow his own belief that one should buy land but never sell it. Although Lee probably never gave them such advice, the family knew him, and King named one of his sons after the famous general. Over the years the family came to believe that it was following the old Southern tradition that land should be owned and not bartered in the market place. Supposedly, too, King remarked later in life to his former partner in steamboating that while boats fell prey to wrecks and decay, land and livestock increased in value.

Whatever the cause, King thought of his ranching venture as an investment for the future and plowed into it funds from steamboating and other enterprises. Spanish and Mexican land grants in Southwest Texas received legal confirmation by the Texas legislature in the early 1850's, thus providing King an opportunity to obtain large holdings. His first purchase of 15,500 acres in the forks of the Santa Gertrudis and San Fernando creeks, on part of which the modern town of Kingsville stands, cost him three hundred dollars, and he added to his holdings over the years. As his biographer suggests, friends and lawyers contributed greatly to his success. The former provided business help and capital; the latter checked land titles for him so carefully that later suits contesting his ownership were of no avail. In 1867 he and his most prominent partner, Mifflin Kenedy, divided up their common holdings, and the latter purchased the Laureles grant from the Stillman family. Both men began to fence their land, using creosoted cypress posts and pine planks brought by ship from Louisiana. Elsewhere in Texas and on the plains, open-range ranching was in its infancy and barbed-wire fencing many years in the future. At the end of 1868 Kenedy's thirty miles of heavy post and three-plank fencing enclosed 131,000 acres, the first fenced range of any real size west of the Mississippi River. Of the two, however, King displayed the greater love for land. At his death in 1885 his estate was appraised at $1,061,484—$564,784 in real estate and $496,700 in livestock and other property. In adjusting the ranch to changing conditions, his son-in-law and successor as manager, Robert J. Kleberg, had to sell some land before the upward climb in land ownership could be resumed toward the million-acre enterprise that the ranch ultimately became.[7]

King's land increased greatly in value over the years. Similarly, original investors in some of the great foreign cattle corporations that supposedly lost everything in the hard winter of 1886-1887 actually profited if they held on until their companies sold out at greatly increased prices in the twentieth century. Shareholders in the Prairie Cattle Company who stayed with it in hard times and good until it closed out during World War I made ample profits on their investment. Western Ranches, another cattle corporation, shifted in the direction of a land-mortgage business in the twentieth century. Original investors who retained their stock from the company's formation in 1883 to its termination in 1919 got back double their capital investment and an average dividend of 9 per cent annually over a 37-year period. The Matador Ranch achieved an even better record. It too experienced the ups and downs of ranching but had many prosperous periods. In 1948, for instance, its board chairman announced that the directors had obtained a voluntary agreement among shareholders to limit annual dividends to 30 per cent! Prospects improved still more when the British devalued the pound and a major oil strike occurred within ninety miles of the ranch. In 1950, Lazard Brothers and Company of London paid nineteen million dollars for the Matador and agreed to share any future mineral or oil royalties equally with the vendors. Matador shares thus sold for over thirty times their original cost and after having approximated 15 per cent annual dividends or bonuses during the preceding thirty years. Original Matador shares thus proved a bonanza.[8]

Some ranchers, however, thought it best not to buy grazing land until absolutely necessary. John W. Iliff died before the days of open range passed in his region. Nevertheless, it is worth noting that Iliff owned very little ranch land, even though he could have acquired large amounts at very reasonable prices. Moreover, some time before his death he started investing part of his profits in bank stock and Denver real estate.[9] The latter increased in value far more than would have a similar sum invested in ranch lands. In other words, alternative investment opportunities challenged the skill of any entrepreneur who looked to the future.

Like Goodnight, George W. Littlefield could have purchased outright his LIT range in the Texas Panhandle. As early as 1878 Gunter, Munson and Summerfield offered to sell him 16,800 acres at seventy-five cents an acre. Although this was a reasonable price, Littlefield thought that the open range would last a while longer and preferred to use his capital funds in other ways. In 1881 he sold his LIT herd and his simple range rights to a Scottish syndicate for $253,000. Even had he owned the land, he might not have obtained a better price as agents for foreign syndicates were buying freely and without particularly good judgment as to what they obtained for their money. Littlefield and his nephew shifted their major operations to New Mexico, where they benefited from open range and favorable leases of federal land for a period of years. In 1888, for instance, the Littlefield interests owned only about 15,000 acres near their Four Lakes Ranch, a range which constituted something like a million and a half acres. They bought out an occasional troublesome nester but by 1910 were convinced that it was better to dispose of their range rights and holdings in that region. Their successor found it necessary to buy out additional squatters at prices which bankrupted him, an indication that the Littlefield group knew when to turn loose of a range at a profit. In 1901, Littlefield paid two dollars an acre for 235,858 acres constituting the Yellow House division of the XIT Ranch in Texas. This was more than double the going price for Panhandle land in 1878, but Littlefield had used his capital in the interval to profit by ranching on free or cheap land and in other ways. His Austin bank, the American National, for instance, paid dividends of 20 per cent a year to its stockholders from its start in 1890.[10]

Richard King bought land early and fenced it in; George W. Littlefield bought late, preferring to depend upon open range. Both made money. That alone indicates that entrepreneurial skill perhaps paid the greatest dividends of all.

Although labor costs generally are high and workers scarce in frontier regions, there seems to have been an adequate supply of cowboys as a rule and a wage scale no higher than that prevailing in older communities. For the nation as a whole in 1860, common laborers received about six dollars a week and artisans not quite twice that amount, approximately twenty-five dollars a month for the former and fifty for the latter. By 1880, following readjustments after the Civil War, wages of common labor averaged around thirty-two dollars a month and pay of artisans sixty. From then to 1900 wages advanced slightly for the country as a whole.[11] Writing in the early 1870's, Joseph G. McCoy estimated that wages of cowboys ranged from fifteen to twenty dollars a month in specie, and that Mexicans could be obtained for twelve.[12] They also received board, which perhaps added no more than three to four dollars a month per man. At least, the Spur Ranch in Texas fed its hands at an average cost of eleven cents a day in the period 1889-1910.[13] Such figures indicate that wages were actually lower in the cattle kingdom than in older parts of the country.

One historian of the cattle industry has suggested that during the 1870's and early 1880's, a period of rapid expansion, good hands were relatively scarce and could easily find work. During slack seasons they received no pay but lived by "riding the grub-line," that is, by staying free of cost with some outfit that would take them on when the busy season arrived. After the crash of 1886-1887, jobs became scarce, and some would-be cowboys were driven to rustling in order to survive. The typical ordinary cowboy received $30.00 a month and keep; if very good, his wages ranged from $35.00 to $45.00 a month. Trail bosses received from $50.00 to $65.00 a month, and range foremen $125.00 a month and keep. Over the years, the number of hands declined as the open range gave way to fencing and operations were reduced and simplified.[14]

William Holden's detailed analysis of operations on the Spur Ranch in Texas for the period 1889-1910 shows that wages constituted the single largest item of yearly expenses for that corporation, not counting, of course, payments on invested capital. Between 1885 and 1909, the ranch employed a yearly average of forty men. From December to March it needed only one-third to one-half as many workers as it did for the remainder of the year. On the basis of a yearly average, it employed one worker for every 1250 cattle. Only on one occasion during that spread of years did the ranch find itself shorthanded during the busy season. Significantly, wages on the Spur depended more upon the reliability of the individual and the length of time that he had worked for the ranch that it did on the kind of duties performed. In some types of work wages were fairly well standardized, as in cooking. A wagon cook got the same wage as a top hand; a headquarters cook got $50.00 a month, and thus rated the same pay as a trail boss. Although trail bosses and range foremen were paid in accordance with their work, an ordinary hand and a skilled handler of cattle might work side by side in branding, riding fence, and other duties in spite of difference in their pay. Like so many other ranches, the Spur had an abundance of crude labor but found it advisable to pay considerably better wages to reliable and skilled employees in order to hold them.[15]

In addition to board and lodging, ranchers almost always furnished horses for their mounted employees, partially because the necessarily hard riding at roundup time required that each cowboy have a half-dozen mounts available so he could change to a fresh horse when the one in use became fagged. As a rule, cowboys furnished their own saddles and other riding gear but otherwise were paid only for their labor and skill.

Quite obviously, as a factor of production in the ranching industry, labor was relatively cheap as compared to the prevailing situation in most industries in older sections. As a rule, ranchers found the supply adequate, often abundant, and they needed to spend little or no time and money in recruiting a labor force. Although a seasonal occupation in the sense that the number of employees needed to be sharply increased during part of the year, the men were available when wanted. The ratio of labor to capital invested was attractive. With one hand able to handle, on the average, over a thousand cattle, as Spur records indicate, investors could put generous amounts of their funds in cattle, the immediate source of profits, and relatively small sums in labor. Moreover, in contrast with conditions to the eastward, labor costs seem not to have risen in the closing decades of the nineteenth century, partially because of the declining need for hands. In speaking of the vanishing cowboy, romanticists have failed to note that declining opportunities for employment meant that his wage pattern could not hope to improve relative to that in other industries.

Undoubtedly, the relatively generous labor supply stemmed

Right, Texas cowboys playing cards on a saddle blanket. (Erwin E. Smith Collection, Library of Congress)
Below, Mexican John, XIT cook, during Montana roundup. (L. A. Huffman photo)
At bottom, chuck wagon, about 1885. (L. A. Huffman photo)

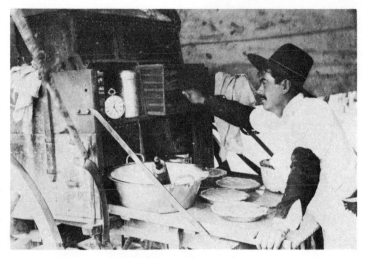

At left, Texas colt fighting the rope. Above, bronc buster at work on Matador Ranch. (Erwin E. Smith Collection, Library of Congress)

Roundup outfit on the move: Chuck wagon with bedrolls on top leads the hooligan wagon, which carries water, branding irons, and other supplies. (New Mexico State Tourist Bureau)

in considerable part from the aura of romance associated with the cattle kingdom. Romanticists were glorifying the Wild West at the very time when the ranching industry was expanding and in need of more workers. Many rank-and-file cowboys looked on their occupation as an opportunity to participate in a colorful era, not as a means of earning a living. George W. Littlefield's biographer mentions his reputation for operating his range out-fits in an almost penurious manner as far as food and lodging were concerned. Apparently, no cowboy selected a Littlefield ranch because of a reputation for good food. On the other hand, Littlefield generously aided employees who wanted to get ahead. He also furnished his cowboys with good quality mounts, which appealed to their pride and derring-do.[16]

The cowboy has been highly praised for loyalty to his employer and to herds of cattle placed in his charge. Supposedly, he never hesitated to risk his life in line of duty, the highest compliment that could be paid him. In the early days of open range, outfits did develop a high sense of group solidarity and a real loyalty to the job at hand. The brand mark demonstrated that *property* concentrated itself in herds of cattle, a situation in which the cow-boy felt a loyalty to the herd and to other members of his outfit who joined with him in protecting it. Owners often were in con-stant touch with their employees.

In the 1880's and after, *property* concentrated itself more in land, and fenced-in acreage became a mark of ownership. Imper-sonal corporations and extensive partnerships appeared. It was more difficult for a man to feel loyal to a fenced ranch than to a herd of cattle dependent upon his protection, and even more difficult to feel a sense of personal loyalty to a corporation. More-over, the numerous organizations of ranchers which soon de-veloped all over the West consisted of owners and managers of ranches, not of cowboys. The latter had no direct interest in the subjects generally discussed by such organizations and yet felt the influence of policies made by them. Although ranchers sel-dom considered working hours and wages at their annual meetings, the very fact that they organized as a group separate from cowboy employees helped sever the earlier feeling of a common bond.

Contrary to romantic rugged individualists who insist that cowboys never thought of striking against their employers, the Knights of Labor included many cowboys in its membership from 1884 to 1887 and local assemblies existed over the entire West Texas plains.[17] During the critical roundup period on a ranch managed by John Clay in 1884, the cowboys struck for higher pay. Although the local ranch manager wanted to compromise with the strikers, Clay refused to bargain with them and, with the help of the hay crew and those who had refused to quit their work, managed to get the herd to market.[18] Even the cowboy was not immune to the stress of the industrial age.

In contrast to a relative abundance of land and labor, capital was scarce, and at times ranchers found it impossible to obtain sufficient funds to meet their needs. Interest rates fluctuated with the times and with the borrower's reputation, but in general surpassed considerably those prevailing in older sections of the country. According to one historian of the cattle industry, interest charges in the 1880's usually ran about 1 per cent a month (12 per cent a year) but commissions on loans might increase the rate to as much as 15 per cent. In Wyoming in the 1870's, rates of 3 per cent a month or 36 per cent a year were quite common. In Denver, as late as 1886, the usual bank rate ran 12 per cent a year.[19] Although such rates should have proved highly remunerative to lenders, they prevailed in part because of the great risk involved. John Clay, who spoke on the basis of extensive financial experience, said that the established interest rate in 1883 ran 10 per cent, with interest compounded every three to six months, and that even then it proved inadequate because of the hazards of the industry.[20]

In early days and in times of financial stringency, ranchers paid exceedingly high interest rates. Immediately after the Civil War, George W. Littlefield concentrated on cotton production with free Negro labor. Reverses in planting between 1868 and

1870 burdened him with a debt on which he was paying interest of 24 per cent a year. Hoping to extricate himself, he drove a herd of cattle to distant Abilene, and acquired enough thereby to pay off his debts. The memory of those early difficulties encouraged him thereafter to maintain a high liquidity of assets and to combine banking with his ranching activities.[21]

As a wholesale and retail butcher in the 1860's, Conrad Kohrs moved his business from one mining strike to another as miners rushed feverishly around to exploit each new discovery. When a strike at Alder Gulch in present-day Montana left him without customers at his old stand, he could not do otherwise than go along. A few days of prospecting for gold without success convinced him that he should resume his business of supplying meat to others. To carry out his plans, he found it necessary to pay a banking house in the new mining camp of Virginia City, Montana, 10 per cent a month (over 100 per cent a year) at times for loans. During the winter of 1864-1865, new discoveries at what became the mining camp of Helena, Montana, convinced him that demands for beef would increase rapidly. As a result, he borrowed twelve thousand dollars at 5 per cent a month to purchase cattle for his butcher shops. Kohrs naturally began to herd cattle on the open range in order to reduce his operating costs. Over the years his excellent reputation as a businessman made it easier for him to obtain needed capital. After he suffered heavy cattle losses in 1886, an acquaintance in Butte, Montana, offered to lend him one hundred thousand dollars without security. In later years he served as president of the Union Bank and Trust Company in Helena,[22] a post from which he must have looked back with considerable satisfaction to the period when he paid interest rates of 50 to 100 per cent a year to finance his business.

When Charles Goodnight and others organized the Stock Growers' Bank of Pueblo, Colorado, in September, 1873, they advertised that they would pay 6 per cent on deposits left with them for three months and 8 per cent on deposits running as long as twelve. Since Goodnight had been paying 1½ to 2 per cent a month to obtain working capital, and had paid at least one of his cowboys 2 per cent a month to leave his accrued wages in Goodnight's hands, the new arrangement advertised by the bank reduced the costs of capital for its promoters to the extent that it attracted time deposits. Nevertheless, when Goodnight borrowed fifty thousand dollars from John George Adair's agent in 1876, he agreed to pay 18 per cent a year for the loan and pledged his Pueblo lands as security.[23] Without doubt, capital was both scarce and costly in the early days of the cattle kingdom.

Moreover, it took time for a banking system to develop to a point where men could even transfer funds from one place to another by bank exchange. While the Plummer gang was operating around Virginia City, Montana, Conrad Kohrs carried as much as five thousand dollars in gold dust on trips to purchase cattle for his local butcher shops. In spite of employing every conceivable ruse to slip out of town unobserved by the gang, Kohrs credited his survival on such trips to sheer good luck. At least, however, such business methods effectively called attention to one's wealth. Shanghai Pierce loved to impress others in his early days of cattle buying by dumping piles of gold and silver on a cloth to pay for herds of cattle. Years later, George Saunders, president of the Old Time Trail Drivers Association, recalled his vivid boyhood impressions of Shang. Since Shang bought fat cattle all over southern Texas immediately following the Civil War, Saunders saw him arrive at a number of cow camps. Large and portly, mounted on a fine horse, and accompanied by his Negro servant leading a pack animal loaded with gold and silver, Shang impressed the assembled men as an empire builder. His Negro servant dumped the sacks of money carelessly on the ground until the cattle were selected. After that, he emptied the sacks on a blanket, from where Shang paid off each cattleman with whom he had closed a deal. Business over, Shang then entertained the boys far into the night with stories of his exciting adventures.[24] No banker ever staged his money rites more effectively, for Shang's power and importance were starkly revealed in the primitive methods necessitated by local conditions. Another early-day Texan, Luther Lawhon, remembered in later life how men often carried gold in belts around their waist but transported silver in "duckin' sacks" on pack horses or mules. According to him, everyone had to know the weight as well as the value of money, and everyone knew that one thousand dollars in silver weighed 62½ pounds.[25]

Quite obviously, a banking system was needed to eliminate such dangerous and time-consuming methods and to provide funds for local development. As businessmen, ranchers saw the need. George W. Littlefield's roadside store was a case in point. Since customers could pay their bills in cattle but not in cash, he acquired considerable livestock that had to be driven to distant markets. Compelled thus to operate over a vast expanse of territory, he recognized the value of some form of commercial exchange. Moreover, local purchases of cattle for cash emphasized the same need. In 1877, for instance, he took two big sacks of gold and silver by buggy from his Gonzales, Texas, store to purchase cattle in the surrounding countryside. His heavily weighted buggy became mired in mud along the way, causing considerable inconvenience and delay. At each point where he bought cattle, he poured out sufficient specie on a blanket to cover the purchase price. Littlefield lacked Shanghai Pierce's histrionic urges and so felt no compunction in wanting to reduce so irksome and dangerous a system of exchange to more businesslike, if less colorful, methods.

Experience very rapidly demonstrated how this could be done. Supposedly, a drummer drove up to the store operated by Littlefield and his partners and requested them to take overnight care of five thousand dollars in specie that he had collected for goods sold to local merchants. The next day he returned and asked if the owners of the store had any money on deposit in New York, the location of his employers and the place to which he must remit any money collected in Texas. It so happened that one of the partners did have money there. He agreed to take the drummer's specie, and for one dollar per hundred dollars involved to give him a draft on his own deposit in New York City, thus making it unnecessary to ship specie. As a consequence, the store added banking to its other functions, keeping its deposits in an old safe that opened with a large key. In time, the partners fenced off their "office" with a railing, and made a "cage" through which an employee transacted financial matters. And so they entered banking.

Too perceptive in financial matters to require that such opportunities be spelled out so explicitly, Littlefield's interest in banking grew to the point where cattlemen thought of him first of all as a banker, though specialized bankers stressed his interest in ranching when speaking of him. In 1890 he established his own bank in Austin, Texas, and twenty-one years later housed it in his newly erected office building. The great bronze doors opening into his banking quarters were embossed with designs of the various Littlefield cattle brands, and murals around the walls depicted various aspects of the ranching industry, indications of the major activity from which the institution had sprung.[26]

Virtually all the ranchers whose names have been mentioned in preceding pages either operated banks of their own or sat on boards of directors of such institutions in their later years. Early in their careers they learned how dearly one paid for borrowed capital, how powerful bankers were in shaping the welfare of borrowers, and how much ranchers had to depend on banking institutions. Motives of prestige and profit alike persuaded them to take a direct part in banking in their own communities. Writing in 1915, C. F. Coffee, early-day Wyoming rancher, humorously explained why he shifted almost wholly to banking in later life. Population pressure forced him to move his ranching operations farther and farther out on the frontier, until finally the Northwestern Railroad attracted so many grangers to the region where he was making his last stand that he had to give up. Since he could not legally shoot the grangers, he decided to get even with them by turning to banking, in which he could live off their labor.[27] Many a rancher must have experienced a similarly wry twist of humor when he became a banker, thinking of earlier times when it had seemed to him that he was working for the bankers rather than for himself in trying to meet his obligations.

Credit and exchange facilities naturally developed most rapidly in livestock marketing centers, which needed them to facilitate transfer of cattle from the ranchers to feeders, speculators, and packers. Joseph G. McCoy discussed the financing of the cattle trade at some length in the early 1870's. Even then, transactions ran as high as one hundred thousand dollars, and those engaged commonly borrowed large sums of money, usually on short time, thirty to ninety days. Banking institutions constituted the most common source of such credit, every market or livestock center having one or more that specialized in cattle loans. At Kansas City the First National Bank handled such business without competition for a period of years. Drovers to that region commonly bought their herds on credit from ranchers and so generally needed loans only for current expenses or to pay off surplus hands. Such small sums could be obtained in Abilene or Junction City, Kansas.

As the volume of trade increased, demands for loans grew rapidly, and competition among drovers for cattle enabled ranchers to demand payment for herds on shorter time. Consequently, many drovers obligated themselves to pay off immediately upon arrival in Abilene. McCoy began to send them to the Kansas City bank, which had opened in 1865. By 1868 it was cultivating loans to drovers, and in 1870 opened a branch in Abilene. At the start of the Panic of 1873 it had over one-half million in notes from livestock men. Although many of these were paid at maturity, the bank had to close its doors. Cattlemen had found its services so essential that they petitioned the owners to remain in business, which they did with increased capitalization, only to fail again in 1877. Howard M. Holden, president of the bank, was a native of Massachusetts, received his training there, and operated a bank in Des Moines, Iowa, before opening the Kansas City institution. The Mastin bank of Kansas City offered some competition to the First National but had to close its doors in 1878. Some of Kansas City's oldest and wealthiest men had backed the Mastin bank.

In the 1870's financial agencies were beginning to develop at points within the cattle-ranching region. Coffeyville, Kansas, had a bank, and at Wichita, in the same state, two institutions competed for the cattleman's business. D. W. Powers of Leavenworth, Kansas, operated a bank at Ellsworth, which financed most of the cattle trade passing over the Kansas Pacific Railroad. A self-made man, Powers migrated from Kentucky to Virginia and then to Missouri, where he engaged in farming, stock dealing, and freighting on the plains. In addition to banking, he operated several ranches of his own, and obviously understood the cattle business.[28] George W. Littlefield began to engage in banking in the same period, and Charles Goodnight and others opened a bank at Pueblo, Colorado, in 1873. Far south in Texas, Daniel Sullivan operated a general mercantile store and made loans to ranchers in his vicinity at 1 per cent a month, compounded monthly. Shanghai Pierce was one of his best customers.[29] With the passage of time, and especially after the crisis of 1886-1887, bankers loaned money somewhat more cautiously and the industry became more stabilized, changes reflected in more moderate rates of interest. New financial agencies, such as livestock commission firms and cattle loan companies financed by the large meat packers,[30] also contributed to easing rates on short-term loans.

Ranchers with a large volume of business were able to make use of banking facilities at distant points as early as the 1870's. When Richard King, for instance, sent one of his foremen, Captain John Fitch, up the trail in 1875 with a herd, he instructed Fitch where to look for help in case of financial need and in remitting funds from sale of the cattle. Swenson, Perkins and Company of New York City, Perkins, Swenson and Company of New Orleans, and the Mechanics Bank of St. Louis were ready to furnish money and to accept remittances on King's behalf. Adams, Burke and Company of the Union Stock Yards in Chicago and Joseph Mulhall of St. Louis were livestock dealers to whom Fitch could look for advice and aid in selling the herd. King also employed a livestock broker and agent, James H. Stevens, who moved according to the direction of herds of cattle sent out from the King ranch, scouting ahead, so to speak, to search out buyers and to keep informed on market trends in various shipping centers.[31] With such widespread financial connections, King could easily handle marketing problems, unless, of course, a national monetary crisis closed the flow of funds everywhere. Smaller operators, however, had to depend on more localized institutions where their financial standing and reputation were known.

Although much of the capital needed for long-term operations came through cattlemen plowing their profits back into their business, European and American investment capital was available. The flow of British capital abroad and to America had been incessant since 1815 in spite of fluctuations. By mid-century investors were actively seeking American outlets, and the California gold discoveries of 1849 precipitated a rush of capital there. During the Civil War the flow of capital lessened, only to resume with increased intensity at its close. The Scots lagged somewhat behind the English in American investments but they too began to display great interest in the 1860's. Although capital exports often went into raw materials necessary to sustain home manufacturing, many investors thought primarily in terms of mines, railroads, and, especially, real estate. This meant that any capable and experienced Westerner might hope to obtain operating capital without having to accumulate it slowly through his own savings. Charles Goodnight, for instance, demonstrated his ability so thoroughly by 1878 that John George Adair gladly supplied the necessary capital to finance the highly successful Panhandle ranching venture.[32]

Between 1844 and 1862 the British Parliament passed a series of corporation laws legalizing and regulating investment trusts, which made it easy for even the small investor to share in foreign opportunities. Thus, the flow of investment capital became still larger through changes in British corporation laws just at the time when the cattleman's frontier was opening in the American West. In the midst of the depression of 1873, the British used the investment trust form to launch several new mortgage and investment companies. The Scottish-American Mortgage Company, Limited, of Edinburgh concentrated on land mortgages in the agricultural section of Illinois. In the east of Scotland, where Dundee became known as the "home of the investment trust" shortly after the first was established in 1873, a group of Dundee capitalists began loaning on real estate in the Pacific Northwest. Some companies paid initial annual dividends of 12½ to 15 per cent because they could loan money in America at much higher than the going rate in Britain. The sudden success of these Edinburgh and Dundee syndicates precipitated an unprecedented flow of Scottish capital to the western United States, a movement duplicated in London where still larger concentrations of capital existed.

By the late 1870's British capital began to move rapidly into the ranching field. Eastern Scotland possessed large reserves of investment capital, which flowed all the more easily to the American West because Scotsmen had specialized at home for generations in animal husbandry. In the British Isles as a whole, notable figures among the landed aristocracy and in politics, industry, and military life attained positions of leadership in the investment and mortgage field and in sponsoring agricultural colonization schemes in the American West, which pointed the way toward investments in ranching. Confidence in such men led clerks, accountants, lawyers, merchants, tradesmen, ministers, and teachers to put their savings in the hands of investment trusts, to be used to purchase range rights, land, and cattle. Awareness that strategic land controlling water rights would soon be gone contributed to the speed with which funds flowed across the ocean.

At least thirty-three limited companies registered in Great Britain between 1879 and 1888 with the primary intention of investing in American ranching. Their capital structure totaled more than thirty-seven million dollars, of which twenty million was paid up and transferred to the United States. They probably also borrowed an additional ten million dollars. The British also loaned money to hard-pressed ranchers, and many invested in and served as directors of companies incorporated under American state laws. One historian estimates that four million dollars or more found its way into the industry through British investments in corporations chartered by individual American states, and that, over-all, the British may have had as much as forty-five million dollars invested in American ranching in the 1880's.[33]

Although Britain furnished by far the greater part of the foreign capital, some came from other countries as well. Pierre Wibaux obtained funds from his own textile-manufacturing family and other French businessmen to underwrite his successful ranching venture in the Dakotas in the 1880's.[34] Attention has been called to the activities of the Marquis de Mores and the Baron de Bonnemains, representatives of the French nobility who popularized the ranching opportunities available to Frenchmen in the American West.

Investment capital also came from older sections of the United States. Younger members of prosperous Eastern families, like Theodore Roosevelt, drew on their inherited wealth to participate. Between September, 1884, and July, 1885, Roosevelt furnished $82,500 to his partners to stock and equip their Dakota ranches,[35] virtually the whole capital sum involved. Dan Dillon Casement's father prospered as a railroad construction engineer but became involved in ranching through his friendship with Charles N. Cox, son of an ex-governor of Ohio, who "located" a ranch in Colorado in 1882. Casement agreed to take a one-third interest in the venture, as did the father of Tot Otis, a wealthy steel manufacturer and mayor of Cleveland, Ohio. In the end, Casement and Otis had to assume the total cost of the project, which their sons operated for a period of years.[36]

At the height of the ranching craze, American capitalists joined the rush to invest in cattle and land. In 1883, for instance, a group of Louisville businessmen formed a Kentucky corporation to operate the Two Buckle Ranch in Texas. Several members of the Tillford family, famous producers of sour mash whiskey, and David Frantz, owner of a Louisville tanning factory, seem to have invested most heavily in the corporation, which maintained a herd of several thousand cattle until 1893. Ultimately, the corporation sold much of its land to farmers and small ranchers, and in 1908 laid out the townsite of Crosbyton, Texas.[37] Similarly, a member of the Chicago firm of Field, Leiten and Company was an officer and heavy investor in the Dubuque Cattle Company, which maintained better than twenty-five thousand head of cattle in New Mexico in the middle 1880's.[38] At the height of the cattle craze, a Santa Fe newspaper commented that many wealthy Eastern men were becoming heavy investors in local ranches. It mentioned the Delano-Dwyer Cattle Company as the latest example, an organization with a capital stock of one million dollars, of which half was paid up. The owners included John S. Delano and Joseph W. Dwyer of New Mexico, Stephen V. White and Adolph H. Boreman of New York, and Columbus Delano of Ohio. According to the paper, these men were well and favorably known around the country, especially White and Columbus Delano. The former was considered one of New York's most successful and shrewdest financiers, second only to Jay Gould in Wall Street, and Delano had served as Secretary of the Interior in President Grant's administration. "Such men are very welcome in the business community of New Mexico," said the reporter,[39] as indeed they were because of the capital that they invested locally.

Of the three factors of production, capital continued to be the most costly during the heyday of the cattle kingdom. Cheap land and open range initiated and sustained the cattle craze, and moonstruck youngsters were willing to work at low wages to bear the fabled name of cowboy. But interest rates remained high throughout the period.

TEN

Poker on Joint-Stock Principles

COMING as they did from so many different parts of the world and from widely varying social backgrounds, ranchers naturally possessed a collective understanding of every conceivable form of business organization. As capitalists, they might prefer individual ownership and operation or choose to enter a partnership with some congenial associate. They might participate in forming a limited liability partnership, become a member of an operating corporation, or cast their lot with an investment trust. All were well-known instruments of capitalistic society, and all found a place on the ranching frontier. Since ranchers varied so widely in personality, they could hardly be expected to agree on the best way to organize their undertakings. As the product of a French manufacturing family, Pierre Wibaux could be expected to voice less objection to the impersonal corporate form of business organization than his fellow Frenchman, the flamboyant Antoine de Vallombrosa, who held the title Marquis de Mores. Of noble blood and with a shadowy claim to the French throne, adventurous and self-willed, the Marquis instituted numerous projects, such as cattle ranching, sheepherding, a stage line, meat packing, and paper ventures in pottery making and the growing of vegetables for early season marketing. He even attempted to create a national consumer cooperative to reduce the cost of meat, with retail outlets in New York City. After his projects failed one by one and his wealthy father-in-law ceased to underwrite his American ventures, he went to India to hunt tigers, and then was killed by tribesmen in Africa while on an expedition that he hoped would further his plans to restore the French monarchy. Such a man had to stand at the very center of command and could not abide having others curb his restless imagination. Although he entered numerous temporary partnerships to carry on his multitudinous activities, he insisted essentially on operating as a free individual. Impersonal corporate structures could have little appeal to such a personality, whatever economic advantages they might offer.

In sharp contrast to the Marquis, Colonel Amos C. Babcock of Chicago preferred teamwork to individual effort. He and his business associates, in return for building the Texas state capitol, received 3,050,000 acres of Texas land, upon which they established the XIT Ranch, the most extensive American range ever placed under one barbed-wire fence. Like the Marquis, Babcock had imagination, but there the resemblance ceased. A merchant, an active Republican, and an investor in railroads and other business ventures,[1] the Colonel looked on the Texas deal simply as another source of profit. He and his associates found corporate organization useful for their purposes and preferred to concentrate on financial problems, leaving the more adventurous side of the Texas project to others. When the Colonel visited Texas to inspect the lands acquired by his Capitol Syndicate, he used an ambulance to tour the holdings, dined on a trunkful of food that he took along to escape cowboy fare, and slept at night on a cot.[2] Quite obviously, personalities accounted in part for the differences that existed between the business organizations developed by the Marquis and the Colonel.

Of course, the nature of ranching itself also influenced the form of organization selected by its various practitioners. Although never able to agree on one form as superior to all others, cattlemen tested each in terms of its applicability to ranching. For instance, they debated at length the question of how large a ranch should be to obtain a maximum rate of profit, and the relation of this to forms of conducting business. Ora Haley, an experienced Wyoming rancher, argued in 1885 that by increasing the number of cattle involved in a ranching operation one could decrease the proportionate expense of raising them for market.[3] A. R. Converse, a banker and ranchman in the same region, was convinced, however, that the future of the industry depended upon improving the quality of livestock, which in his opinion meant that large herds must be subdivided and given proper care in cold weather.[4] Although Converse failed to comment on what this meant for the future of corporate ranching, it obviously suggested the possibility of maximum profits through individual ownership of ṣmaller herds.

Promoters naturally favored large-scale units because of the greater profit from selling them. After the Earl of Airlie, chairman of the Scottish-American Mortgage Company, returned home from an inspection trip to Oregon and Colorado in the early 1880's, he warned British agricultural laborers against moving to America without capital resources. According to him, it would require 325 pounds sterling to move a family of four to Colorado, acquire eighty acres of land, and put half of it in cultivation. As to ranching, he thought no person should enter that occupation with less than four thousand pounds sterling in capital and a minimum herd of one thousand cattle.[5] Similarly, Richtofen's promotional book of 1885 emphasized the advantages of large-scale investments, although he granted that small ranches could be profitable. In his opinion, the big rancher had the necessary money to hold cattle for top market prices, obtained reduced railroad rates, and benefited from savings in labor costs.[6]

Without doubt, the larger ranches did have some advantages. Access to capital provided them with staying power in depression periods or when some catastrophe decimated herds. Thus, Scottish capitalists who hung on after the hard winter of 1886-1887 profited in many cases from rising land values and better cattle prices in the twentieth century. Size also gave power. The great XIT spread in Texas could afford to hire former Texas Rangers to guard its exposed position, men who by their very reputations struck fear into rustlers. Size enabled the Spur Ranch to operate a mercantile establishment, thereby obtaining its supplies at wholesale prices.[7] Large ranchers also received rebates from stockyards and railroads until government regulation curbed such practices. Records of the huge Matador Ranch indicate that the packers and the railroads hesitated to deal arbitrarily with the larger ranches. Moreover, the larger spreads could use Texas lands for breeding grounds and fatten their stock on the more nutritious grasses of Northern ranges. Ample financial resources permitted them to experiment with newer methods of handling livestock and to select the most efficient.

Bigness alone did not insure profitable operations, however. Corporate ranches floated by promoters often began their existence burdened with excessive costs. If promoters agreed to accept part of their profits from future earnings, they often insisted on marketing more cattle than the annual increase of the herds justified, thereby thwarting sound management. Moreover, investors learned that in paying huge sums for "range rights" they had bought nothing more than token permission to use the land until purchasers or homesteaders wanted it. When Rufus Hatch, American promoter and speculator, disposed of the Cattle Ranche and Land Company to Scottish businessmen, he charged them fifty thousand pounds sterling for "range rights" included in the deal. Disillusioned within a few years, the purchasers decided that range rights in reality descended from Adam and that claimants were as numerous as his progeny.[8] At times, foreign and Eastern investors demanded greater dividends than operations justified, thereby preventing local managers from making necessary repairs or additions to ranch property. Thus, slippery speculative practices, policies based on inadequate or misleading information, and problems of management from a distance militated against cattle corporations owned by outside interests compiling sufficiently good records to justify the contention that corporate ranching paid off because of its efficient size.

Although most of the large American ranchers like King, Iliff, and Littlefield maintained direct control of their business, they too found that bigness had an unpleasant and crippling side. Most often when such a man heard himself called a "cattle king" or a "cattle baron," the term carried a derogatory meaning. In part, ranchers brought such condemnation upon themselves. When a member of the Kountze banking family joined Shanghai Pierce in buying two hundred thousand acres of land, he knew that Shang would skirt the law wherever possible. In buying land, Shang's agents enclosed a number of small owners within the circle of their purchases. When one of them asked Shang to pay him five cents an acre annual rental on enclosed land, Shang supposedly told him he could move his land to a more pleasant location if he did not like its current position. Moreover, Shang hired a member of the Texas legislature to fight efforts of the smaller men to prevent land engrossment.[9] Although he and others like him failed to win their point in the legislature, they did cut the heart out of free range by bluffing, trading, buying, and enclosing land without the consent of those who were using it.

Depressed farming conditions in the post-Civil War period provided a natural setting for hostility toward Eastern and foreign capital on the part of agrarians intent on redressing their wrongs. At the same time, British investors in American railroads were learning that financial pirates could wreck a supposedly sound business. Although they disliked for railroads built by their capital to fall into hands of men like Gould, Fisk, and Vanderbilt, they had no vote as bondholders. Consequently, when they invested in the American West, they preferred to own outright a majority of all stock involved or to incorporate in the British Isles. They even appointed British managers like John Clay and Murdo Mackenzie to oversee their holdings. That, of course, brought attention directly to the presence of foreign investments far more quickly than if money had been put only in bonds of operating companies.

The Committee on Public Lands in the United States House of Representatives responded to complaints of foreign monopolies by sponsoring a bill forbidding alien ownership of land in territories of the United States. In this manner the legislators proposed to prevent landlordism from swamping America's free institutions. In the Cleveland-Blaine presidential contest of 1884 both parties favored legislation to eliminate such dangers, the Republican slogan of "America for Americans" sounding even more ominous than promises made by the Democrats. In 1887 Congress passed, with Cleveland's approval, a law prohibiting alien ownership of land in the territories of the United States except by inheritance or in collection of debts. Similar prohibitions ran against corporations in which more than 20 per cent of the stock was owned by non-Americans.

States also enacted legislation to curb foreign ownership of land. In Texas, Governor James S. Hogg's crusade in behalf of the "common people" played up the "English lords, syndicates and corporations" with "vast" estates which in time would be leased to "serfs and peons" from the old world. He stressed this danger especially in his inaugural address in 1893. A Texas alien land law of 1892 forbade ownership of land by foreigners and ordered current owners to sell their holdings or become American citizens within ten years. The Texas law was not well enforced and the Supreme Court of the United States ultimately declared it unconstitutional. Nevertheless, in Texas and elsewhere, states and territories took various degrees of action on the supposed danger. In some cases, ownership was forbidden; in others, foreign corporations were ordered to incorporate within the governmental unit where they operated and to maintain headquarters there. As a whole, mining and ranching states proved less vindictive than those more heavily devoted to farming, for they realized the need for foreign capital to develop their resources.[10] Although such legislation did not seriously hamper existing investments, it did discourage the flow of additional foreign capital. Perhaps more important, attacks on foreign corporations strengthened the whole crusade against monopoly. Cattle kings, whether American or foreign, thus operated within a framework of suspicion that benefited smaller competitors.

Moreover, although corporate wealth in many fields can be shielded against the public eye, thus avoiding resentment, in ranching the necessarily large landholdings stand out. The larger the ranch, the more likely was resentment to develop. The King Ranch in Texas is a case in point. Involving hundreds of thousands of fenced acres, it seems larger still because so much of its capital investment is in land. At times, the King Ranch has aroused bitter local criticism and a feeling of public hostility. In the 1930's, for instance, its owners opposed construction of a public highway that would traverse their property for some fifty miles in Kenedy County. At the height of the controversy, the *Houston Press* headlined its treatment of the subject with the words "Texas' Walled Kingdom of Kenedy," a phrase that stuck in the public mind as a just judgment on the nature of so huge an enterprise.[11] Granted that arrogance on the part of some of its owners and policies at variance with majority wishes have resulted in just criticism at times, the very bigness of such a ranch makes it highly susceptible to creation of ill will. Because smaller ranches seem more in keeping with democratic American traditions, they have an advantage over mammoth holdings, especially if the latter operate as "soulless" corporations.

In general, individuals or simple partnerships constituted the most prevalent form of business organization in the early history of the cattle kingdom. Then came an influx of outside capital, with a tendency for partnerships to become more complex and corporate organization a common device. Although the latter was almost a necessity for channeling funds from small foreign investors into the cattle kingdom, much was said of the innate advantages of corporate organization. As foreign and Eastern syndicates began to buy up numerous small ranches for consolidation into larger units, many observers must have thought that the day of the individually owned ranch was rapidly disappearing. Orin C. Waid, who had bought and sold a number of ranches himself, and who was operating his own spread on Poison Spider Creek at the time, told an interviewer in the middle 1880's that he knew of only two men in addition to himself in Wyoming who were continuing to operate as individuals. All the rest were in companies of one sort or another. Having failed to sell Waid a set of books, the interviewer recorded in his report that the man was a "pin headed stubborn donkey with small ideas based on coin,"[12] perhaps a key to why he had not succumbed to the lure of greater profits by joining a syndicate or promoting one of his own.

But preferences were soon to change. The hard winter of 1886-1887 terminated the already wavering craze for ranching investments, and thereafter one heard less of syndicates and corporations. Although large corporate ranches still exist, the family enterprise far outnumbers them, as it always did in spite of promotional efforts on behalf of bigness. On lands suitable only for grazing, ranches of one hundred thousand acres and more are not uncommon, but in 1950 the average operator ran less than 150 head,[13] a sharp contrast to estimates in the 1880's that spoke in terms of one thousand cattle as a minimum for efficient operation. As one observer has said, it is now good business

and the best kind of insurance for a ranchman to raise his own feed, but the practice goes further than that. Mixed farming and ranching are extremely common. In fact, it has become so difficult to draw the line between farm and ranch that only the most courageous agricultural economists will attempt it. The staff of New Mexico A. and M. College distinguish between the stock ranch and the stock farm. A ranch is not a ranch, they say, unless it has "ten acres or more of grazing land to each acre in crops."[14]

The same observer has also pointed out the tendency toward specialization within ranching. Today's specialists include those who produce pure blood animals; commercial breeders; pasture cattlemen, who feed grass and hay to calves and yearlings; and finally the feeder or finisher, who prepares the animal directly for market.

When James S. Brisbin published his promotional book, *The Beef Bonanza,* in 1881, he listed names of ranch outfits and the number of cattle held by each in various parts of the West. In Lincoln County in western Nebraska, for instance, the sixteen outfits mentioned ranged from a low of seventy to a high of 6,500 in number of cattle. In Wyoming Territory Brisbin listed seventy outfits, with herds varying from sixty cattle to 7,000. Jack Abney on Crow Creek had 60; F. C. Dixon on Pole Creek had 70; and B. A. Sheidly on Horseshoe Creek 3,000.[15] Although Brisbin favored operating on a large scale, his figures revealed the prevalence of the small, individually owned ranch.

Perhaps the lonely nature of ranching strengthened the tendency toward family partnerships. Charles Goodnight started his ranching career in Texas in collaboration with a stepbrother, and both were aided in their efforts by a brother-in-law. George W. Littlefield depended heavily upon three of his nephews, Shelton Dowell and the White brothers, in developing his ranching empire, a connection strengthened all the more by the absence of children of his own. In Colorado, John R. and W. A. Towers combined their resources to establish a highly profitable business. Malcolm Moncrieffe, son of a titled English family, ranched by himself in Wyoming but was pleased to have a younger brother come from England to join him.[16] Joseph M. Carey moved to Wyoming Territory as United States District Attorney in 1869 and shortly thereafter entered the ranching partnership of J. M. Carey and Brother with a relative who followed him West. Such illustrations could easily be multiplied, an indication that family ties contributed heavily to the popularity of the partnership form of ranching.

The need for capital resources also played a prominent part in stimulating partnership agreements. John Chisum was holding the elective post of county clerk in Lamar County, Texas, in 1853 but wanted to shift to ranching and an outdoor life for reasons of health. His chance came when S. K. Fowles of New York City visited Paris, the county seat of Lamar, looking for a suitable person with whom to invest money in livestock. Fowles put up six thousand dollars to purchase cattle, Chisum agreeing to manage the project for a share in the profits. He invested the money in stock cattle and established a range in Denton County, part of which occupied the present site of Fort Worth. Shortly thereafter settlers pushed Chisum still farther out on the frontier, but he and his partner did well in spite of Chisum's refusal to renew their partnership at the termination of their first agreement in 1864.[17] He preferred to go it alone, and his later fame as cattle king of the Pecos in New Mexico indicates that he made no mistake in doing so. Only a need for capital could persuade Chisum to work jointly with others.

Successful partnership ventures in the 1870's undoubtedly contributed to the increasing flow of Eastern and European capital into ranching and the rise of large corporate organizations. Henry Campbell, for instance, moved to Texas with his parents in 1840 while still a boy. There he spent only a few months in school, devoting his time instead to hauling cotton to market for neighboring farmers with his father's ox team. Then followed a period of managing a herd of cattle for one-fourth the profits, which proved discouragingly meager. He and his brothers fought in the Civil War, and in 1869 he agreed to drive a herd of cattle to California for their owner at a salary of seventy-five dollars a month, only to have to sell them in Nevada because drouth ruined the grass along the way.[18] Other drives to New Orleans and Dodge City turned out better. By speculation and small drives he acquired his own herd, which he sold in Chicago in 1878.

While in Chicago, Campbell was invited along with other cattlemen to a luncheon sponsored by a group of bankers. During the meal he mentioned that his cattle had cost him nine dollars a head in Texas and had sold for twenty-three in Chicago, information that greatly impressed Colonel Alfred Markham Britton, one of his hosts. Britton agreed to finance the purchase of a herd of cattle to be managed by Campbell, and the latter hurried home to carry out the assignment and to acquire acreage south of Goodnight's range in the Panhandle. In 1879 Britton and he incorporated their holdings as the Matador Cattle Company under Texas law, with Fort Worth and New York men also included in the deal. Campbell's first home as manager for the new company was a dugout, from where he rapidly acquired herds and land for the group. On September 28, 1882, they sold out to the Matador Land and Cattle Company, Limited, of Scotland for $1,250,000, and Campbell became first manager for the new organization.[19] Thus, starting out as partner with an outside capitalist to obtain funds to expand, Campbell found himself catapulted into management of one of the great corporate ranching spreads of the American West.

On the other hand, Charles Goodnight and John George Adair displayed no great interest in the possibility of selling their successful organization to eager investors or corporate groups. Goodnight entered the partnership to obtain working capital and sufficient funds to hire men to sustain and protect his property on the new frontier. As to Adair, Goodnight's excellent reputation as a cattleman convinced him that he could not hope to find a better partner to manage his funds. Under the partnership arrangement, Adair agreed to finance the project and Goodnight to furnish the foundation herd and to serve as manager. For the latter service Goodnight received twenty-five hundred dollars a year which, with operating expenses, came out of current income. Adair's investment, with ten per cent interest, was to be repaid in full at the end of five years, and the residual property was then to be divided, one-third to Goodnight and two-thirds to Adair. The partnership lasted until Adair's death in 1885,[20] and proved highly profitable for both men.

Richard King made a variety of partnership agreements preceding the Civil War as a means of acquiring capital to develop his ranch. All involved business associates in Texas rather than out-of-state capital. In 1860, on the eve of the Civil War, he and Mifflin Kenedy joined forces in ranching as well as in steamboat operations, the firm of R. King and Company involving three-eighths' ownership each to King and Kenedy and two-eighths to a mutual friend, James Walworth. Although the agreement simplified management problems, it appealed to King most of all because it provided the necessary funds to consolidate ranch titles.[21] As soon as he made a stake in Civil War trade, King could afford to proceed on his own, which he did after 1867 when he and Kenedy terminated their ranching partnership.

The partnerships just described all involved businessmen, of whom at least one was an experienced cattleman. Consequently, they fared much better than the numerous ventures undertaken by those who lacked previous contact with the industry. Teddy Roosevelt was a good example of such men, although he was more fortunate than some in picking honest partners. Indeed, they seem to have fretted over the welfare of his investments more than he. His partners at the Maltese Cross Ranch, Sylvane Ferris and William Merrifield, came west on the Nothern Pacific Railroad, which carried immigrants to the frontier for nothing but charged five cents a mile for a return ticket. They were honest and enterprising men who worked hard to succeed, but their experience in the cattle business scarcely surpassed that of Roosevelt. On still another ranch, Roosevelt installed two of his former hunting guides from the state of Maine who knew nothing of Western ranching.[22] To the credit of his partners, Roosevelt would have suffered less of a financial loss if he had taken their advice, but to him the greatest rewards lay elsewhere than in making money. After his partnership ventures failed, he incorporated his ranch properties, but even then he did no better financially. He did gain renewed health and vigor and an appreciation of the problem of conservation, a real contribution to a career that lay beyond the confines of business.

For the serious businessman, partnerships also proved valuable in the field of management. Early in his career, George W. Littlefield used J. C. Dilworth and Hugh Lewis as partners in his Texas store, where they looked after local trade and cattle acquisitions, thus enabling him to move freely around buying and selling livestock. Over the years, J. P. White, Sr., served him well as manager of his larger ranches, an arrangement so satisfactory that Littlefield felt safe in visiting them only at intervals.[23] Similarly, Richard King formed a partnership with Gideon K. Lewis, captain of a company of Texas Rangers, at the beginning of his ranching ventures. Exactly the same age, the two men were much alike in their daring, an important attribute in the lawless region where they proposed to operate. Apparently, Lewis was supposed to serve as armed guard and direct overseer of the ranch while King concentrated on raising funds through his steamboat operations on the Rio Grande. Such a distribution of duties made sense even though King found ranching so much to his liking that he assumed active management of the project.[24]

Ranchers also formed partnerships to cover single ventures of short duration. John W. Iliff, for instance, made an ingenious contract in 1877 with D. H. and J. W. Snyder to purchase and deliver fifteen thousand Texas cattle to his Weld County, Colorado, ranch. Iliff agreed to pay nine-tenths of the cost of buying and delivering the stock, the Snyders being responsible for one-tenth. On delivery at his ranch, Iliff was to pay a set price for the cattle, with the Snyders receiving one-tenth of the difference betwen that price and what they paid for the cattle as compensation for their investment. After subtracting a sum necessary to cover losses and expenses from the difference between the purchase price and Iliff's agreed price for receiving the cattle, the remaining nine-tenths of the price spread was to be divided equally between Iliff and the Snyders as compensation for their services. If the venture resulted in a loss, the contracting parties agreed to share it in the same proportions as specified in other parts of the contract. Such agreements encouraged drovers to buy carefully, to handle stock properly on the road, and to economize in all phases of their operations.[25]

Richard King made similar contracts with his trail bosses instead of paying them a salary. Most of them came from his own ranch foremen. They purchased trail herds from him on a note at the ranch for a set price, hired and paid hands needed for the drive, and took care of all expenses along the way. After herds were sold, King and his contractors split the profits. This protected him to the amount of the herd's value when it left the range and encouraged careful handling along the way. In 1875 Captain John Fitch, one of his foremen, gave him a note for $62,251 for 4,737 head of cattle, necessary equipment, and five hundred dollars in cash advanced to him at 8 per cent interest. The contract was signed on March 12 and the two men settled on November

27. King made a profit of some fifty thousand dollars on the drive, and Fitch received $5,366.38 as his share,[26] far more than the usual salary for such work.

In spite of their usefulness, partnerships also caused much trouble, a major reason why many ranchers operated independently. Even large-scale speculators who needed partners in their multitudinous schemes became impatient at conflicts and delays that resulted from working with others. Stephen W. Dorsey, for instance, spent a lifetime looking for speculative opportunities. With that in mind, he migrated from his native Vermont to Ohio, from where he served as a colonel in the Civil War. Carpetbag days in Arkansas found him occupying a seat in the United States Senate from that state and speculating in railroads. From there he moved on to New Mexico in the 1870's, where he acquired options on huge quantities of land for sale to foreign investors. When interviewed in 1885, Dorsey was in the process of dissolving the Palo Blanco Cattle Company, of which he owned nine-twentieths, because he found some of his partners so disagreeable that he refused to continue working with them. At the moment, he felt that he would never enter another partnership.[27]

Partnerships were especially galling to ranchers with an independent turn of mind. When Oliver Loving, Charles Goodnight's partner on some of his pioneer cattle drives, lay dying from a wound received in an Indian attack in 1867, he asked Goodnight as a fellow Mason to continue their business arrangement two years longer so that Loving's family might not be left destitute. Goodnight agreed at considerable financial cost, turning over to Loving's heirs in 1869 half of the seventy-two thousand dollars in profits realized since his partner's death. On another occasion his need for funds encouraged him to take on a partner whose niggardly attitude soon made him regret his decision. Although highly profitable, his partnership with arrogant John George Adair so galled his sense of pride and independence that he wondered late in life why he ever put up with the man. When Adair's wife sent her son by an earlier marriage to work on the ranch, Goodnight had to relieve him of all responsibility because of his bad habits. When Adair died, Goodnight found the widow reluctant, slow and demanding in her attitude concerning division of property, and accepted a settlement on less favorable terms than his holdings justified in order to terminate the partnership. Even then, Mrs. Adair felt free to call on him for advice and service concerning her part of the property.[28] Although Goodnight used the JA brand, based on Adair's initials, to identify the stock which ranged their joint holdings, it seems unfair in retrospect that so able a cattleman had to run some of his greatest herds under the initials of another man.

Richard King's first ranching partner, Gideon K. "Legs" Lewis, furnished him with ample evidence of the uncertainties of partnerships. Deciding to run for Congress in 1855, Lewis was murdered while attempting to recover damaging letters that he had written to a mistress. He had no heirs and left no will, thus putting King in a difficult position concerning their joint ownership of two principal properties essential to the ranch. Through Major W. W. Chapman of the regular army, King succeeded in buying a clear title to the land in question, although at considerable cost. Chapman apparently furnished part of the purchase money. Soon, however, he received unexpected orders to report to a new army assignment in California, making it necessary once again for King to scramble to obtain money necessary to hold his venture together.[29] As soon as possible, he ceased to rely on partnerships that could jeopardize his basic operations, using them instead for temporary ventures.

More complex forms of business organization became necessary to serve the needs of promoters of ranch properties during the speculative craze that swept the industry. Investors were widely scattered, huge sums were involved, and ownership and management necessarily became separate functions. Corporations, syndicates, and investment trusts provided the necessary capital and organizational structure to handle such problems, no matter how extensive they might be. In 1881 a Scottish syndicate had no trouble in financing the purchase of George W. Littlefield's LIT holdings in Texas for $253,000. In 1882, Mifflin Kenedy sold his Los Laureles ranch to the Texas Land and Cattle Company, Limited, of Scotland, for $1,100,000. Even Richard King, who loved his ranch devotedly, considered dealing with the "Johnny Bulls," as he labeled the Britishers, in 1883. Dry weather, his own declining health, and the death of his son, Robert E. Lee King, perhaps temporarily weakened his resolve never to sell his ranching empire. According to one account, King priced his ranch to a foreign syndicate at $6,500,000, but for some unexplained reason the deal fell through.[30] Possibly his asking price was too high even for those feverish customers who were acquiring cattle and range rights at prices far above their real worth all over the West.

By then, Westerners with some experience in ranching and a flair for promotion were seeking prospective purchasers for their promising but capital-starved projects. Alexander Hamilton Swan typified the rapidity with which such men built and lost ranching empires. At the height of his financial power in the mid-1880's he summarized his career and his views for the benefit of an interviewer. Born in Pennsylvania in 1831 and reared on a farm in that state, he acquired a common school and academy education. In 1855 he moved to Ohio for seven years and then on to Iowa, from where he migrated to Wyoming in 1872. Since Iowa and Wyoming Territory were sparsely populated when Swan first visited them, they surpassed the Eastern states in hardships and privations, but Swan loved the "more perfect freedom" of new country. His fondest dream had been to "rear" and handle cattle, but it could not be realized until he reached the great grazing region of Wyoming, where there was room enough to satisfy the most ambitious. During his first six years in that territory he spent most of his time on ranches among the cowboys, and obviously liked to think of himself as one of them.

Swan was willing to leave the decision as to how well he had done to others, limiting his own account to the "facts" of his career. At the moment, he was general manager of the Swan Land and Cattle Company, Limited, a corporation controlled mostly by Scottish capital. The Company's herd totaled 120,000 cattle and covered a range fifty by 150 miles in extent. Previous to December, 1882, it had consisted of three separate herds, "controlled" by Swan and his associates. In 1883 he went to Scotland and consolidated the three herds into one under the ownership of the corporation, of which he became general manager. Swan had "other large interests" in Wyoming and Nebraska as well. He helped establish the Wyoming Hereford Association in 1883, and at the moment owned seven hundred pure blood Herefords on a ranch six miles from Cheyenne, of which five hundred were imported from England, according to him probably the largest herd of its kind in the world. He had connections with the Ogallala Land and Cattle Company of Nebraska, owner of some ninety thousand cattle. In addition, he possessed over four thousand acres of land and fifteen hundred cattle and horses in Iowa where he had formerly lived. He was one of the founders of the Union Stock Yards in Omaha, Nebraska, and was currently president of the South Omaha Land Syndicate, a corporation which purchased a large body of land in 1883, subdivided it, and started the rapidly growing town of South Omaha. He had served in the legislature of both Iowa and Wyoming, his politics being those of the "great national" Republican party.[31] Such was the manner in which one of the great promoters of the cattle kingdom described himself.

Others were much impressed by Swan during the height of his power. According to one observer at that time, Swan's history was written all over the Territory of Wyoming and should have a proud and commanding place in its future chronicles. Another, writing in 1884, mentioned his fine home in Cheyenne, built in 1878, and his liberality. He gave the local Presbyterian Church $3500, subscribed to stock in the local opera house and in the Cheyenne Club, and freely aided the schools in that vicinity. His daughter Louisa attended school in Europe and his son helped out with Swan's many local activities. The observer estimated that Swan started in life with a thousand dollars but was now worth two to three million, and that he had never missed a day's business in thirty years because of illness.[32] Scottish investors to whom

Swan sold his Wyoming holdings were equally enamored with his charm and ability. At the first general meeting of the Swan Land and Cattle Company, Limited, in Edinburgh on July 30, 1883, Mr. George Prentice assured the stockholders that the property had been a good buy, and went on to say

And of Mr. Swan himself I would like to tell you, that it is impossible to hear anything in that country but a favorable opinion of him. The whole way from Chicago to Cheyenne Mr. Swan is as well known on the road as any one who travels on it; and you never hear his name mentioned without an encomium passed upon him. The more I have seen him the more I respect him.[33]

In less than another five years Swan was bankrupt, and the stockholders who applauded Prentice's tribute to him in 1883 voted to dismiss him as general manager. According to John Clay, who succeeded him in that post, Swan left Cheyenne for Ogden after his failure and ultimately died virtually forgotten in an asylum. He had overexpanded his credit and pyramided his business to the point where bad weather, falling cattle prices, or any one of the problems common among cattlemen would bring him down. Scottish investors in the Swan Company suffered heavy losses. In 1892 they voted to write off eight pounds sterling out of every ten-pound share of the ordinary stock and to sell a considerable amount of land. Unlike a number of other Scottish companies, the corporation failed to repay capital investments to its stockholders who held on to their original investment. In 1925 the business was transferred to an American board wholly independent of Scottish management, although the Scots retained a financial interest. A new Swan Company was incorporated in Delaware with an authorized capitalization of $750,000, and as late as 1956 was still trying to dispose of its landholdings on favorable terms.[34]

Even those who disliked Swan remembered his forceful personality, and there were others who never lost their sense of loyalty to him. John Clay recalled him as a reckless and slippery promoter, commenting that the mercantile agencies rated him as worth a million dollars when it was doubtful if he ever owned an honest dollar. Clay recognized his skill and resourcefulness as a promoter and that his statements commanded respect. He had simply played for big stakes and lost. Moreover, Clay emphasized his personal weaknesses, but still remembered his striking personality. As Clay recalled him around the mid-1880's, he was about fifty years old, over six feet tall, with a Duke of Wellington nose, gold teeth, and an imposing figure. Casual but magnetic in manner, he attracted a great following, who sat around in his office and worshiped at his feet. Bankers, commission men, and breeders of fine stock courted him. As a vain and jealous man, he was driven to attempt to do big things.[35] In 1944, F. W. Lafrentz, a successful New York businessman and former employee of Swan's in the 1880's, presented a far more kindly picture of him. While keeping books in 1881 for a group of Chicago bankers who were involved in business dealings with Swan, Lafrentz became acquainted with his many activities and met him personally. Shortly thereafter, Swan persuaded him to come to Cheyenne and join his staff at double his existing salary "as a start." Lafrentz remembered his employer as looking like Uncle Sam—lank, gaunt, a long face, a beard, gray hair, knock-knees, and fine blue eyes, a personality whose failure he regretted deeply. In retrospect, Lafrentz still fretted that his own business judgment had not been great enough to save Swan from ruin.[36]

Without doubt, it took promotional skill and ability to dispose of the holdings that Swan, his chief partner Joseph Frank, and their associates sold to the Scots for $2,387,675, and to have himself named manager of the new company at a salary of $10,000 a year. Moreover, since he and Frank subscribed one-sixth of the corporation's stock, they did not think of it simply as unloading a promotional scheme on foreigners. Seemingly, Swan believed so firmly in the future of Wyoming ranching and in his own skill that he dared the impossible. He did help breed up Western cattle, and his Omaha venture had real merit. Even his failure was on a scale comparable to the grandiose pattern that had been his trademark all the way.

Of course, Swan's Scottish deal of 1883 came at a time when formation of large cattle corporations was something of a rage, and he was only one of the striking personalities involved. There was, for instance, Rufus Hatch, a leader in the creation of the Cattle Ranche and Land Company in 1882, capitalized at 200,000 pounds sterling. John Clay, then a young man, vividly remembered the personalities on both sides of the Atlantic involved in that deal. His pen sketches confirm the truth of a comment by a contemporary Scottish newspaper that "Cattle ranching is, after all, only poker on joint-stock principles." According to Clay, Rufus Hatch and two younger men, Earl W. Spencer and Francis Drew, acquired cattle and a range extending from western Kansas into Texas which they proposed to sell. Webster, Hoare and Company handled the deal for the Scottish group, with Hume Webster of that firm in charge of the negotiations. Thus Webster represented Lombard Street in Britain; Hatch represented Wall Street in America—at least in a symbolic sense. Clay was the young Scot on whose judgment of the property's worth his fellow Scots would rely.

In retrospect, Clay pictured Hume Webster as a promoter and genteel pawnbroker who stood ready to try his hand at anything. Suave and with a good presence, he was at the same time unscrupulous and already slightly dissipated. Several years after completion of the ranching deal, he killed himself at his country place to avoid criminal prosecution for some of his business dealings. Webster received a large block of common stock for his work in floating the company, part of which he distributed among his aides. For visiting and reporting on the ranch properties, Clay was promised $1250 and expenses, but if the deal went through he was to receive an additional $2500 in common stock: "This meant of course an indirect bribe, the first and the last I ever received. I was roped and tied down before I knew it." Another recipient of Webster's favors in all probability was the chairman of the board of the new organization, a Mr. Moore, who was socially delightful, something of a dandy in dress, and a man of perfect manners, although apparently devoid of real business experience. Clay knew that at least some of the directors of the new company benefited by gifts of stock for their services in recommending the organization to the public, a service made all the easier by distribution of a prospectus of "gilded glory."

In carrying out his assignment, Clay met Rufus Hatch at Dodge City, Kansas, in May, 1882, and in company with four others. they traveled by buggy and a four-seated wagon ninety miles south to examine the ranch property. Clay found Spencer a delightful companion, but Drew impressed him as a miserable specimen, lacking in honor, guilty of an evil tongue, an adventurer whose later dissipation of all his property followed naturally from his inclinations. "Uncle Rufus" Hatch was a Wall Street operator, with the reputation of a demon, but in the West his kindly personality drew men to him. Squat, well built, with a noble head and a mobile face, he easily won the liking and sympathy of young Clay. A passionate love of music on his part proved that he was no mere business machine, although he could press an issue as strongly as any man. A few weeks after their visit to the ranch, Hatch invited Clay to accompany him west on his own private train, consisting of a dining car, Pullman, and a combination Pullman and observation car, a trip motivated by his desire to examine Northern Pacific Railroad property, in whose stock he was speculating. Until financial misfortune made it impossible, Hatch traveled in the best available style. On that particular trip, Hatch proposed the formation of a company to lease the transportation and hotel business of Yellowstone Park and also to run cattle there. Clay joined thirty others in putting up a thousand dollars each to finance the project, but the Federal government rejected their proposition.

Everything turned sour for Hatch within a short time—his ranching venture, his Yellowstone project, and his railroad speculations alike. Fighting desperately to realize something, he attended the director's meeting of the Cattle Ranche and Land Company in London in 1885, where, having fortified himself with a pint of champagne before each session, he demanded that dividends be declared in spite of the sorry plight of the corporation. For emphasis, Hatch pounded on the conference table with the handle of his cane so violently as to disturb clerks working in the Rothschild banking house across the way. Staid Britishers, according to Clay, were not accustomed to the free and easy language of Wall Street.[37] All the pounding and strong talk in the world, however, could not prevent thousands of livestock from freezing to death in bitter plains weather and a disheartening decline in cattle prices. High finance of the type exemplified by Swan and Hatch provided only a superstructure of paper companies and paper profits to burden an industry struggling for survival even where good management and sound capitalization prevailed.

Some of the corporate ranching enterprises seemed almost fantastic in origin and size, the XIT syndicate being a case in point. The Texas state constitution of 1875 authorized the building of a new capitol through sale of state lands. In 1879 the legislature appropriated 3,050,000 acres to underwrite construction, and in 1880 authorized bids on 50,000 acres to cover costs of surveys. Since cattle syndicates were just becoming popular, some difficulty arose in finding a bidder willing to pay a fair price for the land. That problem was solved, however, and by the time the old capitol building burned in 1881, thereby making a new structure imperative, architectural plans had been drawn. On January 1, 1882, when bids for construction of the new capitol were opened, the contract went to Matthias Schnell of Rock Island, Illinois. In February, 1882, with consent of the Texas legislature, he assigned a three-fourths interest in the contract to Taylor, Babcock and Company, to whom he also turned over the remaining fourth the following May. In return for the three million acres of land, their syndicate constructed a building costing $3,334,593.45, which still serves as the capitol of Texas.

Taylor, Babcock and Company consisted of A. C. Babcock of Chicago, Abner Taylor, and John V. and Charles B. Farwell, all of the same city. They were merchants and speculators, the latter three being connected with the wholesale firm of J. V. Farwell and Company of Chicago. Since that firm maintained offices in Paris, Manchester, and London to obtain merchandise, and was already known to English capitalists, it facilitated negotiations to form the Capitol Freehold Land and Investment Company, Limited, of England in 1885, which supplied necessary capital to the American group. The Marquis of Tweeddale, governor of the Commercial Bank of Scotland, became chairman of the board, and the four additional Englishmen who served with him consisted of an English Lord, a lesser member of the nobility, a London merchant, and a member of Parliament. The two Farwells, Abner Taylor, and a Boston banker completed the nine-member board. In reality, the XIT was not an English institution. It consisted of the American syndicate, which sold its land to the English corporation, and the latter in turn used the land as security to obtain funds from English investors for a period of years. The English group leased the land back to the American corporation, which constituted the managing and operating company in building the Texas state capitol and in developing the great XIT Ranch.[38]

Before the speculative craze ran its course, corporate ranching organizations of every conceivable variety were formed. Westerners, Easterners, and Europeans combined forces regionally, internationally, by nationality, and across all such lines. They incorporated their ventures in Britain, in some Eastern state, or directly in the state or territory where they intended to operate. Some were formed for the primary purpose of selling stock to the public; others furnished all necessary investment capital from their own funds and never issued a prospectus or listed their stock for sale.

Nevertheless, insofar as foreign investments were concerned, a somewhat common pattern of creating new corporate organizations developed by 1882. British investments in America over a long period of time had given rise to American agents who brought lender and borrower together and performed administrative services of other sorts. The Kansas City Directory of 1880, for instance, listed the firm of Underwood, Clark and Company, financial brokers, headed by Frank L. Underwood, who served additionally as president of the Merchant's National Bank.[39] Since Underwood's company placed numerous real estate loans in Iowa, Kansas, and Missouri for the Scottish-American Mortgage Company, it kept well informed on possible land investments in all parts of the country. In 1880 Underwood convinced the board of the Scottish company that ranching would be highly profitable, and this resulted in the formation of the Prairie Cattle Company, Limited. J. Duncan Smith, managing director of the Scottish Mortgage Company, frequently visited America on business, and he became the first of his group to agree with Underwood's ideas as well as the foremost Scottish promoter of the new company. Occasionally, information on ranching opportunities came directly through a Britisher sent out to evaluate the market for foreign loans. And, of course, American promoters frequently turned up in England to solicit financial help or to sell their holdings, generally having acquired such properties with foreign sales in mind.

The second step in the process consisted of organizing a joint-stock company under a British board of directors, the issuance of a prospectus describing the project, and the taking of public subscriptions to stock. In the meantime, an inspector was sent out to examine the property, John Clay being an example of such an agent, and until he reported nothing was settled definitely.

Once a favorable report was received, things moved rapidly through the third and fourth steps. In the third step, the new company purchased the range and herd involved, and frequently retained the original vendor as manager. The Company sometimes also created an American board to advise the British directors. The fourth step involved detailed financial arrangements with the American vendors. In early years, American promoters demanded a share in annual profits, but it soon became customary to give them a "deferred interest," to be paid only after shareholders received specified annual dividends and upon return of the original capital. Even then vendors profited by selling their holdings to the new company at considerable markups over the original cost to them. Occasionally, the agreement specified that vendors could not dispose of their interest for a definite period of years, and some vendor-managers worked without salary until the ranch property attained a specified degree of success. The British thus tried to intertwine the interests of British owners and investors with those of the American vendors and managers as a means of encouraging devoted service.

In spite of efforts to safeguard their investments, the foreign-owned cattle corporations found themselves involved in mounting problems as early as 1884. Part of their difficulties lay in long-distance management by remote control. Conflicts developed between British directors and American managers over contracts and policies. Companies that had purchased herds by "book count" found themselves short of cattle; English quarantine regulations on American beef sharply curtailed marketing possibilities. By then, too, legislative agencies were thinking of measures to curb foreign ownership of American land. Declining markets, agrarian encroachments on land occupied by foreign-owned corporations only because they had bought rights to "the accustomed range," and losses of cattle from severe climatic conditions added to the mounting problems.

In 1888 a British periodical summarized in an exaggerated way, but with considerable insight, the reasons why investors found themselves in trouble. Corporations paid four times too much for lands and herds and had operated on a falling cattle market for the past seven or eight years. They had foolishly bought herds by estimated book count, not taking the trouble to demand an actual check. Since a majority of ranches were located on public domain, increasing population pressure had forced them to sell off cattle that should have been retained. Ranches on the prairies of the Dakotas, Wyoming, and Montana, a land of blizzards, were too far north for raising cattle on open range. Moreover, management had used shareholders' money to build "castles on the prairies," thus burdening a sick industry with needless extravagance.[40]

Foreign critics thus mixed together explanations for failure that applied to the ranching industry as a whole, no matter what type of business organization was involved, with others that related primarily to large-scale corporate schemes of operation. Obviously, however, sound policy and good management rather than organizational patterns furnished the greater measure of protection to an investor's dollar.

ELEVEN

The Vanguard of Change

As RUGGED individualists, ranchers liked to emphasize the importance of frugality and hard work.
In a society which prized the self-made man, it paid dividends to
work with one's hands and to live frugally in early life. John B.
Kendrick benefited greatly from the fact that he had once punched
cattle with rank-and-file cowboys when he campaigned for governor and United States senator from Wyoming. One of his con-
stituents recalled Kendrick's early responsibility for driving cattle
to Lusk, the most important shipping point on the Northwestern
Railroad. Once the cattle were delivered most of the hands caroused for two or three days, drinking, gambling, and even shooting up the small community. But not Kendrick. While waiting for
the others to finish their spree, he returned to the roundup wagon
to read and study the books that he always carried in his saddle-
bags. At that period, cowboys bought "round-up socks" at the rate
of twelve pairs for a dollar, and threw them away as soon as they
became soiled. Kendrick, however, refused to be so wasteful,
darning and washing his socks and underwear in order to save
money.[1] Such stories not only helped the politically ambitious;
they made it easier for many a rancher to obtain a loan at his local
bank when in need of money. But frugality and hard work alone
never made a United States senator any more than they did a cattle king.

If any one word explains or offers a universal key to how so many men started without inherited money and became cattle kings, that word would be "trader." Instead of relying simply on the natural increase from a small herd of cattle to make them wealthy, such men traded in cattle, in mines, in beef, in store goods—in anything that came to hand and yielded a profit by being passed on to someone else in the channels of trade. By such means they obtained the capital resources that they concentrated in herds of cattle. Many gained most of their wealth from ranching, it is true, but they acquired their basic capital for foundation herds through trading enterprises. As one studies the careers of the cattle kings, he becomes impressed with the flexibility of their operations and their sense of timing. Like other good entrepreneurs, they were innovators in the sense of taking a lead in changing policies rather than imitators of well-established practices. According to one theory, American businessmen have generally built their wealth on one major innovation or discovery, shaping all their later activities around it, and prospering unless some other entrepreneur destroys their advantage by a still more effective program. Such did not hold true of the cattle kings. In general, they were in the vanguard of change and often so close to it as to receive credit for being the originator of a new idea. More important than originality, however, was a willingness to consider new ideas and to judge their immediate applicability to conditions at hand.

In reality, such men employed methods that characterized what economic historians have called the Age of the Commercial Revolution. Antonio, the merchant of Venice in Shakespeare's play, would have understood their basic scheme of operation. Antonio sent his ships to distant ports to search out products for exchange in world markets. In his age, trading rather than manufacturing, swapping rather than concentration on changing the form of raw products, tended to dominate the thinking of businessmen. Discoveries of vast new frontiers in Antonio's age fired man's imagination with the idea of exploiting resources of virgin regions. Adventurers extracted the raw products of such lands and traded them at a profit in the more highly developed parts of the world.

Furs and precious metals and the hides of hoofed animals attracted their attention in frontier regions. The working-up of such raw products could be left to artisans at points of consumer demand. The greatest volume of profit lay in exchanging merchandise for the raw products of frontier regions, and not until the Industrial Revolution got under way did manufacturing surpass trading or swapping on a grand scale as a way to wealth. Thus, it has been said that in the Age of the Commercial Revolution, commerce dominated industry; but in the Age of the Industrial Revolution, industry dominated commerce.

At the close of the Civil War, the cattle kingdom lay virtually undeveloped, a frontier region still to be probed except for the furs and minerals that had already received attention. Mining, ranching, farming—the extractive industries—would characterize the economy of that region for years to come. In ranching, butchering, mining, freighting, and merchandising, entrepreneurs displayed a common pattern of exchanging raw products for capital assets or goods. Unlike Antonio, they had no ships to suffer delays and perils of distant voyages, but long drives to dispose of cattle in uncertain and distant markets proved quite as hazardous and quite as capable of bringing riches or bankruptcy. Nor was it strained hyperbole to speak of ships of the desert when referring to pioneer means of crossing the plains. Those blessed with skill and insight into the opportunities available, and also with a measure of good fortune, rapidly acquired the capital necessary to launch careers as cattle kings. Probing and trading, they surpassed their less imaginative or less interested contemporaries who thought of ranching either in terms of relying simply on the natural increase of herds or as a job from which one acquired funds for a spree in some cowtown.

The skill with which men like Goodnight, Iliff, Kohrs, Littlefield, Story, and a host of others combined the commonly recognized factors of production—land, labor and capital—certainly substantiates the argument of those economists who insist on recognizing a fourth factor, namely, entrepreneurship. Littlefield, for instance, bartered merchandise for cattle at his roadside store and acquired others on credit for drives to Kansas cowtowns. In 1871 he made his initial and highly successful drive to Abilene. Thereafter, for fourteen years Littlefield herds went up the trail in charge of others while he looked after the purchasing of additional Texas cattle or moved on ahead of his drovers by commercial transportation to seek out the best markets—to Abilene, Kansas City, Council Bluffs, Ogallala, Dodge City, and so on. Contemporaries said that he could scent the location of an active trade—that is, a market where prices were good—as easily as a Texas longhorn could scent water. After fourteen years of trail driving, Littlefield explained his success in the same terms as Shanghai Pierce: "I have only one rule in business: When everybody is wanting to sell, I buy; when everybody is wanting to buy, I sell."[2] Littlefield continued to operate his store and home plantation, carefully supervising every aspect of his business. In his estimation, economy and industry guided by good judgment assured success; as they did, if good judgment included a capacity to *trade* at a profit. Certainly, the basis of the Littlefield fortune lay in his early trading ventures.

When the *Rocky Mountain News* announced the death of John W. Iliff in 1878, his obituary bore the caption "Death of the Cattle King of the Plains," and described him as the West's most successful "cattle merchant,"[3] a term which aptly characterized his career. Stimulated by accounts of Western opportunities, Iliff left Ohio for Kansas in 1857, where he helped to start the town of Princeton. Iliff operated Princeton's first store on money raised by popular subscription, bought a farm of 160 acres, and pre-empted 154 more. In 1859 he sold his store and invested in an ox-train of provisions, with the idea of opening a mercantile establishment in Denver to profit from the mining rush then taking place. The Denver directory for 1859 listed "Fenton, Auld and Iliff, Merchants" in groceries, provisions, and clothing. Although Iliff concentrated primarily on merchandising for some eighteen months, he and Fenton soon began to buy cattle from work trains passing through Denver, and fattened them on nearby grass for sale to mining camps, local butcher shops, and slaughtering establishments.

Iliff quickly sensed the profits inherent in cattle trading. With that in mind, he established a herd on the South Platte River in northeastern Colorado, an advantageous location for buying, selling, and reconditioning work cattle and for ranching. Iliff did not depend simply on the increase from his own herd to sustain his business plans, his listing as a "Stock Dealer" in the Denver directory for 1866 reflecting the nature of his operations. In 1865, for instance, he and his partner, Fenton, purchased thirteen hundred head of cattle in the Cherokee Nation and drove them to Fort Union, New Mexico, to supply a government contract. On June 13, 1868, the *Rocky Mountain News* reported that Iliff was furnishing beef for workmen engaged in constructing the transcontinental railroad and also for the troops and Indians in that vicinity —some five thousand head a year, all bought in southern Colorado. Already he had shipped some beef in iced cars to Chicago dealers. In addition to handling his own cattle, he served as agent for the sale of Texas longhorns coming up the trail. Iliff bought part of the first herd driven north by Charles Goodnight and Oliver Loving, trailmakers from Texas to the Northern plains.

Iliff continued to buy ten to fifteen thousand Texas cattle yearly at a cost of ten to fifteen dollars a head. These he fattened for a year or two on grass and then sold at thirty to thirty-seven dollars a head. Steers produced from his own herd of six to seven thousand breeding cows sold at thirty-eight to fifty dollars a head. Always seeking the best markets for his stock, Iliff established cow camps near the "hell on wheels," temporary centers for construction workers, on the transcontinental railroad in order to have beef ready for delivery under contract to feed the crews. He sold to government depots that provisioned forts over a wide region, to builders of telegraph lines, and to agents in charge of Indian reservations.[4] Merchandising provided the capital with which he launched his larger operations, and, like Littlefield, the basis for his fortune lay in his early trading ventures. Moreover, like Littlefield, he remained a trader throughout his career.

Conrad Kohrs and Ora Haley represented the same pattern of trading or merchandising, the basic capital for their ranching ventures coming from the operation of wholesale and retail butcher

shops in mining camps.[5] As Texas Ranger, trail breaker and frontier ranchman, Charles Goodnight represents to a remarkable degree what the popular imagination visualizes a ranchman to have
been. Nevertheless, as a boy he engaged in freighting and in hauling goods in the vicinity of Waco, Texas. To make out during his
first partnership venture in ranching, he freighted in goods for
settlers while his partner looked after their herd. Moreover, he
established the early Goodnight and Loving trails from Texas to
the Northern plains shortly after the Civil War basically as a trading route for marketing Texas cattle. Sales to government contractors at Santa Fe, to Indian agents at Fort Sumner, to Iliff in Colorado, and elsewhere on the Plains proved highly profitable. By
1873, he was able to establish himself as a rancher and businessman at Pueblo, a position resulting from his trading activities over
a wide expanse of territory, not from ranching as such.[6]

Similarly, Richard King acquired the means to build his ranching empire through trading activities. At age eleven he escaped
from an apprenticeship to a New York jeweler by stowing away
on a sailing ship bound for Mobile, Alabama. When discovered
by the master, King managed to wangle a job as cabin boy, and
at journey's end entered a new apprenticeship on Southern river
boats. By age nineteen he had earned his pilot's license. King
signed on for government service as a pilot on the Rio Grande
during the Mexican War. At the termination of hostilities, he ran
a combination grog shop and flophouse while waiting for an opportunity to purchase one of the steamboats soon to be released
from government service. In 1849 he bought one of them for $750,
a vessel for which the government had paid $14,000 three years
previously. After hauling merchandise on the Rio Grande on his
own for a short time, King joined Mifflin Kenedy and Charles
Stillman, a local banker and later on a prominent New York
banker, in a partnership to operate river boats. This firm made as
much as a 50 per cent return on capital investment during some
years.

Stillman soon became a silent partner, and both King and
Kenedy gave up direct command of boats to handle the business

affairs of the partnership ashore. Both of them engaged in ventures outside the firm's major business of hauling freight. At times they bought cargoes of wool, hides, bones, tallow, or livestock to sell down river. Usually they pursued such ventures separately, often with outside partners, and the profits were their own. After Stillman withdrew from the business to move to New York City, King and Kenedy continued a joint ownership of the firm until 1874. Profits from that business helped both men acquire ranches.

During the Civil War King made a great deal of money. With the Federal blockade strangling the Confederacy along most of its coastline, the Rio Grande became an important back door for imports and exports. Cotton wagons traversed King's Santa Gertrudis Ranch and moved to the decks of his steamboats on the Rio Grande. He quickly became an adviser to cotton-owning strangers, an assistant to Confederate agents, a contractor to haul cotton on the river, and a cotton speculator himself. When the Federal government tightened the blockade, King and his partners put their boats under the flag of Mexico and continued to operate. Millions of dollars worth of munitions and supplies entered Matamoros in exchange for cotton. The partners contracted with the Confederacy to handle sales, their commission and shipping charges paying them exceedingly well. During the closing months of the war King did especially well buying and selling cotton, supplying Confederate troops, and running wagon trains and steamboats. He profited tremendously from the war and was shrewd enough to take pay in sound money. His big gold stake from the Civil War Matamoros trade enabled him to survive the vicissitudes of Reconstruction and to make his Santa Gertrudis Ranch into a great enterprise.[7] Quite obviously King laid the basis for his ranching empire as a trader.

Colonel Dudley H. Snyder of the famous Texas ranching family displayed remarkable ingenuity as a trader even before he and his brothers established their reputation as drovers. His father's death and loss of the family property in the hard times of the 1840's caused Snyder to seek out every opportunity. In 1851 he collected mercantile accounts for his grandfather's store at Round Rock, Texas. The next year he engaged in farming and hauling. Although

accounts vary, several speak of his hauling apples and other delica-
cies from Missouri to trade in Texas. He also supposedly swapped
Texas ponies for the larger Missouri horses and sold the latter to
Texans. In 1862 he contracted with a wealthy planter to deliver
beef to the Confederate forces. Such activities prepared him and
his relatives for their careers as drovers of Texas longhorns to
Northern markets, the basis for their ranching wealth.[8]

One of Montana's pioneer ranchmen, Nelson Story, obviously
preferred ranching to all other occupations, and did well at it, selling out his cattle and horses in 1889 for some half million dollars.
Nevertheless, he started out as a trader. At age eighteen he left his
native Ohio, virtually penniless, and spent two years cutting, hauling, and selling posts and wood in Kansas. A chance to buy condemned government wagons enabled him to shift to freighting
merchandise to Denver. Story also tried his hand at mining, but
without great success, and in the spring of 1863 he moved to Bannack City, Montana, only to discover that the local population had
just departed for the newly discovered diggings at Alder Gulch.
Story opened a store at the new camp and also rented out his pack
train of eleven jacks to those in need of transportation. By then
his parents had joined him, his father spending his time prospecting and the mother baking and selling pies to miners at Story's
store. In 1866 Story obtained thirty thousand dollars in gold dust
from a mining claim, took it east and exchanged it at a very favorable ratio for greenbacks, and purchased a stock of merchandise.
On the same trip he bought a thousand Texas cattle and then transferred all his enterprises to Bozeman, Montana,[9] where his reputation as a cattleman overshadowed his other economic activities.
With him, as with so many others, it was possible to move into the
upper echelons of the ranching fraternity through skillful trading.

In addition to trading widely, such men shifted easily from
one occupation to another as the opportunity offered. Worden P.
Noble, Indian trader at the Shoshone Agency in Wyoming, came
west as a bookkeeper, from which he soon turned to merchandising
and the provisioning of forts. Freighting and operation of a quartz
mill also occupied his attention. By the middle 1880's he was

heavily engaged in ranching.[10] Similarly, Morton E. Post, who started west in 1860 with only twenty-five dollars, had by the mid-1880's already engaged in hunting, trapping, the provisioning of government forts, itinerant merchandising, freighting, speculation in town lots, coal mining, and banking. In 1872 he began to participate in ranching, much of his time being devoted to buying and selling sheep and wool. By the middle 1880's he claimed to have three thousand brood mares on his horse ranch, consisting of an original forty thousand acres acquired early in his career and an additional fifty thousand purchased from railroad holdings, all under fence.[11] A contemporary of Post, William Van Gasken, in his early years engaged in mining and freighting in Utah, chopped wood for steamboats, and ranched on a small scale. By the middle eighties he claimed to have the largest wholesale and retail slaughtering business in the Miles City, Montana, region, an occupation that naturally caused him to extend and intensify his ranching activities.[12] John Donegan, Irish immigrant, worked for eight years in New York City and an additional seven in the Illinois lead mines before moving west to Salt Lake City. There he bought a stock of merchandise, disposed of it in the Montana mining region, and engaged in mining for four years. At the end of that time he had cleared three thousand dollars, which he invested in ranching.[13]

Of course, one would expect considerable shifting and experimentation in the early days of ranching and among young men. As a young man in new country, Charles Goodnight naturally experimented in laying out his early cattle trails but, of more significance, he continued in the vanguard of change. Sensing the importance of foreign investment capital, of barbed wire, of improved breeds of cattle, of artificial watering facilities, and of permanent and outright ownership of range, he moved ahead in all these respects. When the *Galveston News* sent a reporter to his ranch in the winter of 1885 to see what he had accomplished, the writer claimed that Goodnight's work stood a century ahead of the free-grass longhorn ranch of the past few years. The reporter called him a bold pioneer and a man of native genius, who with great energy had set a new

Left, the windmill, a chief source of water for cattle. (New Mexico State Tourist Bureau)

Below, haying scenes became familiar when winter feeding proved necessary. (University of Wyoming Library)

Cowboy herding cattle to feed on cactus after spines have been burned off. (New Mexico State Tourist Bureau)
Below, manager of Spur Ranch and wife. (Erwin E. Smith Collection, Library of Congress)

Tenderfoot visitors to the JA Ranch: a writer from Boston and the nephew of President Faure of France. (Erwin E. Smith Collection, Library of Congress)

pattern for the industry. He commented on the houses; the water tanks; the miles of barbed wire; the fine hay farm; the corrals; the dairy, which made and stored enough butter during the summer to last the year; the poultry flock; the tinware shop for supplying ranch needs; the blacksmith shop, and so on. Many of the employees were saving their wages, the owner having on deposit for them some twenty-six thousand dollars.[14] Although almost fifty years of age, Goodnight obviously stood in the vanguard of progressive ranchers just as when laying out his first cattle trails in the 1860's. Goodnight's success stemmed from his curiosity as to possible avenues of change, his daring in adopting new paths, and his ability to inspire confidence in others, rather than in infallible judgment. The Panic of 1873 wiped out his earliest successes, and he lost considerable money in a Mexican mining venture still later in life. Knowledge resulting from curiosity tempered his daring sufficiently, however, to make his career almost prophetic of the changes in which he participated.

Quite obviously, land, labor, and capital could be combined on the ranching frontier in a manner conducive to extraordinary profits. Quite obviously, too, the proper combination for maximum profits shifted rapidly over the years. By luck alone one might profit greatly from a single venture of short duration, but only an entrepreneur possessed of daring, flexibility, curiosity, and a willingness to change procedures could hope to retain his place among the cattle kings for any extended period of time.

Although responsible for policy-making decisions, entrepreneurial leaders in the cattle kingdom also devoted a great deal of time to management. Unless faithfully executed, the best of policies were of no avail. In ranching, however, it was physically impossible to oversee directly every activity. Ranges covered a vast extent of territory and markets were hundreds of miles away. Partnerships and corporate organizations placed an additional premium on management if distant investors wished to have any degree of control over their property.

In spite of the need for managerial talent to meet such demands, the cattle kingdom failed to produce an adequate supply of good

managers. A shortage of reliable trail bosses and range foremen
on the Spur Ranch in Texas seems to have been fairly common
everywhere, although the industry was amply supplied with cowhands. Like other ranches, the Spur paid foremen from two to four
times as much as an experienced cowhand but still had trouble
finding an adequate number. Like others, it recruited most of them
by a process of trial and error from the general run of employees.[15]
The relative scarcity of such men stemmed from the unwillingness
of cowboys to assume responsibility, partly because they had little
interest in getting ahead economically and partly because the authority of such a person rested basically on his ability to prove his
competence to those under him. In a society based on achieved
status, employees respected the man more than the title. Those
higher up the ladder of management could discharge unsatisfac-
tory employees, but at the level where boss and cowboy came in
daily contact, the man directly in charge needed a combination of
aggressiveness and restraint, of leadership and initiative in keeping his associates constantly at work that few individuals working
for wages in the cattle kingdom seemed to possess. If they did have
such abilities, it was relatively easy to move to a still higher managerial post within a few years, thus necessitating constant replace-
ments. Out of the few men who stuck by John Clay during a cowboy strike in 1884 came a ranch manager, a ranch owner, a bank
president, and a successful sheepman.[16] For the ambitious, the
managerial path lay open.

The managerial shortage was also due in part to the heavy responsibilities faced at all levels. In 1882, for instance, Jim Flood
took a herd of three thousand cattle from the Rio Grande in Texas
to the Blackfoot Agency in Montana, a trip requiring five months
and close to three thousand miles of travel. His employer had other
herds and other business problems to look after, thus leaving Flood
wholly in charge of the drive. That meant responsibility for three
thousand cattle, a chuck wagon, fourteen cowboys, and a remuda
of 150 horses. Moreover, in accepting the assignment, Flood knew
there could be no hope of obtaining advice from anyone higher up
in the organization during most of the trip, his job by its very

nature preventing the close supervision that many a less confident man in the lower echelons of management would have welcomed. He also knew that his decisions could not be strictly of a routine nature, for no two problems on the trail were identically alike. During the drive he had to contend with stampedes, rustlers, Indians, unexpected shortages of water for long distances, and the fording of a variety of rivers and lesser streams along the way. Poor judgment in selecting a ford or in meeting similarly dangerous problems could cost his life or that of one of his men. There were sure to be occasions on so long a drive when man and beast alike would flag in spirit, necessitating on Flood's part a fine sense of balance in regard to how much he could demand of them.[17] Such responsibilities caused many a well-trained cowhand in the technical sense to reject an assignment as trail boss.

Good ranch managers were also relatively scarce, especially if one judges them in terms of success achieved. Many self-made ranchers continued to manage their spreads in later life, partly because they loved such work but also from distrust of the available managerial talent. Richard King, for instance, covered his ranch property frequently in a spring wagon, with a Winchester rifle and a jug of his favorite Rose Bud whiskey at his side. King's ranch foremen and trail bosses knew that he might turn up at an unexpected moment to check on them.[18] Until 1877 George W. Littlefield assumed virtually the whole burden of managing his range and marketing activities. Charles S. McCarty served him as a trail boss in the 1870's, brought in the herd that established the LIT spread, and remained with his employer for many years. As a range manager he could care for a herd of cattle, but had little ability in keeping books and at times drank heavily. When Littlefield sold the LIT to a syndicate, McCarty's accounts were two thousand dollars short, but since he had served long and well, Littlefield overlooked the shortage and gave him an additional two thousand dollars. According to rumor, McCarty spent the next winter in Las Vegas squandering the money. Still another LIT employee, Bob Robinson, became an able cattleman and good executive in spite of scanty education. When Littlefield sold the

LIT, Robinson remained with the new organization as range manager, started a herd of his own, and ultimately became a wealthy banker. Like so many other able men, he moved from managerial work to business activities of his own.

J. Phelps White, Sr., Littlefield's young nephew, also had a hand in building the LIT spread, and in time became his uncle's chief reliance in all ranching ventures. Stocky, congenial, observant, and conservative, White knew cattle and also could handle business matters. Although he admired his uncle's business ability, he fretted at times over what he considered needless supervision. White's obituary sketches in the Roswell, New Mexico, papers credit him with policy decisions as well as with good management in his joint ventures with Littlefield. As White put it, he would have preferred for Littlefield to say in his will "Phelps White helped me make my money" than to have been left the whole fortune. Others may have felt the same way. After Littlefield started his Austin, Texas, bank, he required foremen of his nearby farms and ranches to draw checks directly on him for operating expenses. Every Sunday morning they had to meet him at the bank, where he checked over their accounts for the past week and conferred with them on plans for the immediate future.[19] Necessity had compelled him to supervise closely in the early days and his love of business seems to have encouraged a continuation of that practice after the need lessened.

Most ranch managers were native Americans with considerable ranching experience behind them before they acquired jobs with the larger outfits. Some of them moved up through the lower echelons of management; others did so well in managing small herds of their own that they found ready employment by promoters engaged in consolidating smaller ranches. A. G. Boyce, Colonel B. H. Campbell, Charles Goodnight, R. G. Head, and others fitted that pattern. Colonel B. H. Campbell, first general manager of the XIT spread, for instance, obtained considerable experience as a cattleman in Indian Territory before the XIT hired him as manager. A. G. Boyce, Campbell's successor, and general manager of the XIT for eighteen years, first visited that ranch as trail boss in charge of a herd sold to it by the famous Snyder brothers. Already seasoned and knowledgeable from association with skilled Texas cattlemen, Boyce proved invaluable to the XIT owners.[20] R. G. Head, who became manager of the Prairie Cattle Company in 1883, grew up in Texas ranch country and started his career as a hand on one of the early drives to Abilene. Within three years he became a trail boss and during a seven-year span delivered cattle at points all over the plains. In 1875 he became general manager for Ellison, Dewes and Bishop of San Antonio, Texas, handling for them thirty to fifty thousand head of cattle a year. From 1878 to 1883 he operated in partnership with Bishop alone, and then accepted his post with the Prairie syndicate.[21]

A few managers came from foreign backgrounds, worked as cowboys for a period of years, and then assumed greater responsibilities. Fred G. S. Hesse, for instance, was born in Essex, England, studied law briefly in his native country, and then decided to join two of his brothers in Australia. He stopped briefly in New York City in 1872, changed his plans, and went to Texas for a few years, working as a cowboy and at other jobs. In 1876 he took a herd north as trail boss for John Slaughter, noted cattleman and drover. At his destination in Cheyenne, Wyoming, Hesse went to work for John Sparks, a prominent stockman and later governor of Nevada. In 1878 the Frewen brothers of England hired him to manage their Wyoming ranch, a job that he held for ten years. Ultimately, Hesse built a considerable ranching enterprise on his own.[22]

During the ranching craze of the 1880's, a good many managers came from American speculative groups who sold their holdings to foreigners, with one of them assuming management of the new corporation. Alexander Swan both promoted and managed a large cattle company. Swan apparently had greater previous experience with cattle than Spottswood Lomax, who served as first manager of the Spur Ranch (the Espuela) from 1884 to 1889. Lomax belonged to a group of American promoters who obtained control of range and cattle holdings and then marketed them to English investors as the Spur and the Matador spreads.

Another source of managers lay in the desire of some foreign-owned corporations to put one of their fellow countrymen directly in charge of their American holdings. Although never numerous, this group contributed some of the most successful managers. Some brought to America from their native Scotland considerable experience in stock raising. John Clay's father, for instance, was a prosperous and successful stockman and farmer, and Clay himself first visited America in 1872 on profits acquired from successfully settling the landed estate of a Scotchman. During the next decade he gained much knowledge of American ranching while serving British corporations in various capacities, and they naturally turned to him as manager when hard times destroyed their faith in American employees.

Murdo Mackenzie, probably the greatest of all ranch managers, knew the Scottish livestock industry at firsthand before the Prairie Cattle Company persuaded him to join their American managerial staff in 1885 at age thirty-five. At the time he held a managerial post on the Scottish Balganown estate of Sir Charles Ross at a salary that had risen from five to twelve hundred dollars a year. The Balganown estate covered five hundred thousand acres of land, had a flock of twelve thousand sheep, two hundred tenant farms, and a game preserve of nine thousand acres.[23] Thus Mackenzie brought to America extensive experience in financial management and livestock breeding from a job that even the largest American ranching corporations could not dwarf to insignificance.

Salaries in the higher echelons of management varied widely. Although such differences stemmed partially from the varying degrees of responsibility given to managers, they must have arisen in part from variations in usage of the word "salary." For instance, some managers were furnished living quarters for themselves and their families. Many also owned stock in the organizations for which they worked and shared in the profits. Occasionally, they had the privilege of running cattle on their own. Some reported these perquisites as part of their salary; others mentioned only the cash payment made to them by their employers. Harry Oelrichs, manager of the Anglo-American Cattle Company, told an interviewer in 1885 that he received a salary of two thousand dollars a month. This Eastern playboy took more interest in the famous actress Sarah Bernhardt than in ranching problems and was known as a "character" from coast to coast because of his extravagance.[24] Since Oelrichs owned stock in the ranch, he may well have included returns other than strict salary in telling his interviewer how much he made. Similarly, R. G. Head's salary of twenty thousand dollars a year as manager of the Prairie Cattle Company[25] probably included income that should not have been reported as salary. When Alexander H. Swan sold his Wyoming holdings to a British syndicate, he became manager of the new organization under a five-year appointment at ten thousand dollars a year, but he and his partner had also subscribed to one-sixth of the stock of the new company. At the height of the cattle boom, managerial salaries undoubtedly reflected the prevailing optimism, but even then straight cash payments for such services seldom if ever equaled figures such as those mentioned by Head and Oelrichs.

The more business-like foreign corporations kept managerial salaries below the level reported by some of the less cautious companies during the boom years. From its establishment in 1884 until 1889 the Spur Ranch paid Spottswood Lomax $7,500 a year as general manager. Hard times caused the home board to cut his salary to $3,750 in 1889, although they offered to restore it to $5,000 when Lomax threatened to resign. During the negotiations, a bank at Vernon, Texas, offered Lomax a job, and he decided to accept it rather than take any salary cut from the Spur. In 1886 the Spur sent over a Scotsman, Fred Horsbrugh, at a salary of $125 a month as a sort of general agent to look after investments. When Lomax left in 1889, Horsbrugh applied for his job on the grounds that during the past three years he had become well acquainted with company business. The Spur appointed him at two thousand dollars a year, and he continued in that post until 1904.[26] Managerial salaries of Lomax and Horsbrugh probably reflected the prevailing scale much more accurately than did the larger payments reported by a few men during the boom period.

Murdo Mackenzie's twelve hundred dollars a year on the Balganown estate fell considerably below what an experienced manager could hope to receive in America. He and his family liked Scotland, however, and he was approaching middle life when an offer came to join the managerial staff of the Prairie Company. From that he moved on to management of the Matador organization. Except for an interlude as manager of an enormous South American ranch from 1911 to 1919, he spent the remainder of his life with the Matador. No moneygrubber, Mackenzie refused to let salary alone determine his choice of job, and his abilities were such that he had considerable freedom in making a selection. His family lived well, his children attended college, and all of them traveled abroad. Bonuses and income from ownership of stock added to his substantial salary from the organizations fortunate enough to obtain his services.

As to the characteristics of a good manager, it seems axiomatic that they should have been both honest and reliable, but some otherwise well-equipped men fell short in those respects. Colonel B. H. Campbell, first manager of the XIT, practiced strict economy when ranging cattle on his own but showed less consideration in handling property belonging to others. In stocking the XIT Ranch, he arranged for a cousin to supply inferior Texas cattle, a deal from which both profited personally. Campbell also neglected his supervisory duties, thus permitting the ranch to become a rendezvous for rustlers, outlaws, and loafers. Suspecting him of failing to meet his responsibilities, the owners sent their agent and a Texas lawyer to the ranch in the summer of 1887 to investigate, and there the lawyer immediately recognized, among those present, men with criminal records, some of whom he had defended in earlier court actions. He and the agent agreed that a new manager must be employed, and so A. G. Boyce began his long and faithful career by running out the toughs who had congregated under Campbell's regime.[27] Although less numerous than TV shows would have us believe, venal managers did exist, in part because the isolated nature of ranching tempted men to steal.

Top managerial posts required much travel and an ability to negotiate at all levels of society. Murdo Mackenzie covered thousands of miles yearly and associated with people ranging from line riders to heads of state. Part of his travels in 1897 involved: a ranch inspection in company with the local manager; negotiations in Kansas to rent pasturage; a meeting of stock growers in Fort Worth; a cattleman's convention in San Antonio; an Austin conference on leasing of school lands; sale of a herd of cattle in Kansas; a Kansas City business trip; a court session at Childress, Texas; a conference in Denver with railroad officials on shipping rates; purchase of purebred heifers in Kansas; supervision of the sale of several carloads of cattle in Chicago; and purchase of a carload of bulls in Topeka.[28] From his seat in a buggy or a spring wagon, such a manager conferred with mounted cowhands scattered across the range, seemingly intent only on passing the time of day but learning from such conversations how well his organization was functioning. The next day he left for a business appointment in a distant city or to testify before a Congressional committee in Washington, D. C.

Although courage sustained a manager during the occasional trouble with a dissatisfied cowhand or dissident element, his success depended fundamentally upon his capacity to handle people. As previously mentioned, Murdo Mackenzie never carried a gun, relying instead on his ability to put matters so clearly and so cogently as to persuade those who would do him bodily injury that they were making a serious mistake. Only a courageous man could hope to succeed as a manager in the cattle industry, it is true, but courage was only the base from which his talents could operate.

And, of course, a good manager must know enough concerning the breeding and care of cattle to judge how well his subordinates carried out instructions. When A. G. Boyce appeared at the XIT Ranch to deliver a trail herd, B. H. Campbell asked him to assist in separating the steers according to age, which could be done by looking at their teeth. Many a cowboy could make that decision, but Boyce knew cattle so well that he could go still further in shaping up a herd according to specifications given him. As a ranch manager, he needed knowledge beyond that inherent in the skills of a top cowhand.

Even within comparable grades, managerial freedom of action varied greatly. As a whole, the home offices of Scottish cattle corporations exercised closer supervision than did English groups. In some promotional companies, the managerial ranch force had virtually complete freedom of action; in others, distant investors meddled to the point where employees in responsible posts were severely handicapped. Some managers shared in making policy; others were expected only to carry out decisions from above. Investors and home-office officials criticized field management for extravagance, and the latter thought of employers as stingy to the point of hampering company welfare. John Clay worked for his fellow Scots many years as agent and ranch manager before concentrating on his own livestock and commission firm. In answer to a request for business advice in 1907, Clay commented that long ago he had quit working for Scottish boards: "Their ideas of remuneration & mine were so far apart that I gave up without a murmur."[29]

The history of the Matador Company illustrates the complexities of managerial organization, the personal dissatisfactions experienced by those involved on both sides of the Atlantic, and the degree to which an exceptionally able manager like Murdo Mackenzie could free himself from restrictions. As soon as the American promoters relinquished title to the Scots, company control shifted from the Ballard Springs ranch quarters in Texas to Dundee, Scotland. From Dundee came policy decisions and also supervision through an efficient communications system and occasional visits by board members. All official correspondence passed through the firm of Alexander Mackay and William Mess, chartered accountants and secretaries of the board. As head of the firm, Mackay gave personal attention to Matador affairs, interpreted board decisions and relayed them to officers in America. He served as secretary of the Matador board for thirty-three years and then became its chairman. John Clay rated him head and shoulders above all other Britishers who visited America in connection with the land and livestock business. He became familiar with range problems, showed good judgment in choosing among

various proposals, and employed first-rate men to carry out decisions. Without doubt, his guiding hand contributed greatly to the
welfare of the Matador Company.[30]

John Paton and Company of New York City and Thomas De-
Witt Cuyler, Philadelphia attorney, represented the syndicate in
America. Paton and Company handled the transfer of all funds,
and Cuyler furnished information as to the effects of American
laws on company affairs. His primary responsibility, however, was
the examination of land titles, his sanction being necessary on all
real estate purchases. Immediately below Mackay was the office
of manager in Fort Worth. A. M. Britton of the original American
promotional group held that job from 1882 to 1885, but from the
first a Scot, William F. Sommerville, did the work. Deeply loyal
to his employers, Sommerville possessed considerable knowledge
of the cattle business based on experience in northern Britain, although his lack of familiarity with American range conditions
created some difficulty at first between him and the general ranch
manager, H. H. Campbell.

Books of the Ballard Springs and Fort Worth offices closed
yearly on November 30. Sommerville then summarized the work
for the past year so that Mackay could prepare a report for the
board. On the basis of his report, the board reviewed accomplishments for the past year, set dividend rates, and formulated policies
for the next twelve months. Sommerville also furnished Mackay
with monthly copies of the ranch accounts, which reached Dundee
by registered mail within two weeks. If discrepancies appeared, the
manager was asked for an explanation and correction, even if the
change cost more than it saved. The company used cable service to
expedite communication when speed was important. Messages
were sent in code beginning in 1888, both to save money and to
maintain secrecy. Every cable had to be confirmed in a return letter quoting it and giving its meaning. In all these ways the home
office maintained close supervision over its American employees.

Although the board appointed Henry H. Campbell as general
manager of the ranch because of his intimate knowledge of the
range and ranching in general, it curbed him so much that he was

never happy in the job. Preoccupied with duties of local super-vision and often absent from headquarters on such work, he dis-liked the extensive and set system of bookkeeping and reporting that the company imposed upon him. Campbell even had to ob-tain Sommerville's approval before making any contract involving more than five hundred dollars. Such regulations made it difficult for him to bargain effectively or to act with dispatch. Because of these irritations he resigned in 1890. Thereafter he operated a small ranch of his own and served several terms as a county judge. Years later, his son recalled that Campbell had never gotten along well with the Scots, resenting what he considered to be foolish restrictions on their part. They had, for instance, instructed him to pay no more than ten cents an acre for land. Contrary to orders, he bought several sections at fifty cents an acre to prevent another rancher from obtaining the land and moving a herd of cattle di-rectly into the heart of the Matador range. When some of the direc-tors visited the ranch that fall, they severely criticized Campbell for his action. Although he offered to keep the land himself and let them pay taxes on it in return for grazing rights, they mag-nanimously approved the purchase, warning him at the same time not to take such action again without previous consent.[32] To the Scots, it made sense to check closely on expenditures thousands of miles from home; to Campbell, such a policy hampered sound action and reflected on his honesty.

When Murdo Mackenzie became general manager in 1890 he removed the Fort Worth office to Trinidad, Colorado, primarily because he wished to live there, although the transfer fitted in with the growing tendency of the company to feed out its cattle on Northern ranges. Mackenzie's insistence on continuing to live at Trinidad contrary to the wishes of some of the company directors presaged the greater freedom of action, even in policy making, that he would take over the years. His appointment of Henry H. Johnstone as accountant, and soon as assistant manager, and of Arthur G. Ligertwood as Campbell's successor as ranch manager, both of whom had worked under Mackenzie while he managed the Prairie Cattle Company, also indicated the role that he intended to play in the Matador. Nevertheless, the home board continued to advise him, even on small matters. They suggested savings by eliminating needless words in messages sent by cable and by asking cattlemen's associations to pay Mackenzie's traveling expenses when as president he represented them on matters of interest to the cattle industry as a whole. In turn, Mackenzie balked at making long written reports, although his assistants supplied detailed information to the home office as long as he did not object.

The Matador stockholders realized that they were fortunate to obtain Mackenzie's services, and their confidence in him increased steadily. Although the home board still made final decisions on major policies, Mackenzie initiated and won acceptance of many of them. In 1902, for instance, he went directly to England and presented to the annual stockholders' meeting a recommendation to purchase 210,000 acres of land from the XIT holdings at two dollars an acre, which they approved. He and Mackay jointly recommended the leasing of grazing lands in Canada. When Mackenzie learned that Indian lands in South Dakota totaling seven hundred thousand acres would shortly be open to lease for grazing purposes, he rushed to investigate and then by telegraph obtained board support to bid for use of the land. Their approval showed that they had changed a great deal from the days when they quarreled with Campbell over acquiring a few sections.

Over the years, Mackenzie displayed great skill in shaping the breeding program, in land acquisitions, and in public relations for the Matador. When he left for South America in 1911 to manage the huge Brazil Land, Cattle and Packing Company project, the Matador directors appointed his nephew John McBain to succeed him. McBain had been with the Matador since 1898, had served for nine years as Mackenzie's assistant in the Trinidad office, and had supervised operations during Mackenzie's frequent visits to Scotland. Mackenzie took to South America with him some of the young men whom he had trained in the Matador organization, and some of them remained with the Brazil company on his return to the United States in 1918. Since Mackenzie held stock in the Matador, he was elected to its board of directors in 1918, and in

1923 he became manager once again following McBain's death, a position that he held until retirement in 1937. His son, John, who became an assistant manager in 1947, succeeded him as head of the American office and held that post until the Matador sold out in 1951.[33]

Although Mackenzie made a distinguished record in the field of management, his increasing influence on Matador policy and the presence of his relatives in executive jobs, able as they were, pointed up in cattle ranching, as in so many other economic fields, the increasing separation of ownership and operation, even in policy matters. In a way, Mackenzie won through to a victory that would have pleased and amazed many an early-day cattleman. He proved that it was possible to employ capital resources belonging to others without having them meddle to the point where a man would prefer to go it alone.

TWELVE

Cattleman and Cowboy: Fact and Fancy

THE cowboy constitutes the best known and possibly the most significant contribution of the cattle kingdom, and his fame grows even greater as his environmental surroundings recede into history. Ironically, the cattleman rather than the cowboy was the central character on the ranching frontier. Without him, there would have been no cowboys, and he set the bounds within which they lived. Nevertheless, novelists, dramatists, and other practitioners of the arts have generally relegated the rancher to a shadowy, background role for the main hero of their imaginative creations, the American cowboy. And yet, what a magnificent cast of characters lies ready at hand for the creative artist! Conrad Kohrs, George W. Littlefield, Shanghai Pierce, Charles Goodnight, Alexander H. Swan, the Lang family, John Chisum, Murdo Mackenzie, the Marquis de Mores, George W. Miller, and a host of others were colorful, complicated personalities who deeply impressed contemporary observers.

In contrast, the few novelists using cattlemen as central characters have generally pictured them as wooden types devoid of individuality. In Harold Bindloss' novel, *The Cattle-Baron's Daughter*, written early in the twentieth century, "Torrance, the Cattle-Baron, of Cedar Range" is a stiff-necked, stupid old man who cannot see that nesters are sure to take over his feudal domain. He and his fellow cattlemen use their loyal henchmen, the cowboys, to fight against the inevitable triumph of agriculture. Bind-loss' lone horseman, etched dimly against the horizon, watching the drift of smoke from the iron horse, symbolizes the pitifully noble but arrogant and uncomprehending nature of the cattle bar-ons. Naturally, their passing takes place only after the reader has experienced an overgenerous supply of the drumming, beating, hammering, and thudding of hoofs.[1] The main character of Andy Adams' novel, *Reed Anthony, Cowman*, seems little more than a business machine, whose whole interest centers in a constant buy-ing and selling of cattle.[2] Of the two novels, Adams' surpasses Bindloss' by far in veracity, but neither probes successfully the personalities and motivations of cattlemen.

Of more recent vintage, A. B. Guthrie's *These Thousand Hills* portrays the satisfactions of the cattleman's way of life as well as the price paid for these. In this story of the rise of Lat Evans to membership in the Montana ranching fraternity of the 1880's, Guthrie deals with motivations differentiating ranchers from cow-boys. Callie Kash, the beauty from the red-light district, whose love Lat turns aside in his drive for power, riches, and respectability, lacks reality, but Guthrie has in general displayed remarkable understanding for that era without typing his characters as symbols rather than flesh-and-blood people.[3] Certainly, Guthrie's novel points the way to a rich vein of literary ore that remains largely unexploited.

There is, of course, an equal paucity of good books on the cow-boy, but not from want of hundreds of practitioners who have writ-ten what purports to be his story. The market for such material seems insatiable. For instance, Zane Grey, a New York dentist who turned to writing Westerns, produced fifty-four books during his career which sold over fifty million copies and were translated into several foreign languages. Radio and television lean heavily on Western themes, with cowboys as central characters. Basket-ball and baseball games alone have surpassed rodeos in recent years in attendance figures. Indeed, the cowboy theme is so popular in modern-day culture that it needs no documentary proof.

In reality, the cowboy's life involved so much drudgery and loneliness and so little in the way of satisfaction that he drank and caroused to excess on his infrequent visits to the shoddy little cow-towns that dotted the West. A drifter whose work and economic status made it difficult for him to marry and rear a family, he sought female companionship among prostitutes. Most of his physical dangers scarcely bordered on the heroic, necessary as they were in caring for other men's cattle, and they served primarily to retire him from cowpunching, not to glorify his career. Older men could not endure the rigors of such a life, the major reason for the youth-fulness of the group. In the true economic sense, rank-and-file cowboys were hired hands on horseback, and very unromantic ones at that. Realistic observers during the cowboy era agreed with Bruce Siberts' evaluation. While living in the Dakotas in the 1890's as a cowhand and small rancher, Siberts concluded that most of the old-time cowhands were a scrubby lot, and that many of them suffered with a dose of the clap or pox: "Only the few good ones got into the cow business and made good."[4]

Siberts was speaking of the rank-and-file cowboys, for he and other observers did see individuals who measured up to Owen Wister's famous character, the Virginian, who came to personify the cowboy in American imagination. But, of course, Wister had his hero marry the schoolteacher, accept a foreman's job, and obviously move in the direction of becoming a rancher on his own. Ordinary cowhands simply lacked the traits out of which national heroic types could be expected to emerge. And yet, the cowboy became an American hero.

Since the gaucho, a South American counterpart of the Ameri-can cowboy, achieved an equally exalted status in the minds of later generations, one is tempted to seek an explanation inherent in frontier conditions. After the gaucho helped liberate the Plata lands from Spanish rule, the gaucho theme blossomed into one of His-panic America's contributions to world art, literature, and music. As one authority has pointed out, Latin Americans honor the gaucho as settler of the wilderness, soldier defender, and conqueror of the Indian. They praise him as a hide collector, for many gen-erations the source of the Argentine's economic life. Although much of the gaucho literature is trash, this same authority pays tribute to the poesy of the Santos Vega theme, the quaintness of the gaucho folk song and dance, the dry humor of riddle and proverb, and the realism of such descriptions of pastoral life as are found in Ascasubi's *Santos Vegas*. Through accounts of gaucho life and literature, the Plata peoples have come to accept certain ideals as their own: independent self-sufficiency, stoic courage, and pride in worthy national achievement. In actuality, however, the gaucho was a colonial bootlegger of hides and of exceedingly low social status, first despised and then feared by the upper classes as he grew in numbers. How he became the symbol of the dashing cavalryman, the successful lover, the singing minstrel of the plains, and the noble defender of the poor[5] constitutes as fascinating a riddle as explaining the rise of his North American brother, the cowboy, to an equally exalted status.

The answer does not lie in universal, mystical frontier influences. No such class developed out of the Boer economy on the South African frontier, perhaps because the Boers used native herdsmen. In Australia, shepherds and hut-keepers lived a monotonous existence looking after flocks of sheep for wealthy owners, and sought forgetfulness of such drudgery in the same careless squandering of their earnings that characterized American cowboys. There were also second-generation boys from small settlers' families whose horsemanship and familiarity with the bush country fitted them for more exciting tasks than herding sheep. They became the drovers, bullock-drivers, and horse-breakers, and their lives paralleled most closely of all that of the American cowboy. Apparently, however, they were more inclined to marry and settle down in their own districts after a few years of wandering.[6] There were also "lawless bushrangers" who managed to carry on their depredations because of frontier conditions,[7] and who seemingly had many characteristics in common with desperadoes on the American frontier. And yet, Australia seems not to have centered attention on such groups, leaving to the United States and South America the deification of the horsemen of the plains.

That process within the United States lacks any tangible or

easily seen key, such as the important boost to his popularity which the gaucho received through participation in the wars of liberation. Cause and effect in the story of the American cowboy's rise to fame cannot be sharply separated, although plausible explanations abound. Why, for instance, should an employee of a conservatively inclined rancher become a symbol of freedom and individualism? Possibly an emphasis on a philosophy of live and let live, which characterized the ranching frontier, accounts for that seemingly incongruous development. Social restraints rested lightly on a land where acreage far outnumbered population, where the cosmopolitan background of inhabitants necessitated recognition of the right of others to self-expression, and where a desire to make money or to live from day to day—depending on whether one wanted to be a rancher or a cowboy—encouraged individualistic expression more than if the inhabitants had been trying to create a Utopian society. Perhaps the growing distrust of big business in the late nineteenth century prevented the rancher from achieving heroic stature. Instead, the public thought of him as a cattle king, who, like his fellow moguls elsewhere, oppressed the little fellow, in his case the squatters or homesteaders who competed with him for land and water rights. And so the cowboy became the hero of the ranching frontier.

In achieving that status he passed through a variety of interpretations at the hands of the dime novelists, whose mass audience could make of him a folk hero. Apparently, there was no "typical" cowboy dime novel but rather a progression in interpretation toward the position ultimately held. Joseph E. Badger, one of the earlier dime novelists, would have completely baffled modern-day readers of pulp literature by refusing to type his characters. His heroes often had faults; his villains were not wholly bad. If his point of view had prevailed over the years, the quality of cowboy literature would have improved immeasurably. Another dime novelist, Captain Frederick Whittaker, condemned the cowboy as a reversion to primitive man in a lawless West. Since Whittaker served in the Union army during the Civil War, memories of that conflict may well have influenced his interpretation of Texas cowboys. To him, the cowboy was no folk hero. Colonel Prentiss Ingraham supposedly wrote more dime novels than any other man, more than one hundred on Buffalo Bill's exploits alone. His cowboys embodied the same traits as all his other heroes: blood would tell. In his books cowboy heroes exemplified the medieval tradition of knight-errantry—heroes who spent their time redressing wrongs and protecting the weak. That interpretation has never quite passed away. The elevation of the cowboy from a subordinate role to the central spot in stories, however, and from vilification to heroism, achieved fullest expression in the writings of William G. Patten, probably the most glib of all dime novelists. Patten pictured cowboys as men of action and as nature's noblemen. Thus, briefly put, the dime novelists moved through a series of stages to a final deification of the cowboy—from cowboys as morally unpredictable to cowboys as depraved, to cowboys as moral defenders of a transplanted medieval tradition, and to cowboys as nature's noblemen.[8]

In 1902 Owen Wister wrote *The Virginian*, the most famous of all cowboy novels, and thereby gave concrete expression to a legend for a host of readers. The novel went through fifteen printings its first year and as late as 1924 rated eighth on a reader survey to pick the ten best books published since 1900.[9] Wister graduated from Harvard Law School in 1888 but found it both necessary and pleasant to spend much time in the West because of his health. Having hunted and rambled from Washington Territory to the state of Texas, he knew much of the West firsthand, and for him it had an enduring charm.

Wister's *Virginian* typified the better grade of cowboy. He was a slim young giant, reticent to strangers, given to swearing, a practical joker, sang off-color songs, loved his horse dearly, and easily won the favors of women of frail virtue. He had never begged nor stolen, and he defended the purity of womanhood and the rights of the downtrodden. One could approach him only on the basis of equality because he was subservient to no man. There was also the schoolmarm from Vermont whose ancestry traced back to the American Revolution and whose family thought of cowboys as inferior beings. Although at first she ignored the Virginian, she

soon sensed his innate greatness of mind and character. By study-
ing the books which she loaned him, he became her equal in the
literary arts. But only his rich endowments of heart and soul could
have made him the rewarding companion that he proved to be
when it came to discussing Shakespeare and Browning, the Virginian being the first man in the schoolmarm's life with sufficient
insight to point out possible flaws in her favorite poet, Browning.

Basically, of course, the Virginian was a man of action, and the
story reached its peak in his classic gun battle with his mortal
enemy, Trampas, on the very eve of his wedding. But Wister made
it clear that such violence on the part of the Virginian arose only
from the necessity of the environment in which he lived, not from
personal preference. His skill with the six-shooter gave him no
hankering to build a reputation as a gunslinger. The schoolmarm's
Eastern relatives had to recognize the greatness of such a man, and,
by implication, so did all other Easterners. Sired in old Virginia,
winner of the hand of a Vermont descendant of Revolutionary War
heroes, and master of every challenge posed by America's last great
land frontier, the Virginian could well expect every man to obey
when he uttered his famous warning, "When you call me that,
smile."

Of course, the American cowboy was already undergoing a
process of glorification when Wister wrote his novel, and its mass
appeal only strengthened and shaped that trend. Over the years,
the cowboy has become America's folk hero in a particularly intimate and unique sense, and one can only speculate as to the factors
involved in that development.

Part of the explanation may lie in the cowboy's nameless state.
Observers like Theodore Roosevelt described ranchers as far more
individualistic than cowboys in personality and background. Some
spoke of "good" and "bad" cowboys, but beyond that generalized
classification they seemed unable to go. On the other hand, virtually any schoolboy can name Daniel Boone as the symbol of the
wilderness Indian fighter, Mike Fink and Davy Crockett as kings
of the wild frontier, and Paul Bunyan as hero of the lumber camps.
All of these characters, except possibly Boone, have been raised

to the stature of Beowulfs of old—folk heroes, yes, but credited with feats that put them above the emulation of mortal man. But who is *the* great American cowboy? In answer, one must recognize that he continues to be a composite of many men, a nameless hero in recognition of the fact that his deeds were not beyond the powers of virtually anyone willing to exert his energies. His feats were great but not miraculous, and Americans have been reluctant to endow him with a superhuman personality. As a hero of the American folk, he is truly all of them in one.

Of course, there is Pecos Bill, "the greatest cowboy of all time," who was raised by the coyotes, gentled the wonder-horse Pegasus, established the perpetual-motion ranch and performed other truly miraculous feats. Supporters identify him as *the* American cowboy and claim that stories attached to his mythical name were actually told by cowboys during their contests to produce the biggest yarn of all. Some stories may well have originated in that manner. To a considerable extent, however, Pecos Bill is the creation of writers who seem to feel that the cattle kingdom must have a character comparable to Mike Fink or Paul Bunyan, although a true folk hero needs no press agent to trumpet his claims.[10] Perhaps that explains why Pecos Bill has never quite caught on, charming and illuminating as some of his mythical exploits are.

Perhaps the cowboy became famous partially because he reached his peak of activity at a proper *time* to be canonized as a folk hero. In the 1890's commentators everywhere were beginning to worry about the disappearance of land frontiers. In Europe, advocates of the new school of geopolitics talked about the doctrine of "closed space" and how countries should reshape their policies according to that concept. In America, Frederick Jackson Turner spoke of the end of free land and cited the census of 1890 as proof that frontier days were gone. In Turner's opinion, the American frontier had created many of our prized values, democracy, individualism, and so on, and its disappearance boded ill for the future. Still another observer, Alfred Thayer Mahan, in *The Influence of Sea Power upon History,* urged fellow Americans to become strong on the sea and to seek out new frontiers in the Far East. Average citizens recognized that the old days of great open spaces were passing away and thus felt hemmed in for all time to come by cities and factories. Railroad connections with the West still made it easy for travelers crossing the plains to observe cowboys at work. Such a startling contrast to their own existence increased their inclination to believe that worries never existed in the simple and uncomplicated life of the range. The fears thus engendered by a rapidly burgeoning industrial and urban age encouraged people to idealize the life of the American cowboy.

Moreover, as the last representatives of the westward movement, cowboys gained in stature by becoming something of a composite of all preceding frontiersmen. On TV today they fight Indians just as Daniel Boone did, hunt for lost mines as once did the prospectors, and even trap furs in the tradition of the mountain men. They belonged to "outfits," which exemplified many of the characteristics of youth. Those small, closely knit groups of young males emphasized gang loyalties rather than more mature social relationships. Thus, they came to personify all the past youth of the American nation, an essential characteristic of the folk hero, who must come from an earlier and idealized period.

Changes in literary conventions also gave the cowboy a greater role than heroes of earlier frontiers. As Henry Nash Smith has so well pointed out, class traditions governing the pre-Civil War genteel novel required the hero to be an upper-class person exemplifying the virtues of civilization, which supposedly surpassed those of more primitive societies.[11] Thus, Uncas in Cooper's *Last of the Mohicans* and his faithful friend Leatherstocking could not hope to win the hand of a beautiful girl whom they rescued from a fate worse than death. In the background, Cooper maintained a shadowy aristocrat who in the end married the girl, although his futile ways on the frontier where the story took place proved that he did not deserve her. By the time the cowboy reached his peak, literary traditions had changed. Edward Eggleston, Hamlin Garland, and others developed a more realistic attitude toward society. In the leading cowboy novel, *The Virginian*, the hero married the heroine, and thus suffered no diminution in the minds of readers.

The cowboy might not choose to marry, but literary convention no longer blocked his range of choice as it had for many of his frontier predecessors.

Moreover, the cowboy demands little cerebration on the part of his admirers. Most stories concerning him emphasize action rather than subtle character analysis, thus posing few problems for readers. They constitute escape literature for many people, a way of getting free from conventional patterns and problems of living. And, again, they represent a simple formula of good versus evil without any shading in between. A noted theologian who is addicted to reading Westerns has explained his interest in exactly those terms:

If just once I could stand in the dust of the frontier main street facing an indubitably bad man who really deserved extermination, and with smoking six-gun actually exterminate him—shoot him once and see him drop dead. Just once to face real and unqualified evil, plug it and see it drop. . . .[12]

Those who struggle hardest to destroy evil, and yet find it difficult because they injure the good in the same action, may well indeed find release from their frustration in the cowboy Western. When the Virginian killed Trampas, he eliminated a wholly evil man.

In usurping the center of the stage from his employer, the rancher, the cowboy has become a folk hero, but his victory has imprisoned him in the formula that necessarily applies to such a character. In reality, the cowboy would make an inadequate hero for the yet-to-be-written great novel on American ranching, even could he break the bonds that imprison him. In many respects, his career consisted of running away from life or of adjusting to it at the lowest common denominator. The cattleman, with all his faults, provides better insight into the motivations, struggles, defeats, and triumphs that constituted life in the cattle kingdom.

Nevertheless, the highly popular Western continues to repeat its well-known formula. A critic has outlined the characteristics of such a story, elements of which extend back to the 1880's, and suggests that the rules for its composition are almost as clearly defined as those for writing French tragedy in the seventeenth century. Such a story must stress high moral standards, in spite of superficial deviations from conventional behavior, and must rigidly classify its characters as "good" or "bad." It must express a romantic and chivalrous attitude toward women. It must involve an abundance of action: shooting or killing; lynching or near lynching; crime or attempted crime; conspiracy of the bad against the good, with the latter winning the final victory. It must have a noble heroine, duped to side temporarily with the villain but turning in the end to the noble hero, a man of superior strength, skill, honesty, and courage.[13] Such plots revolve around a variety of topics: cattle feuds; conflicts involving sheepherders, Indians, and homesteaders; disputed titles to ranches or mines; railroad rivalries; attempts of crooks to cheat innocent white owners, Indians, or the government; efforts to identify and punish cattle thieves and other desperadoes; and exposure and punishment of corrupt government officials. Writers like Zane Grey, who remained most faithful to the formula, found ready sale for their work, but they also failed to produce literature of a high order.

Some practitioners have shown a superior craftsmanship and sufficient insight to lift them well above the level of much that passes for Western literature. O. Henry and Hamlin Garland tried their hands at Western stories with a fair measure of literary success. Among those who centered their attention more fully on Western themes, Eugene Manlove Rhodes and Owen Wister produced stories that far surpassed the usual run of such literature in their day, and Wister's *The Virginian* achieved a fine sales record as well. More recently, writers like Dorothy Scarborough, Conrad Richter, Tom Lea, Walter Van Tilburg Clark, Jack W. Schaefer, and A. B. Guthrie have demonstrated superior skill in overcoming the handicaps placed on creative writers by the time-honored formula governing the production of Westerns.[14]

Nevertheless, any creative writer who dares to tamper with the formula faces considerable peril because of its association with the cowboy folk hero. Even the critic can expect little mercy for daring to point out the unrealistic nature of much that passes for Western literature. The intensity of feeling surrounding the whole subject found ample expression in a controversy involving Emerson Hough's popular novel, *North of 36*, which appeared in 1923. Born in Newton, Iowa, Hough taught school and took a law degree at the University of Iowa before transferring to New Mexico in the early 1880's. In 1897 he published *The Story of the Cowboy*, the outgrowth of his interest in Western life. Although well received, it achieved much less popularity than his later novels, such as *North of 36*. The latter story appeared in the *Saturday Evening Post*, in book form, and as a motion picture produced by Paramount Studios. No author could wish for more in the way of general public recognition.

Hough's plot concerned the driving of a herd of cattle from Texas to Abilene, Kansas, in 1867, and included a generous amount of violent action, as well as the beautiful heroine, Taisie Lockhart, who accompanied her loyal cowboys on their hazardous trip. In explaining his intentions in regard to the story, Hough wrote on April 20, 1923:

Of course, you know that in writing such a book as "North of 36", we are dealing with fiction absolutely and the characters are all strictly imaginary as well as most of the incidents. All I can attempt to do is to give general fidelity to the historical facts of that long-ago period, without claiming to write history at all. Indeed history is rather dull reading, don't you think?[15]

In November, 1923, *The Literary Digest International Book Review* printed a review of *North of 36* by Stuart Henry under the caption "Faults of our Wild West Stories." Henry opened on a favorable note by commenting that readers of Hough's *The Covered Wagon* could now enjoy this new story of Taisie Lockhart and her cowboys and 4500 steers:

As a thriller, none but fair and complimentary words can be said for this last romance of Mr. Hough's. It has all the tearing action provided by hostile Indians, raging floods, cattle-stampedes, fatal contests with pistols, rough cow-punchers on woolly mustangs, and a conventional

Mary Pickford love-story developed amid the excitements and spectac-
ular hardships of a long cattle drive.[16]

But then, stimulated in part by a prefatory note to the book and
comments on the jacket that it intended to give the coloring and
"feel" of acual existence—to pen the essential truth, Henry opened
a barrage of adverse criticism:

Yet, after all merited praise is awarded, may not one protest against the
giving-out of the idea that such narratives reflect the real history and
life of the West that was?

In his opinion, the book suffered from faulty chronology and factual distortions, examples of which he listed at considerable length.

As a historical romance, however, Hough's book suffered most
grievously from following the usual Western formula in which
characters were so strongly typed as to lose individuality. It was
little more than the usual account of the "good" guys versus the
"bad," with the good, of course, winning out. But Henry was more
concerned with truth in its literal form. He criticized the language
spoken by the characters in the book as a mixture of earlier and
latter-day forms. Most of all,

Gloss and glamour can not well be harmonized with the grim life of
these wiry frontiersmen of the cattle camp and "prairie schooner." They
were gaunt, homely, hungry, leading a rawbone and rawhide existence.
Many excellent traits had they, but their life was necessarily hard, even
to sordidness. They and their few women-folk furnished figures too
weazened, weary, forlorn, for the buoyant pages of adolescent pag-
eantry. They would not feel at home in the West that Mr. Hough depicts.

The editors of the magazine must have considered Henry highly
competent to review Hough's book, both from historical background and literary experience. Born at Clifton Springs, New York,
in 1860, he moved to Abilene, Kansas, in 1868 at the age of seven,
his older brother having preceded him and the rest of the family
there in 1867. Young Stuart saw at first hand the great days of the
Texas-Abilene cattle trade, and his brother, Theodore, served as

the town's first mayor. Stuart took A.B. and M.A. degrees at the University of Kansas, and then studied for six years in Germany and Italy, and at the Sorbonne. In later years, his business interests kept him in touch with both Eastern and Western sections of the country, although he resided at the Century Club in New York City. He also wrote a number of books praising French and Continental society: *Paris Days and Evenings*, 1896; *Hours With Famous Parisians*, 1897; *Romance of a French Salon*, 1903; and *French Essays and Profiles*, 1921.[17]

But Henry "placed his powder on a stove," according to George W. Saunders of the Old Time Trail Drivers' Association, when he dared to criticize Hough's book. Saunders solicited rebuttals from a wide variety of sources, and these appeared in *The Pioneer Magazine of Texas* over a period of several months in 1924.[18] Saunders himself wrote a vehement denunciation of Henry's criticisms, including evidence of the historical soundness of Hough's story. His ire surpassed all bounds, however, when he spoke of Henry's characterization of the people involved in Hough's book as wizened, gaunt, and homely. That "stupendous Parisian ass," said Saunders, must have been reared in a hothouse not to understand the deeper and finer emotions that were the birthright of people of the open, of God's own. Their womenfolk were daughters of proud Virginia ancestors. Because they did not drink bootleg whiskey, use rouge to attract the kisses of libertines, indulge in cigarettes and promiscuous cursing, and bore children instead of poodle dogs and monkeys, they appeared hideous to perverted critics like Henry.

John R. Blocker, a participant in the long drives, also testified to the authenticity of Hough's book. The Abilene dance halls were as he described them, and, if Henry could have seen (as he apparently did) lean, hungry cowboys in those dance halls, he would not have thought of them as weary and wizened and forlorn. Moreover, Henry's strictures on Wild Bill Hickok failed to credit him with killing off the worst characters and of making as good a marshal as times and conditions allowed.

The Honorable E. C. Little, congressman from Kansas, who spent his childhood in Abilene in the early 1870's along with

Henry, and who, having visited Paris, felt as well qualified as Henry to judge degrees of civilization, entered the fray with a letter stating that he remembered one Abilene mother and her four daughters who easily ranked with anyone that he or Henry ever saw in Paris. He especially deplored Henry's comment that frontier life was so grim as to approach sordidness. Instead of memories of wizened and weary people, he recalled the bright, bold, fearless, adventurous boys, and the sweet, fearless, rosy and fragrant girls of his youth. He was indeed sorry that Henry did not remember things as they were in that fairyland of adventure and romance, of stirring events and stirring men:

> When all the world was young, lad,
> And all the trees were green,
> And all the geese were swans, lad,
> And every lass a queen.

But Henry, unfortunately, preferred to pick his heroes and heroines from dusty theatres and soiled drawing rooms of the French capital.

Western authors also testified to the general soundness of Hough's novel. William MacLeod Raine, Andy Adams, and Charles Siringo, for instance, commented on its historical spirit or offered bits of evidence to bolster its reputation. Even more impressive were the comments of Philip Ashton Rollins because of his geographical background and honors. In June, 1924, Princeton University, his alma mater, conferred an honorary degree upon him for distinguished legal work and for showing that the "making and blending" of the West from the Missouri river to the Californian mountains was largely done by cowboys, that virile race of tireless horsemen. As a result of having resided in the cattle kingdom for a time in the 1880's, Rollins wrote what he called an unconventional history of civilization on the old-time cattle range. As a Princeton man and an Easterner, honored by Princeton for his cowboy writings, he was living proof that even Ivy League circles revered the cowboy tradition in American culture. In a letter on July 4, 1924, Independence Day, Rollins assured the editor of *The Pioneer Magazine of Texas* that every patriotic American owed him and George W. Saunders a debt of gratitude for their "virile" refutation of Stuart Henry's libel against the pioneers of Texas and the West. According to Rollins, if those pioneers were wizened, so were the men who fought the French and Indians, many members of the Continental Congress, many of the signers of the Declaration of Independence, and all of Washington's soldiers at Valley Forge.

Walter Prescott Webb of the University of Texas, who ultimately rose to the presidency of the American Historical Association, also affirmed the over-all soundness of Hough's book insofar as the spirit of history was concerned, and rebutted a number of Henry's specific historical criticisms.[19] On June 7, 1924, a *Saturday Evening Post* editorial praised Emerson Hough and his supporters,[20] thereby greatly increasing the volume of criticism of Stuart Henry's point of view. *The Literary Digest International Book Review,* in which Henry's review had appeared, also took cognizance of the storm of controversy. In its July, 1924, issue, it cited some of the criticism of Henry, including one of Congressman Little's questions that he at least must have considered strictly rhetorical, "How could a man who wants to write books leave Abilene and go to Paris looking for adventures and romance and wonderful people?" The article lamely concluded that two things were evident after the "Texans" got through with Henry: *The International Book Review* was widely read in that part of the country, and Hough's novels were highly esteemed as history by men whose early life they depicted.[21]

In 1930 Stuart Henry published his last book, *Conquering Our Great American Plains,* an appraisal of the early history of Abilene and of the West as he recalled it. The book made it abundantly clear that he still held the point of view expressed in his earlier review of Hough's story, and contained additional evidence to substantiate his position. Even the most casual reading of the book will convince most students that Henry developed a marked distaste for Abilene during his childhood. He and his family disliked the hellfire sermons preached in its earliest church, although they supported religion as a civilizing force. Henry vividly recalled the cruelty involved in crowding Texas longhorns into inadequately equipped cattle cars for their trip to the slaughterhouse. The dirty, drab, provincial aspects of early pioneering disgusted Henry, who had no desire to be a cowboy or to conquer the West by brawn alone. Nor did conditions improve overnight:

This dickering, swapping, spreadeagle species of frontier Yankee was the natural successor to the talkative species of first squatters on that border—the latter accustomed to sun themselves while chockfull of opinions as to all they had "seed an' heerd" and vociferous about the "mighty" curious country where they had now "tied up at."[22]

In the controversy over Hough's book, both sides displayed a marked sensitivity concerning the standing of American culture. Some looked to other cultures for the highest values; others fiercely proclaimed the supremacy of our own. That attitude has accounted in considerable part for the low quality of cowboy literature. The harshness of frontier life repels some authors, and they look elsewhere for themes. Others glorify that epoch out of all proportion. Those who would like to depict it without apology or defense hesitate because of the danger of cruel attack from one or the other of the extreme poles of feeling. And so, the formula writing continues, ignored by those interested in human personality rather than stereotypes, and proclaimed by those who glamorize our past or prefer a story that imposes few demands on their thinking.

In addition to the great quantity of novels and short stories featuring the cowboy theme, there are many supposedly sober accounts of cowboy life written by actual participants or first-hand observers. Some of them, like Hough's *Story of the Cowboy* and, best of all, Andy Adams' *Log of a Cowboy* provide a good picture of that bygone era. Even the best, however, suffer from an overly descriptive approach and a concern with minute matters. They debate whether cowboys carried one gun or two; whether they named their horses or not; whether they valued their horse or their saddle most of all; whether they preferred bright colors, and so on.

Still less rewarding, however, are those books turned out by participants and observers of frontier days who embroidered or modified truth in the interest of attracting a large reading audience. In that field, Charley Siringo won much attention. In 1912, for instance, one of his paperbacks bore the title *A Cowboy Detective. A True Story of Twenty-two Years with a World-Famous Detective Agency* [The Pinkerton, thinly disguised]. *Giving the Inside Facts of the Bloody Couer d'Alene Labor Riots, and the many Ups and Downs of the Author throughout the United States, Alaska, British Columbia and Old Mexico. Also Exciting Scenes among Moonshiners of Kentucky and Virginia.* By Charles A. Siringo, Author of "A Texas Cowboy." Those interested in obtaining a copy were invited to get in touch with Siringo at Santa Fe, New Mexico, where he was residing. Quite obviously, Siringo had come a long way from his earlier cowpunching days. By claiming to have been a secret employee of the Pinkerton agency, he could assert that he had participated in everything from searching out cattle thieves to trapping moonshiners in Virginia. Such were the devices to which authors of his type resorted.

The ranching frontier also influenced American life through its cowboy songs. Cowboys sang to the herds of cattle on long drives and at roundup time as a means of calming them and of lessening the danger of stampedes. They also sang of evenings in the bunkhouse or around the campfire for entertainment. Even the lonely chore of line-riding could be eased by singing to one's self the ballads popular in the particular region where a cowboy happened to be employed.

Fortunately, collectors began to assemble and preserve such songs while many old-time cowhands were still alive. In 1910, for instance, John A. Lomax published the first edition of his *Cowboy Songs and Other Frontier Ballads*, which was reprinted and enlarged over the years. The story of the most famous of all cowboy songs, "Home on the Range," provides a fascinating illustration of how such contributions were preserved and grew in popularity. As John A. Lomax tells the story:

Some one told me that in San Antonio, Texas, lived a Negro singer and cook, who had first plied the latter art in the rear of a chuck wagon which followed many a herd of long-horned cattle up the trail from Texas to Fort Dodge, Kansas. I found him in 1908 leaning against a stunted mulberry tree at the rear of his place of business, a low drinking dive.

"I'se too drunk to sing today. Come back tomorrow," he muttered.

On the following morning among other songs he gave me the words and tune of "Home on the Range." Both the words and the tune sung today were first printed in the 1910 edition of "Cowboy Songs," and attracted no attention for nearly twenty years. Then two sheet-music arrangements—one pirated—helped the tune to a radio audience. Lawrence Tibbett and other singers included it among their concert numbers. A group of newspaper reporters is said to have sung it on the doorstep of Governor Franklin D. Roosevelt the night he was elected to the Presidency. It has since become a White House favorite, and it is said that the President sometimes leads the chorus. . . .

Finally two Arizona claimants to its authorship lost a suit against the National Broadcasting Company and others for $500,000. The humble and modest cowboy song has at last rippled the sea of American music.[23]

The highly cosmopolitan nature of the ranching frontier caused influences to play on it from many sources. That being true, cowboy songs had characteristics of Negro music from the American South and of English ballads, sung perhaps by some younger son of an English family who had been attracted to the cattle kingdom. Like the over-all culture of the cattleman's frontier, its songs were derivative in nature, but in content and spirit they became peculiarly American in a remarkably short time. Lomax described the process well in an introductory note to his first edition in 1910:

Out in the wild, far-away places of the big and still unpeopled West—in the cañons along the Rocky Mountains, among the mining camps of Nevada and Montana, and on the remote cattle ranches of Texas, New Mexico, and Arizona—yet survives the Anglo-Saxon ballad spirit that was active in secluded districts in England and Scotland even after the coming of Tennyson and Browning. This spirit is manifested both in the preservation of the English ballad and in the creation of local songs. Illiterate people, and people cut off from newspapers and books, isolated and lonely folk—thrown back on primal resources for entertainment and for the expression of emotion—express themselves through somewhat the same character of songs as did their forefathers of perhaps a thousand years ago. In some such way have been made and preserved the cowboy songs and other frontier ballads contained in this volume.[24]

Although these songs reflect primarily a nostalgia for the past, they may well strengthen American addiction to certain values expressed in them.

The ranching frontier also produced a surprisingly large number of "cowboy artists" who painted scenes of that rapidly disappearing age. In Wyoming, for instance, E. W. Gallings won widespread attention as the "Cowboy Artist" before his death in 1932. He actually punched cattle for big outfits in South Dakota, Montana, and Wyoming, using his spare time for drawing, before winning a scholarship at the Chicago Academy of Fine Arts. By 1909 he had a studio at Sheridan, Wyoming, and began to attract attention both in America and abroad with his Western paintings. Four of his pictures hang in the state capitol of Wyoming at Cheyenne— "The Smoke Signal," "Indian Attack on Overland Stage," "Emigrants on the Platte," and "The Wagon Box Fight."[25]

Frederic Remington gained still greater fame as an illustrator, reporter, and recorder of Western life. Born at Canton, New York, in 1861, he studied at the Yale School of Fine Arts and the Art Student's League in New York City. At age nineteen he made his first trip west, where he ran a sheep and mule ranch, made some money, lost it, and was helped to return east by Emerson Hough. Determined to report and record life in the raw, preferably men near nature, he traveled widely in North America and abroad. Indians, cowboys, frontiersmen, and especially horses were favorite subjects for his pen and brush. Some critics rate him as the outstanding delineator of the American West.[26]

Another cowboy artist, Will James, wrote and illustrated a number of autobiographical works, living and working for a consider-

able period of time at a four-thousand-acre ranch on the Crow reservation south of Billings, Montana. James was a protegé of
Charles M. Russell, perhaps the most famous of all cowboy artists
who actually lived in the West during the cattle kingdom era. Born
into a prosperous St. Louis family, Russell insisted on modeling
and painting Western scenes in spite of family hopes that he would
turn to something else.

Although Russell never considered himself a first-rate cowboy,
he did actually participate in ranch work. In his earlier years he
gave many of his paintings and pieces of statuary to friends or sold
them for whatever purchasers wished to pay. After marriage his
wife, an astute businesswoman, began to handle sales of his paintings, turned out at a studio in Great Falls, Montana, and built for
him by his father, for sums running into the thousands of dollars.
Nevertheless, he actually sent his most famous work, called "Waiting for a Chinook" or "The Last of the Five Thousand," as a post-
card sketch during the disastrous winter of 1886-1887 to a rancher
who wanted to know how his cattle were faring. Russell's sketch of
a lone cow standing knee-deep in snow, tail and ears frozen, the
glassy stare of death in her eyes, with wolves circling in anticipa-
tion of her death, expressed as no amount of writing has ever done
the horrible destruction of vast herds of cattle in a debacle that
proved once and for all the weakness of open-range ranching on
the Northern plains.[27]

Russell displayed both the strength and the limitations of cowboy artists as a whole. Visitors to the collection of his works at the
State Historical Society of Montana in Helena see before them a
vivid panorama of the ranching frontier. He possessed great skill
as a draftsman, used color effectively, and generally achieved complete historical accuracy in every detail of his paintings. They are
indeed magnificent reproductions of life in the Old West. At the
same time, they stress action to the sacrifice of other elements, and
they never quite escape being illustrations. Genre in nature, they
achieve Russell's desire to preserve the passing era faithfully for
later generations even more than to individualize his work. In ac-
complishing that end, he proved his great talent.

The ranching frontier has also greatly influenced American society in the field of dress. Everywhere one sees people wearing clothing reminiscent of that era, a fact too obvious to need illustration.

Lastly, the rancher and the cowboy have influenced the American language. Philip Ashton Rollins called attention to the large number of words and phrases which entered common usage through the medium of cowboy language and literature, expressions such as stampeded, roped in, rounded up, hog-tied, milling around, buffaloed, throw the bull, and butted in.[28] Maverick, rustler, locoed, and many another word achieved popularity because they seem so fittingly American to those who prize our cowboy heritage.

THIRTEEN

The Cattleman's Role in American Culture

O**N THE** surface, the cattle kingdom seemingly lacked sufficient unity of outlook and the continuity necessary to influence national character. Since ranchers eased the tensions of working with people of greatly different backgrounds and culture by granting every man's right to his own way of thinking and doing as long as he applied the same rule in his relationships with others, pressures favoring uniformity were lightly felt. Nor did any strong central authority attempt to coerce that cosmopolitan group of men, the nature of their occupation often placing them even beyond the surveillance of regular courts of law. Moreover, since open-range ranching could not compete against occupations that used the land more intensively, it lasted scarcely more than a generation. Farms and towns were its mortal enemies. With the introduction of fencing and blooded livestock, ranching assumed patterns common in older communities, losing thereby its most distinctive characteristics. Increasing absorption into the national agricultural pattern thus lessened the possibility of any unique influence on American culture.

Nevertheless, the cattlemen did develop a significant culture and a common role during the period of open-range ranching, modified though it was by latter-day forces. Although symbolic in part rather than concrete, differing only in degree of intensity from patterns elsewhere in America, their scale of values did influence the directional course of American culture. Cultural influences seldom admit of exact measurements, and this has been particularly true of the ranching frontier. The urban, industrial, atomic age naturally takes an ambivalent attitude toward cultural obligations to the cattle kingdom. Because problems have changed sharply and rapidly, some insist on looking elsewhere than to frontier experiences for the historical origin and meaning of modern society. Still others praise pioneer times as the source of all good attributes of national character, traits which they consider essential to national survival. As the last of our real land frontiers, the cattle kingdom and its cowboys naturally appeals to them. And nostalgia for the youthful days of our nation affects all who find current-day problems perplexing. Like the growing child, who must cut the apron strings that bind him to his parents, many deny any significance to a day so different from our own, in part because they are so close in point of time to the American frontier. That same proximity leads still others to magnify our frontier inheritance. Possibly only the future historian can calmly assess the real degree of influence exerted by the cattle kingdom.

As a part of the whole frontier movement, the cattle kingdom shares in the symbolism engendered by it. Cowboy songs illustrate this symbolism if nothing more. In the tremendously popular "Home on the Range" the singer praises agrarian values:

> Oh, give me a home where the buffalo roam,
> Where the deer and the antelope play,
> Where seldom is heard a discouraging word
> And the skies are not cloudy all day.
>
> Where the air is so pure, the zephyrs so free,
> The breezes so balmy and light,
> That I would not exchange my home on the range
> For all the cities so bright.

Still other songs condemn restrictions on personal freedom:

> Let cattle rub my headstone round,
> And coyotes wail their kin,
> Let hosses come and paw the mound,
> But don't you fence it in.

Whether such songs are only sentimental tributes to the past or expressions of deep-seated American convictions, they do exert a wide appeal, and thereby encourage Americans to favor programs to which they seem attuned. As long as they remain popular they will influence American civilization to a degree that only the actual course of future history will reveal. For the moment, they demonstrate the symbolic impact of the cattle kingdom.

This symbolism could scarcely have arisen in an economy marked only by a derivative culture and a cosmopolitan background, requiring instead some unity of thought and action on which to rest its development. In spite of factors militating against such unity, other forces on the ranching frontier created a somewhat common role for cattle kings and cowboys. Selective migration from older communities undoubtedly constituted one such force, perhaps an even more effective one on the ranching frontier than in earlier times because people understood better the challenges awaiting them. Publications ranging from the dime novel to more serious literary efforts had publicized the hazards and opportunities of American frontier life prior to the cattle kingdom. Only the youthful and the adventurous were likely, therefore, to seek out the last land frontier. If they dared to go, they found vast quantities of unoccupied land and a physical environment contrasting sharply with that to the eastward. Such forces modified prevailing cultural patterns rather than establishing new values. Some they strengthened; others were blunted.

The reader will recall many previous illustrations of this process. For instance, ranchers and cowboys alike were active and non-philosophical, American traits mentioned by observers long before the cattle kingdom came into being, but strengthened and prolonged through its own application. Moreover, the cattle kingdom emphasized the characteristics of youthful, male societies so often noticed elsewhere in history. Horseplay, practical jokes, and daring physical activity were much in evidence. Men prided themselves on keeping their word, an outgrowth of personal loyalties common among early-day outfits. As a new society, the cattle kingdom rated men according to their current achievements, not on wealth or rank acquired elsewhere. A philosophy of live and let live permeated the region, although employers and employees alike recognized the right of ranch owners to set rules and regulations touching even the personal lives of cowhands. Even then the close personal relationships and loyalties of early-day outfits mitigated any feeling of subservience. Ranchers were hospitable because they liked company and because they knew hospitality's value in a country where all sooner or later were likely to need the friendly assistance of others. They idolized "good" women, and accorded them high social status, but were thoroughly cognizant of prostitutes in cowtowns everywhere. If they married, they honored their vows and gave to family life a stability that was lacking on many another frontier.

Those who rose to positions of wealth or leadership in the cattle kingdom came in quest of wealth or power, in contrast to the ordinary cowboy who valued money only for temporary pleasures. Adventurous by necessity, ranchers nevertheless looked first of all to the protection of their property, and they favored the development of law and order, albeit according to their own interpretation. Quite obviously, their motivations were similar to those of businessmen elsewhere in America at the time, and they also used the forms of business organization common in older communities.

In seeking wealth, however, ranchers penetrated regions having only rudimentary governmental agencies or none at all. In such circumstances, they depended upon themselves and their employees for protection of life and property. Self-reliance thus being a necessity, those who amassed wealth were sorely tempted to attribute their success strictly to their own abilities. Few indeed escaped the conviction that blood would tell. Ranchers could affirm that principle by pointing to the superiority of blooded cattle with which they replaced the longhorns of earlier years. They had no desire, however, to cast off the bonds of organized society, as social anarchy made no appeal to them. They dressed alike without feeling cramped in personality and they cooperated eagerly with others in forming cattlemen's associations for common purposes. They stressed prescriptive claims to grazing territory and opposed government interference with their activities. At the same time they welcomed government action to remove the Indians, curb monopolistic railroad rates, and regulate the packers. They were rugged individualists like businessmen elsewhere but especially vehement in their discipleship because so many of them were self-made. Undoubtedly, they strengthened the hold of rugged individualism on American culture. They had no illusions concerning equality of ability among men. Although willing to recognize achieved status, they were conscious of class lines, fluid as these might be. In none of these value judgments were they unique among their fellow Americans; in all of them they provided what seemed to be fresh proof of their eternal verity and an enthusiasm for their application that older parts of the country found exhilarating.

Rancher and cowboy alike felt no urge to create Utopias for the common man or to reform society. Although Wyoming, the state most completely involved in ranching, led the nation in granting suffrage to women, and that cause fared well in the region as a whole, ranchers thought of their womenfolk as individuals, not as reformers who would change life for the better through use of the ballot. Undoubtedly, the scarcity of women and the premium placed on them in the upper plains contributed to their success in gaining voting rights. Farther south, as in Texas, ranchers doubted if women should vote. Other reform measures, such as initiative, referendum, and recall, owed more to farmers and urban elements than to ranchers in gaining relatively early popularity in some of the states noted for cattle production.

As a matter of fact, the ranching frontier everywhere has been conservatively inclined in political matters. A student of comparative frontiers has pointed to political conservatism as a natural corollary of the cattle-raising economy of South African Boers.[1] Similarly, an Australian historian has noted a predilection for conservatism on the part of ranching interests in that continent. In his words: "The landowners (and the average size of holdings was large) were conservative. The city dwellers, whether rich or poor, tended to be liberal or even radical."[2] Nor did political and social reform in South America come from the owners of large landed estates. Although ranching frontiers have differed greatly in many ways—American ranchers, for example, being progressive and highly adaptable in business methods and those of South America conservative even in that respect—the bulk of the evidence indicates that democratic and social reforms everywhere have owed less to the ranching fraternity than to other classes. A relatively isolated position, personal control over broad acres, and a concomitant liking for rugged individualism made the American rancher a natural ally of conservative forces.

His political strength coincided pretty largely with the relative importance of his occupation in the economy. He was neither a master strategist in the field of politics nor a neophyte to be manipulated by more cunning men. Since ranching dominated the Territory and State of Wyoming for many years, the Wyoming Stockgrowers Association played a dominant role there.[3] Francis E. Warren, Joseph M. Carey, and John B. Kendrick of the ranching fraternity represented Wyoming in the United States Senate and exerted strong influence locally. In Montana, ranchers like Conrad Kohrs found it harder to defend the cattleman's interests when elected to public office because of the power exerted by mining nabobs in the western part of that state.

Ranchers tended to view issues in terms of their own economic interests, in keeping with prevalent standards of the day, and their political conduct was as shoddy as that of the contemporary forces with which they came in conflict. They reflected the cynicism and selfishness of the post-Civil War Tragic Era, Gilded Age, or Great Barbecue—whichever label one prefers for that crass period—quite as faithfully as business interests elsewhere in the country. When Andy Adams, perhaps the most reliable of all cowboy interpreters, wrote his semifictional *Reed Anthony, Cowman,* he centered his story around the rancher rather than the cowboy. He pictured Reed Anthony's constant travels and his immersion in the business of buying and selling cattle, which, as previously indicated, characterized the careers of many of the cattle kings. Anthony believed in the cattleman's code, including the sacred nature of the pledged word, and displayed many admirable characteristics. He was also a realist who used money to bend a legislature to "my will and wish." He and his partner "bought" a seat in the United States Senate from the state of Kansas as a means of promoting cattle sales to Indian reservations, for otherwise they could not hope to influence venal government agents in charge of contracts.[4] As an author, Adams was realistic rather than imaginative, and it is significant that his book, one of the few among the multitudinous stories on ranching that emphasized cattlemen rather than cowboys, recognized the cynical manner in which such men played the game of politics.

In keeping with that philosophy, Shanghai Pierce paid a member of the Texas legislature to promote legislation favorable to his business, and Charles Goodnight rewarded professional lobbyists for work of a similar nature. Richard King and his friends used their financial power to support their aims in counties and towns adjacent to their ranches. When racial animosity, fanned by acquisition of large tracts of land by King and others, flared on the eve of the Civil War, King furnished horses and supplies to the Texas Rangers to repel raids by Mexican dissidents when the United States government failed to act.[5]

George W. Littlefield's political methods indicated how devastating the shoddy practices of the Reconstruction era in Texas could be in suppressing idealistic urges. From that period on, "practical politics" made sense to him. Littlefield let himself be badgered into accepting dubious election bets because of his fanatical convictions and then, as a means of protecting his investment, went out and bought votes. The morality of such action seems not to have bothered him in the slightest. Devoted to Thomas Jefferson, the Democratic party, the Lost Cause, and State Rights, he could always find some historical antecedent to justify his zigzag stand on issues of the day. He opposed popular election of United States senators and the primary system, preferring convention methods instead, but at times supported very liberal candidates.[6] In his case, excellent business judgment did not carry over into the field of politics, and he failed to display the same cool reasoning as other ranchers in playing the game of "practical politics." He conformed to the general pattern in methods alone.

As to religion, a society of widely scattered young males could scarcely be expected to emphasize formal and regular worship services. And yet, virtually all believed in a just God, a mild kind of deism that paid scant heed to creedal distinctions. Recognizing as they did only achieved status and the self-made man concept in secular affairs, they questioned the doctrine of salvation by grace alone, and scoffed at ideas of the total depravity of humanity. Since they expected men to practice their convictions, church members felt a special responsibility to worship publicly and to exemplify moral principles in their personal lives. Any good Baptist, Methodist, Catholic, or other denominational adherent received sympathetic treatment at the hands of those less religiously inclined as long as he granted others the privilege of their convictions and consistently practiced his own religious beliefs.

Ranchers recognized the value of education. As businessmen, they needed reading, writing, and arithmetic in their daily work and there were many vocational skills to be learned in the proper care of land and livestock. A scattered, heavily male population could not be expected to feel the need for a system of common schools, which found greater support from the agricultural population that followed ranchers into new country. Cattlemen contributed to the founding and maintenance of church colleges and vocational schools, however, because they wanted their sons to have such an education and as a part of their philanthropy. Their daughters more often attended girls' finishing schools, for womenfolk were expected to exemplify the finer and less utilitarian traits.

In philanthropy, ranchers gave most often to churches, colleges, and hospitals, church-connected schools being their favorite. Since they believed in the self-made man concept, they naturally preferred to support activities that opened the way for able but temporarily unfortunate individuals. They had less interest in the chronically weak. To a considerable degree, they hedged their contributions with restrictions on how they were to be spent and expected to be consulted in administering them. In doing so, they followed a pattern quite common elsewhere in America but with an intensity of conviction bolstered by the personalized relationships common in all phases of ranching economy.

As time passed, this young society, with its accent on youth and daring, its insistence on the right of the individual to live his own life, its modifications resulting from selective migrations and a somewhat distinctive environment, came closer to the national pattern that had always found expression through its derivative nature. As older men, those who had participated in open-range, trail-driving activities realized that great changes had occurred. In 1915 George W. Saunders of that group promoted the establishment of the Old Time Trail Drivers' Association to keep alive memories of a day that even then seemed far in the past. In 1925 the organization published biographical sketches of participants in the long drives, and Saunders contributed a summary of their contributions. According to him, the early cattlemen rescued a huge wilderness area from the Indians and the wild animals, stocking, peopling, and developing sixteen states and territories within a twenty-eight year period following 1867—western Indian Territory; western Kansas, Nebraska, Montana, North Dakota, South Dakota, Colorado, Idaho, Nevada, Oregon, Washington, New Mexico, Arizona, Wyoming, Utah and northwestern Texas. By 1890 all this "wilderness" had changed greatly. By then the Indians were on reservations, fine cattle had replaced the buffalo, the iron horse had arrived, and towns, churches, and schools dotted the landscape. Although Saunders granted that governmental and other agencies helped bring about the transformation, he insisted that "to the old trail drivers belongs the glory and honor for having blazed the way that made this great development possible."[7] Such were the contributions of the early-day cattlemen as seen by an organization founded to commemorate their work.

Since trappers, hunters, miners, and farmers also probed the frontier regions of which Saunders spoke, the question of the relative importance of the various groups involved in blazing the way probably will never be settled to the satisfaction of all. That ranchers played a prominent role in such work cannot be denied, however. In vast stretches of the West they tested soil and climate by ranging herds of cattle on new land with only a minimum of protection against the dangers involved. By trial and error they learned what could and could not be done in the way of producing commercial foodstuffs for outside markets. Overgrazing of public lands and damage to moral standards resulted from some of their activity, but even there they provided a body of information on which sounder public policy could rest once the nation saw fit to act.

Moreover, their contribution extended beyond experimentation in ranching alone. In 1860, Granville Stuart raised and sold a small quantity of wheat in what is modern-day Montana. Charles Goodnight grew corn, set out an orchard, and promoted irrigation projects near Pueblo, Colorado, in the early 1870's. If one project proved wrong, ranchers tried another, and thereby built a body of practical information on which still sounder economic foundations could be laid. In the mid-1880's, for instance, N. B. Stoneroad operated a cattle ranch in San Miguel County in New Mexico Territory. Already he had experimented with stock raising, farming, and the raising of wheat in California. Then he turned to sheep raising, driving ten thousand head across the Mojave desert to his New Mexico location. Although he did well with sheep for several years, tariff changes on wool caused him to transfer to cattle in 1882.[8] Thus, through the work of small and large ranchers alike, a vast body of information became available concerning the American West. In that sense they were trail blazers for the civilization that followed.

Ranchers naturally contributed to the breeding up of livestock herds. John Clay paid high tribute to Kohrs of Montana, Swan of Wyoming, and Goodnight of Texas for such work. The only recognized new breed of cattle to come into existence upon the shores of the New World, the Santa Gertrudis, was developed on the King Ranch in Texas. A cross between Brahman cattle and the Short-horn, this big, strong, red creature was recognized officially by the United States Department of Agriculture as a true breed in 1940. Santa Gertrudis bulls have sold for as much as forty thousand dollars because of the breed's superior qualities under certain climatic conditions.

Large ranches could more easily afford to carry on long-range scientific experimentation. Richard Kleberg, for instance, displayed continuous interest in such work during his long tenure as head of the King Ranch. He employed trained personnel to conduct local studies, encouraged the Federal government and agricultural colleges to attack basic problems, and furnished money and quarters to specialists working on them. From 1889 to 1928 the ranch cooperated with the Federal government in a program to eradicate the ticks that caused the cattle fever so common in that region. In the early 1890's Kleberg became convinced that buzzards feeding upon dead cattle spread anthrax. Once his theory was proved, a campaign of elimination was launched.

Kleberg also took an active part in efforts to control the spread of mesquite which threatened to destroy much good grazing territory. Four decades of operation on the King Ranch had brought marked changes in the character of the prairie. When nature was undisturbed, the bean pods of the mesquite bush fell naturally to the ground and almost always rotted. When taken into the digestive system of horses, however, the hulls of the pods cracked in the digestive juices and the seeds germinated in the droppings left by the animals. Grass fires no longer burned off the thickets as in Indian days. Intensive grazing of the land also played a part, for the heavier grass mat of earlier days had kept the mesquite seed from reaching the soil to germinate. Kleberg used labor gangs to clear off the mesquite in hard times but it was difficult to control the menace in so primitive a manner. In time, the ranch developed a custom-built machine that could destroy four acres of brush jungle an hour at a cost of only four dollars an acre.

The King Ranch also maintained a constant search for new sources of livestock forage. Within recent years a trained agronomist at the ranch has developed two new grasses, the KR bluestem and Kleberg grass. Ranchers had long known that the leaf of the prickly pear contained nutritious cattle food, but vicious thorns protected the big, thick plate-like leaves. In dry seasons, ranchers sometimes hacked away the thorns with hand labor to let their starving cattle reach the edible parts of the plants. On the King Ranch today a four-man crew with a pear burner developed for that specific purpose can destroy the thorny covering on enough prickly pear in one day to enable eight hundred cattle to feed on it.

Since water constituted a major problem in ranch country, cattlemen made every effort to increase the available supply. Its importance was reflected in Kleberg's action in 1891 in providing one thousand dollars to test the possibility of creating greater rainfall in his region by explosive concussion. In 1898 Kleberg decided to bore for artesian water, and succeeded in hitting a strong subterranean flow at depths of 402 to 704 feet. Until then his drilling equipment had been inadequate for his purposes.[9] By constructing natural tanks, installing windmills, and searching out artesian sources ranchers eased but did not eliminate the water problem.

Much of the cattlemen's accumulated experience and scientific knowledge applied primarily to local conditions, but they could and did contribute to ranching developments elsewhere. When investors established an enormous South American ranch, in part to set a pattern for additional expansion there, they turned to Murdo Mackenzie, an outstanding American ranch manager, to supervise their project in its formative years. Mackenzie brought to America with him considerable experience in livestock management from his native Scotland, but knowledge is always cumulative, and he acquired a wealth of new information during his years in the United States. The King Ranch of Texas has engaged in joint ventures with citizens of Cuba, Australia, and Brazil in developing a scientific type of ranching in those countries based on the Santa Gertrudis breed.[10] Conservative though they were in many ways, American ranchers displayed commendable daring, skill, and willingness to seek new methods when it came to the development of the livestock industry. Whether they operated on a simple trial-and-error basis or with greater scientific methodology, they helped blaze the way for a more rational management of America's last great land frontier.

Moreover, they helped establish law and order in a region that seriously needed it if it were to develop its full potential economically and socially. As men of property or in quest of it, they knew how uncertain its possession would be if the rule of gunslingers were allowed to prevail. Many went about their business completely unarmed; and if it became necessary to resort to weapons, they preferred double-barreled shotguns or Winchester rifles to the heavy and less accurate six-shooters. They were natural enemies of the desperadoes and saloon riffraff that gave the ranching frontier a reputation for violence, and had generally cleared out such elements in their localities before later immigrants arrived in numbers.

Their contributions in that respect have been clouded by the natural hostility of ranching to agriculture and the reluctance of many cattlemen to give way to the farmer. When Joseph G. McCoy promoted Abilene, Kansas, as the first of the cowtown terminals for the long drives from Texas in the 1860's, the scattered farming population near Abilene opposed the project. To allay their fears, McCoy pointed out that they could sell their crops of vegetables and grain to the drovers and also buy reasonably priced cattle to feed out locally. McCoy claimed that by prearrangement with some of the drovers who arrived early he started a lively bartering for eggs, butter, onions, oats, and corn, thereby persuading local farmers that his project would benefit them.[11] But ranching and farming could have only an uneasy truce since farmers could make the more intensive use of land. The arrival of the farmer in a new region meant the end of open range and a higher land cost for the cattleman.

Even those with greater security of land tenure took little interest in developing towns, churches, and schools, contributions that Saunders, by implication at least, credited to the early cattle-men. The great Matador Ranch in Texas, for instance, seems to have taken little part in organizing county governments in its vicinity. Once these were created, however, taxes soared, thus forcing the ranch to enter local politics. At times it managed to win an election and to obtain tax reductions, only to lose the next time around and undergo increased assessments. News of the establishment of the town of Matador near ranch headquarters aroused neither elation nor regret on the part of the company. A new town might encourage increased local settlement, but the Matador management was too absorbed in raising cattle to think of colonization schemes.[12]

Of course, the Matador was an enormous spread financed by foreign capital, but its viewpoint was the logical one for any rancher so long as he concentrated wholly on cattle raising. Some, like George W. Littlefield, quickly cut up their ranch holdings for sale to prospective farmers, and profited thereby. But that meant the end of large-scale ranching for Littlefield in that immediate locality.

Cattlemen did contribute to other Western enterprises by investing ranching profits in them. As previously shown, ranchers liked banking, and they supplied management and much of the capital for banks in small communities all over the West. As one rancher, turned banker, wryly remarked, he could not defeat the grangers outright and so he turned from ranching to banking as a means of getting even with them. Some, like Iliff and Story, invested in city real estate. Senator Francis E. Warren of Wyoming invested in some thirty different enterprises, such as gold and silver mines, petroleum developments, electric and telephone companies, and a phonograph corporation.[13] Ranching profits thus found their way into a variety of other economic activities.

It would be a mistake, however, to credit ranchers with furnishing all, or even most, of the capital to develop the West, for an equally good case could be made that other industries furnished funds to develop ranching. Most of the cattle kings pursued varied careers in their early years, being fundamentally traders first of all. Many transferred small mining stakes into cattle and land. Wyoming concentrated more heavily on ranching than any other Western state, and Cheyenne called itself the cattleman's capital. Nevertheless, many of its leading citizens obtained their start in life from occupations other than ranching and then transferred to it. Dwight Fisk, mayor of Cheyenne in 1877, followed placer mining, freighting, and government contracting before settling there in 1867. At Cheyenne he continued his freighting business, built many of the early homes, and constructed some fourteen blocks of brick buildings, all of which he owned at one time. He also benefited from contracts to furnish ties for railroads. Naturally Fisk acquired a ranch, but capital funds to purchase it came from other industries.[14] A. H. Reel, mayor of Cheyenne in 1885, engaged in placer mining and merchandising early in his career, furnished slaughter cattle to mining camps, and freighted for several years on the plains. When he moved to Cheyenne in 1867 he turned to the livery business and trading. He also served as one of the incorporators of the local gas company and as an originator of the city water works. After 1870 he engaged heavily in ranching,[15] in keeping with its importance in Wyoming, but, as in Fisk's case, his basic capital came from sources other than ranching. In the post-Civil War West, men shifted their business operations to take advantage of rapidly opening opportunities, and no one occupation furnished the bulk of capital needed for expansion. Without doubt, however, the cattle industry supplied a sizable amount.

Thus, an ephemeral and cosmopolitan frontier helped shape the course of American life to a surprising degree. Despite its brevity and seeming diversity, it came to symbolize much that Americans hold dear in the field of values, and it may serve as a fountainhead to strengthen such concepts as individualism, freedom, and social democracy in the days ahead. Since descendants of men like John D. Rockefeller, once called "Robber Barons," can now be elected to high office in the United States, it may even come to pass that the "Cattle Kings," too, will share in the acclaim showered on their currently more popular employees, the American cowboys. Certainly, thoughtful liberals and conservatives alike can find much to admire in the cattleman's code of values.

Notes

CHAPTER ONE. CHANGE AND CONTINUITY

1. Introductory essay by the editor in Ralph P. Bieber, editor, Joseph G. Mc-Coy, *Historic Sketches of the Cattle Trade of the West and Southwest* (Glendale, California, 1940). McCoy's account in book form first appeared in Kansas City, Missouri, in 1874.

2. The Bancroft interviews are summarized in Maurice Frink, William Turrentine Jackson, and Agnes Wright Spring, *When Grass Was King* (Boulder, Colorado, 1956), p. 20.

3. J. Marvin Hunter, compiler and editor, *The Trail Drivers of Texas*, two volumes in one (Nashville, 1925). This compilation consists almost wholly of biographical data.

4. James Evetts Haley, *The XIT Ranch of Texas and the Early Days of the Llano Estacado* (Norman, Oklahoma, 1953). Chapter three lists the early ranchers in the Panhandle. The term "ranching frontier" as used in the current work applies to that stage in ranching economy characterized by open-range ranching on government land.

5. Frink, Jackson, and Spring, *When Grass Was King*, p. 20.

6. John Clay, "The Cheyenne Club," *Breeder's Gazette*, LXX (December 21, 1916), 1182-1183, 1265.

7. Ernest S. Osgood, *The Day of the Cattleman* (Minneapolis, 1929), pp. 43-44 calls attention to the widespread report of this apocryphal story.

8. McCoy, *Historic Sketches of the Cattle Trade*, pp. 76-77.

9. Theodore Roosevelt, *Ranch Life and the Hunting-Trail* (New York, 1902), p. 6.

10. See Buford Elijah Farris, "An Institutional Approach to the Texas Cattle Ranch," unpublished M.A. dissertation, University of Texas, 1949, for a discussion of Toynbee's comment.

11. S. Daniel Neumark, *Economic Influences on the South African Frontier 1652-1836* (Stanford, California, 1957), pp. 4-5.

12. Roosevelt, *Ranch Life and the Hunting-Trail*, p. 15.

13. Biographical sketch in *Portrait and Biographical Record of Denver and Vicinity* (Chicago, 1898), pp. 1046, 1049.

14. Frink, Jackson, and Spring, *When Grass Was King*, pp. 337-339.

15. Introductory essay by Ralph P. Bieber in McCoy, *Historic Sketches of the Cattle Trade.*

16. *Ibid.*

17. Osgood, *Day of the Cattleman*, p. 23.

18. Paul C. Phillips, ed., *Forty Years on the Frontier, as seen in the Journals and Reminiscenses of Granville Stuart*, two volumes (Cleveland, 1925), II, 97-98.

19. Charles L. Sonnichsen, *Cowboys and Cattle Kings: Life on the Range Today* (Norman, Oklahoma), 1950, p. 30.

20. *Ibid.*, p. 41.

21. *Ibid.*, pp. 32-33.

22. *Ibid.*, p. xiv.

23. *Ibid.*, Chapter 4.

24. *Ibid.*, pp. 6-7.

CHAPTER TWO. WHY BE A CATTLEMAN?

1. Ralph P. Bieber, editor, Joseph G. McCoy, *Historic Sketches of the Cattle Trade of the West and Southwest* (Glendale, California, 1940), pp. 315-321.

2. Michael Slattery interview at Bell Ranch in New Mexico Territory, July 18, 1885, Bancroft Library.

3. Baron de Bonnemains interview at San Francisco, "Stock Raising in Montana," October 18, 1883, Bancroft Library.

4. Letter dated August 27, 1886, in Letters to and from Richard Trimble and his parents, Archives in Western History, University of Wyoming, Laramie. The contents of the letter indicate that the date given above may be in error.

5. William Curry Holden, *The Spur Ranch: A Study of the Inclosed Ranch Phase of the Cattle Industry in Texas* (Boston, 1934), Chapter 6.

6. McCoy, *Historic Sketches of the Cattle Trade*, p. 322.

7. Theodore Roosevelt, *Ranch Life and the Hunting-Trail* (New York, 1902), contains numerous comments on the beauty of the region.

8. Lincoln A. Lang, *Ranching With Roosevelt* (Philadelphia, 1926), p. 46.

9. Paul C. Phillips, editor, *Forty Years on the Frontier, as seen in the Journals and Reminiscences of Granville Stuart*, two volumes (Cleveland, 1925), I, 23-29; 58-59.

10. J. Evetts Haley, *Charles Goodnight: Cowman and Plainsman* (New York, 1936), p. 142.

11. *Ibid.*, pp. 42-43.

12. John Clay, *My Life on the Range* (Chicago, 1924), Chapter 1.

13. Hermann Hagedorn, *Roosevelt in the Bad Lands* (Boston, 1921), and Lang, *Ranching With Roosevelt* both contain the story of Gregor Lang's career and his relations with Roosevelt.

14. J. Evetts Haley, *George W. Littlefield, Texan* (Norman, Oklahoma, 1943), Chapters 1 and 2.

15. Letter Joseph M. Carey, Wyoming Territory, to R. Davis Carey, Philadelphia, October 24, 1869, Archives in Western History, University of Wyoming, Laramie.

16. Haley, *Charles Goodnight*, Chapter 18; Herbert O. Brayer, "Moreton Frewen, Cattleman," *The Westerners' Brand Book* (Denver), V (July, 1949), 1-21.

17. Maurice Frink, William Turrentine Jackson, and Agnes Wright Spring, *When Grass Was King* (Boulder, Colorado, 1956), pp. 367-368.

18. *Ibid.*, p. 91.

19. *Ibid.*, p. 47.

20. *Ibid.*, p. 60.

21. *Ibid.*, p. 215.

22. General James S. Brisbin, *The Beef Bonanza: or, How to Get Rich on the Plains. Being a Description of Cattle-Growing, Sheep-Farming, Horse-Raising, and Dairying in the West* (Philadelphia, 1881), Preface by author.

23. *Ibid.*, p. 200.

24. Walter Baron von Richtofen, *Cattle Raising on the Plains of North America* (New York, 1885).

25. Frink, Jackson, and Spring, *When Grass Was King*, pp. 138-142. Quotation on pp. 141-142.

CHAPTER THREE. CODE OF THE WEST

1. Joe B. Frantz and Julian Ernest Choate, Jr., *The American Cowboy: The Myth and the Reality* (Norman, Oklahoma, 1955), p. 15.

2. Philip Ashton Rollins, *The Cowboy: An Unconventional History of Civilization on the Old-Time Range* (New York, 1936), p. 96.

3. Ralph P. Bieber, editor, Joseph G. McCoy, *Historic Sketches of the Cattle Trade of the West and Southwest* (Glendale, California, 1940), author's preface.

4. J. Evetts Haley, *George W. Littlefield, Texan* (Norman, Oklahoma, 1943), pp. 215-217.

5. Undated autobiographical sketch by George W. Littlefield, Bancroft Library.

6. Hermann Hagedorn, *Roosevelt in the Bad Lands* (Boston, 1921), p. 136.

7. "Across the United States 1885," a twenty-three-page typed account of Mackay's trip of that year, Southwest Collection, Texas Technological College, Lubbock.

8. J. Evetts Haley, *Charles Goodnight: Cowman and Plainsman* (New York, 1936), pp. 286, 290, 336, 343-344.

9. Hagedorn, *Roosevelt in the Bad Lands*, pp. 125-126.

10. McCoy, *Historic Sketches of the Cattle Trade*, p. 85.

11. Theodore Roosevelt, *Ranch Life and the Hunting-Trail* (New York, 1902), p. 126.

12. The material on Abilene, Kansas, comes from McCoy, *Historic Sketches of the Cattle Trade*, primarily Chapter 8 and footnote information supplied by the editor, Ralph P. Bieber, for that chapter.

13. *Ibid.*, Chapter 8.

14. Hagedorn, *Roosevelt in the Bad Lands*, pp. 128-129. See also Lincoln A. Lang, *Ranching with Roosevelt* (Philadelphia, 1926), for much the same picture.

15. Hagedorn, *Roosevelt in the Bad Lands*, pp. 130-135.

16. Mark Twain, *Roughing It*, two volumes in one (New York, 1932), II, Chapter 7.

17. Owen Wister, *The Virginian* (New York, 1902), pp. 480-485.

18. Dan De Quille, *The Big Bonanza* (New York, 1947), pp. 87-88.

19. Frantz and Choate, *The American Cowboy*, p. 93.

20. Roosevelt, *Ranch Life and the Hunting-Trail*, p. 111.

21. "Last Survivor of Cow Kings Recalls Old Goodnight Trail," Pueblo, Colorado, *Star Journal and the Sunday Chieftain*, March 26, 1939.

22. Neil M. Clark, "Do You Use Fair Play or 'Gun Play' to Gain Your Ends?", *American Magazine*, XCIII (May, 1922), 16, 111, 112, 114, 116. Italics in quotation are mine.

23. Maurice Frink, William Turrentine Jackson, and Agnes Wright Spring, *When Grass Was King* (Boulder, Colorado, 1956), pp. 363-364.

24. C. F. Ward, "John S. Chisum, Pioneer Cattleman of the Valley," Roswell, New Mexico, *Daily Record*, October 7, 1937, mentions that Chisum did not carry a gun, as do virtually all accounts of his life.

25. Personal interview with Tom White, son of J. P. White, Sr., Roswell, New Mexico, June 20, 1958.

26. Chris Emmett, *Shanghai Pierce, A Fair Likeness* (Norman, Oklahoma, 1953), Chapter 17.

27. Mari Sandoz, *The Cattlemen: From the Rio Grande Across the Far Marias* (New York, 1958), p. 319 and *passim*.

28. "Early Day Cowhand Carried no Six-Shooter, Veteran Says," Denver *Post*, March 6, 1938. In personal interviews on June 7 and 8, 1958, with Theodore R. and Herbert T. McSpadden, W. F. "Billy" Friend, and Gordon Hampton Scudder, all of whom live near Claremore, Oklahoma, and participated in open-range ranching, all agreed in principle with the views expressed by Arnot.

29. "TV Westerns Wrong, Says Real Cowboy," Tulsa, Oklahoma, *The Tulsa Tribune*, February 3, 1959.

30. Personal interview with W. F. Friend, June 8, 1958. Friend worked for John Blocker, known for his skill in such work, on one long drive. Friend proudly tells an interviewer that he was elected to the Oklahoma cowboy "Hall of Fame," and did not become a member simply by paying a fee.

31. *Trail Drivers of Texas*, pp. 571-584.

32. Personal interview with Gordon Hampton Scudder, June 8, 1958.

33. Haley, *Charles Goodnight*, p. 258.

34. *Ibid.*, p. 257.

35. *Ibid.*, pp. 350-355. Quotation on page 355.

36. J. Evetts Haley, *The XIT Ranch of Texas and the Early Days of the Llano Estacado* (Norman, Oklahoma, 1953), pp. 111-114.

37. *Ibid.*, pp. 241-245.

38. William C. Holden, *The Spur Ranch: A Study of the Inclosed Ranch Phase of the Cattle Industry in Texas* (Boston, 1934), Chapter 6.

39. Haley, *Charles Goodnight*, p. 339.

40. Sandoz, *The Cattlemen*, p. 274.

41. Tom Lea, *The King Ranch*, two volumes (Boston, 1957), I, Chapter 10.

42. Emmett, *Shanghai Pierce*, Chapter 4. Quotation on page 38.

43. Clark, "Do You Use Fair Play?", 16, 111, 112, 114, 116.

44. John Clay, *My Life on the Range* (Chicago, 1924), pp. 270-272.

45. Sandoz, *The Cattlemen*, p. 117.

46. Haley, *The XIT Ranch*, pp. 194-202.

47. Lang, *Ranching With Roosevelt*, Chapter 3.

48. Sandoz, *The Cattlemen*, pp. 468-469.

49. *Ibid.*, pp. 160-161.

50. Charles A. Siringo, *Riata and Spurs: The Story of a Lifetime Spent in the Saddle as a Cowboy and Ranger* (Boston, 1931), p. 62.

51. J. Evetts Haley, *Early Recollections of J. Phelps White*, twenty-one page printed pamphlet, n.p., n.d. The quotation is from an interview between Haley and White on March 2, 1933. Tom White of Roswell lent me a copy of this pamphlet.

52. Haley, *George W. Littlefield*, pp. 53-55.

53. Frazier Hunt, *Cap Mossman: Last of the Great Cowmen* (New York, 1951), pp. 189-190.

54. *Ibid.*, pp. 177-180, 190-192.

55. Autobiographical sketch of Nathaniel K. Boswell, Laramie City, Wyoming Territory, June 23, 1885, Bancroft Library.

56. Clark, "Do You Use Fair Play?", 16, 111, 112, 114, 116.

57. Sandoz, *The Cattlemen*, p. 479.

58. Haley, *Charles Goodnight*, pp. 375-378.

59. Hagedorn, *Roosevelt in the Bad Lands*, pp. 192-197.

60. Sandoz, *The Cattlemen*, pp. 338-389.

61. Clay, *My Life on the Range*, pp. 272-277.

CHAPTER FOUR. LIVE AND LET LIVE

1. Atlanta, Georgia, *Atlanta Journal*, May 3, 1925, clipping, and other material in folder relating to W. A. Towers, Archives in History, University of Wyoming, Laramie.

2. Emerson Hough, *The Story of the Cowboy* (New York, 1936), Chapters 2 and 3.

3. Lincoln A. Lang, *Ranching With Roosevelt* (Philadelphia, 1926), p. 54.

4. J. Evetts Haley, *Charles Goodnight: Cowman and Plainsman* (New York, 1936), pp. 460-461.

5. William C. Holden, *The Spur Ranch: A Study of the Inclosed Ranch Phase of the Cattle Industry in Texas* (Boston, 1934), Chapter 9.

6. Hermann Hagedorn, *Roosevelt in the Bad Lands* (Boston, 1921), pp. 56-58. Both Hagedorn and Lang refer frequently to the Marquis in their books concerning Roosevelt.

7. Lang, *Ranching With Roosevelt*, pp. 184-186.

8. *Ibid.*, pp. 176-200.

9. Will C. Barnes, "English, Scotch and Irish Cowmen of the Southwest," *The Producer: The National Live Stock Monthly*, XV (August, 1933), 3-7.

10. *Ibid.*

11. Dan Dillon Casement, "The Abbreviated Autobiography of a Joyous Pagan," dated Manhattan, Kansas, March 14, 1944, sixty-two typed pages in Western Range Cattle Industry Study Collection, State Historical Society of Colorado, Denver.

12. Quoted in "The Cheyenne Club," a typed account of the Club compiled by Agnes Wright Spring, Archives in History, University of Wyoming, Laramie.

13. Reports of meetings for October 20, 1881, and September 21 and 22, 1882, in "Club Meetings," a book containing the minutes of the governing board for 1880-1890, Archives in History, University of Wyoming, Laramie. See also clipping from New York *World* for July 6 of an unidentified year in biographical folder on Oelrichs in Archives in History, University of Wyoming, Laramie.

14. Letters to and from Richard Trimble and his parents. Letters dated August 27, 1886, and March 6, 1887, Archives in History, University of Wyoming, Laramie.

15. John Clay, "The Cheyenne Club," *Breeder's Gazette*, LXX (December 21, 1916), 1182-1183, 1265.

16. Helena, Montana, *Helena Weekly Herald*, April 16, 1885. See also *Constitution, Rules, Officers and Members of the Montana Club of Helena, Montana, 1890* (New York, 1890), and later publications under this general title for 1898 and 1902 in State Historical Society of Montana, Helena.

17. I am indebted to Dr. Gene Gressley, Director of the Archives in History, University of Wyoming, Laramie, for calling this collection of books to my attention.

18. Paul C. Phillips, editor, *Forty Years on the Frontier, as seen in the Journals and Reminiscences of Granville Stuart*, two volumes (Cleveland, 1925), I, 170.

19. *Ibid.*, I, 198.

20. Ralph P. Bieber, editor, Joseph G. McCoy, *Historic Sketches of the Cattle Trade of the West and Southwest* (Glendale, California, 1940), pp. 132, 134, 145.

21. *Ibid.*, pp. 213-214.

22. J. Marvin Hunter, compiler and editor, *The Trail Drivers of Texas*, two volumes in one (Nashville, 1925), *passim*.

23. J. F. Hinkle, *A Trip to Panama* (*From Notes Made at the Time*), privately printed pamphlet. I am indebted to Mr. Tom White of Roswell, New Mexico, for permission to use the copy in his possession.

24. Ellsworth Collings (in collaboration with Alma Miller England), *The 101 Ranch* (Norman, Oklahoma, 1937), pp. 4-5, 26.

25. New York *Sun*, October 25, 1927, cited in Collings, *The 101 Ranch*, p. 221.

26. *Ibid.*, p. 165.

27. *Ibid.*, Chapter 11.

CHAPTER FIVE. THE MODERATING HAND OF WOMAN

1. Paul C. Phillips, editor, *Forty Years on the Frontier, as seen in the Journals and Reminiscences of Granville Stuart*, two volumes (Cleveland, 1925), I, 215.

2. *Ibid.*, I, editor's introduction and *passim*.

3. Owen Wister, *The Virginian* (New York, 1902), pp. 46, 49-50.

4. Charles Boone McClure, "A History of Randall County and the T Anchor Ranch," unpublished M.A. thesis, University of Texas, 1930.

5. J. Marvin Hunter, compiler and editor, *The Trail Drivers of Texas*, two volumes in one (Nashville, 1925), pp. 662-665.

6. Lincoln A. Lang, *Ranching With Roosevelt* (Philadelphia, 1926), pp. 161-164.

7. *Ibid.*, pp. 189-191.

8. John Thompson, "In Old Wyoming," unidentified newspaper clipping dated August 7, 1940, Archives in History, University of Wyoming, Laramie.

9. Stuart, *Forty Years on the Frontier*, I, 206, footnote 56.

10. La Junta, Colorado, *Tribune*, December 15, 1933.

11. John Thompson, "In Old Wyoming."

12. Autobiography of Edward Swan, eighty-five typed pages, Archives in History, University of Wyoming, Laramie.

13. Mary W. Clarke, "Murdo Mackenzie, Scotsman Makes Cattle History in Western World," *The Cattleman*, XXXVIII (June, 1951), 23-24, 80, 82, 84, 86. See also Margaret Riordan, "Murdo Mackenzie," *The Westerner*, VI (October, November and December, 1943).

14. Typescript copy of material for preparation for published account of history of Murphy family, Bancroft Library.

15. J. Evetts Haley, *Charles Goodnight: Cowman and Plainsman* (New York, 1936), pp. 296-299, 305.

16. Laura V. Hamner, *Short Grass and Longhorns* (Norman, Oklahoma, 1943), pp. 10-11.

17. Maurice Frink, William Turrentine Jackson, and Agnes Wright Spring, *When Grass Was King* (Boulder, Colorado, 1956), p. 352.

18. Dennis Sheedy, Autobiography, microfilm copy, State Historical Society of Colorado, Denver.

19. Autobiography of Conrad Kohrs, 159 typed pages, Historical Society of Montana, Helena; obituary of Conrad Kohrs, Helena, Montana, *Helena Independent*, July 23, 1921, and of Mrs. Kohrs in Butte, *Montana Standard*, September 30, 1945.

20. Letter by Russell Thorp on John B. Kendrick, dated August 26, 1932; *Cheyenne State Leader*, August 27, 1932; and article in *Denver Post*, April 5, 1931, all in clipping file in Archives in History, University of Wyoming, Laramie.

21. Noel L. Keith, *The Brites of Capote* (Fort Worth, 1950), p. 27.

22. Obituary of James Phelps White, Roswell, New Mexico, *Roswell Daily Record*, October 22, 1934, and interview with Tom White of Roswell, New Mexico, June 20, 1958.

23. Frink, Jackson, and Spring, *When Grass Was King*, pp. 364-365.

24. Tom Lea, *The King Ranch*, two volumes (Boston, 1957), I, *passim*.

25. Lang, *Ranching With Roosevelt*, pp. 156-157.

26. Hermann Hagedorn, *Roosevelt in the Bad Lands* (Boston, 1921), p. 456.

27. William C. Holden, *The Spur Ranch: A Study of the Inclosed Ranch Phase of the Cattle Industry in Texas* (Boston, 1934), Chapter 10.

28. *The Trail Drivers of Texas*, pp. 193-202, 595-602.

29. Ralph P. Bieber, editor, Joseph G. McCoy, *Historic Sketches of the Cattle Trade of the West and Southwest* (Glendale, California, 1940), p. 81.

30. Frink, Jackson, and Spring, *When Grass Was King*, p. 365.

31. Olive K. Dixon, "Packhorses carried Sam Isaac's Possessions When He Came to Plains; Now Owns Ranch," Amarillo, Texas, *Daily News*, May 21, 1937.

32. Ellsworth Collings (in collaboration with Alma Miller England), *The 101 Ranch* (Norman, Oklahoma, 1937), pp. 26-29.

33. Lea, *The King Ranch*, I, Chapters 6 and 11.

34. *Ibid.*, II, Chapter 15.

35. Holden, *The Spur Ranch*, Chapter 2.

36. "A Calf Starts a Kingdom," *The Cattleman*, XXIII (December, 1936), 9-13.

37. Holden, *The Spur Ranch*, Chapter 9.

38. Helena, Montana, *Independent-Record*, November 1, 1945.

39. Lea, *The King Ranch*, I, Chapter 7.

40. Dennis Sheedy, Autobiography.

41. J. Evetts Haley, *George W. Littlefield, Texan* (Norman, Oklahoma, 1943), pp. 76-77.

42. Lea, *The King Ranch*, I, Chapter 11.

43. Mary W. Clarke, "Murdo Mackenzie," pp. 23-24, 80, 82, 84, 86.

44. Chris Emmett, *Shanghai Pierce, A Fair Likeness* (Norman, Oklahoma, 1953), p. 242 and *passim*.

45. *Ibid.*, pp. 243-246.

CHAPTER SIX.   THE CULT OF THE SELF-MADE MAN

1. Booth Mooney, "Mackenzie of the Matador," *Texas Parade*, XII (November, 1951), 35.

2. Dan Dillon Casement, "The Abbreviated Autobiography of a Joyous Pagan," dated Manhattan, Kansas, March 14, 1944, sixty-two typed pages in Western Range Cattle Industry Study Collection, State Historical Society of Colorado, Denver.

3. Ralph P. Bieber, editor, Joseph G. McCoy, *Historic Sketches of the Cattle Trade of the West and Southwest* (Glendale, California, 1940), pp. 339-340.

4. *Ibid.*, pp. 405-406.

5. *Ibid.*, pp. 407-413.

6. Dennis Sheedy, Autobiography, microfilm copy, State Historical Society of Colorado, Denver.

7. Comments in letter of Ed. F. Williams, in folder marked "Miscellaneous," Archives in History, University of Wyoming, Laramie.

8. Manuscript autobiographical material on Jerome Churchill, Bancroft Library.

9. J. Marvin Hunter, compiler and editor, *The Trail Drivers of Texas*, two volumes in one (Nashville, 1925), pp. 26-28. See also biography on pp. 173-182 expressing same theme.

10. Samuel R. Gwin interview, Bancroft Library.

11. Fort Worth, Texas, *Live Stock Journal*, October 21, 1882, cited in footnote on page 80 of McCoy, *Historic Sketches of the Cattle Trade*.

12. Mody C. Boatright, "The American Myth Rides the Range," *Southwest Review*, XXXVI (Summer, 1951), 157-163.

13. *Trail Drivers of Texas*, pp. 476-478.

14. *Ibid.*, pp. 592-594.

15. *Ibid.*, pp. 453, 959-971.

16. John Clay, *My Life on the Range* (Chicago, 1924), pp. 83-84.

17. McCoy, *Historic Sketches of the Cattle Trade*, pp. 213-214.

18. James E. Temple autobiographical sketch, Bancroft Library.

19. J. Evetts Haley, *Charles Goodnight: Cowman and Plainsman* (New York, 1936), pp. 267-268.

20. Tom Lea, *The King Ranch*, two volumes (Boston, 1957), I, 268-269.

21. Ellsworth Collings (in collaboration with Alma Miller England), *The 101 Ranch* (Norman, Oklahoma, 1937), p. 43.

22. Maurice Frink, William Turrentine Jackson, and Agnes Wright Spring, *When Grass Was King* (Boulder, Colorado, 1956), pp. 383-384.

23. Mari Sandoz, *The Cattlemen: From the Rio Grande Across the Far Marias* (New York, 1958), p. 238.

24. Denver, *Tribune*, August 29, 1883.

25. Haley, *Charles Goodnight*, Chapter 22.

26. Lea, *The King Ranch*, I, 244-252.

27. *Ibid.*, II, 623.

28. *Ibid.*, I, 344-345.

29. Chris Emmett, *Shanghai Pierce, A Fair Likeness* (Norman, Oklahoma, 1953), p. 233.

30. J. F. Hinkle, *A Trip to Panama* (*From Notes Made at the Time*), privately printed pamphlet. I am indebted to Mr. Tom White of Roswell, New Mexico, for permission to use the copy in his possession.

31. Clay, *My Life on the Range*, p. 114.

32. Frink, Jackson, and Spring, *When Grass Was King*, pp. 97-98, footnote 7.

33. William Martin Pearce, "A History of the Matador Land and Cattle Company, Limited, From 1882 to 1915," unpublished doctoral dissertation, University of Texas, 1952, Chapter 4.

34. Santa Fe, *Daily New Mexican*, December 10, 1886.

35. Pearce, "A History of the Matador," Chapter 4.

36. William C. Holden, *The Spur Ranch: A Study of the Inclosed Ranch Phase of the Cattle Industry in Texas* (Boston, 1934), Chapter 9.

37. Haley, *Charles Goodnight*, p. 414.

38. Emerson Hough, *The Story of the Cowboy* (New York, 1936), p. 259.

39. Holden, *The Spur Ranch*, Chapter 6.

40. Lea, *The King Ranch*, I, 328.

41. Holden, *The Spur Ranch*, Chapter 10.

42. Personal interview with W. F. Friend, June 8, 1958.

43. Hermann Hagedorn, *Roosevelt in the Bad Lands* (Boston, 1921), p. 264.

44. Theodore Roosevelt, *Ranch Life and the Hunting-Trail* (New York, 1902), p. 11.

45. McCoy, *Historic Sketches of the Cattle Trade*, p. 396.

46. *Trail Drivers of Texas*, pp. 645-646.

47. J. Evetts Haley, *George W. Littlefield, Texan* (Norman, Oklahoma, 1943), pp. 201-202, 272, 281.

48. Emmett, *Shanghai Pierce*, pp. 51-52.

49. Haley, *George W. Littlefield*, pp. 181-186.

50. Collings, *The 101 Ranch*, p. 171.

51. Haley, *Charles Goodnight*, pp. 242-243.

52. Paul C. Phillips, editor, *Forty Years on the Frontier, as seen in the Journals and Reminiscences of Granville Stuart*, two volumes (Cleveland, 1925), II, 148-156.

53. Lincoln A. Lang, *Ranching With Roosevelt* (Philadelphia, 1926), pp. 202-203, 351.

54. Haley, *Charles Goodnight*, pp. 307-308.

55. C. F. Ward, "John S. Chisum, Pioneer Cattleman of the Valley," Roswell, New Mexico, *Daily Record*, October 7, 1937.

56. Manuscript autobiographical material on Jerome Churchill, Bancroft Library.

CHAPTER SEVEN. GOD'S ELECT

1. Theodore Roosevelt, *Ranch Life and the Hunting-Trail* (New York, 1902), p. 90.

2. Buford Elijah Farris, "An Institutional Approach to the Texas Cattle Ranch," unpublished M.A. dissertation, University of Texas, 1939, discusses the religious content of cowboy songs.

3. Personal interview with Mr. Herbert T. McSpadden, Claremore, Oklahoma, June 7, 1958.

4. J. Marvin Hunter, compiler and editor, *The Trail Drivers of Texas*, two volumes in one (Nashville, 1925), pp. 207-212.

5. William C. Holden, *The Spur Ranch: A Study of the Inclosed Ranch Phase of the Cattle Industry in Texas* (Boston, 1934), Chapter 8.

6. Ellsworth Collings (in collaboration with Alma Miller England), *The 101 Ranch* (Norman, Oklahoma, 1937), p. 101.

7. Paul C. Phillips, editor, *Forty Years on the Frontier, as seen in the Journals and Reminiscences of Granville Stuart*, two volumes (Cleveland, 1925), I, 251-252 and *passim*.

8. Personal interview with Mr. W. F. Friend of Oklahoma, June 8, 1958.

9. Owen Wister, *The Virginian* (New York, 1902), p. 170.

10. Hermann Hagedorn, *Roosevelt in the Bad Lands* (Boston, 1921), p. 322.

11. *Ibid.*, p. 328.

12. Obituaries in Denver, *The Daily Rocky Mountain News*, February 10, 1878; *The Daily Tribune*, February 10, 1878.

13. J. Evetts Haley, *Charles Goodnight: Cowman and Plainsman* (New York, 1936), p. 462.

14. Account of career of Nelson Story, *The Rocky Mountain Husbandman*, May 5, 1938.

15. Roosevelt, *Ranch Life and the Hunting-Trail*, p. 55.

16. Hagedorn, *Roosevelt in the Bad Lands*, p. 283.

17. Haley, *Charles Goodnight*, p. 463.

18. Christ Emmett, *Shanghai Pierce, A Fair Likeness* (Norman, Oklahoma, 1953), p. 216.

19. *The Trail Drivers of Texas*, p. 139.

20. Personal interview with Mr. Theodore R. and Mr. Herbert T. McSpadden, Claremore, Oklahoma, June 7, 1958.

21. Haley, *Charles Goodnight*, pp. 348-350.

22. Ralph P. Bieber, editor, Joseph G. McCoy, *Historic Sketches of the Cattle Trade of the West and Southwest* (Glendale, California, 1940), pp. 129 and 213-214.

23. For example, Haley, *Charles Goodnight*, Chapter 13, and C. F. Ward, "John S. Chisum, Pioneer Cattleman of the Valley," Roswell, New Mexico, *Daily Record*, October 7, 1937, draw somewhat different conclusions as to the value of Chisum's word.

24. Emmett, *Shanghai Pierce*, pp. 230-231.

25. John Clay, *My Life on the Range* (Chicago, 1924), pp. 153-154.

26. Holden, *The Spur Ranch*, Chapter 6.

27. Haley, *Charles Goodnight*, pp. 348-350.

28. Hagedorn, *Roosevelt in the Bad Lands*, pp. 68-69.

29. Personal interview with Mr. Tom White, Roswell, New Mexico, June 20, 1958.

30. J. Evetts Haley, *The XIT Ranch of Texas and the Early Days of the Llano Estacado* (Norman, Oklahoma, 1953), p. 217.

31. Manuscript autobiographical material on C. C. Slaughter, Bancroft Library; Slaughter family biographical file, Barker Texas History Center, Austin.

32. Letter of D. H. Snyder to wife, January 2, 1903, Snyder Papers, Barker Texas History Center, Austin, and also material in Snyder family biographical file in same library.

33. Noel L. Keith, *The Brites of Capote* (Ft. Worth, 1950), pp. 29-30; personal interview with Dr. Rupert N. Richardson, Austin, Texas, June 14, 1958.

34. Manuscript autobiographical material on the Murphy family, Bancroft Library.

35. Tom Lea, *The King Ranch*, two volumes (Boston, 1957), I, 345-346.

36. Collings, *The 101 Ranch*, p. 15.

37. Emmett, *Shanghai Pierce*, p. 173.

38. La Junta, Colorado, *La Junta Tribune*, December 15, 1933.

39. Knox Kinard, "A History of the Waggoner Ranch," unpublished M.A. thesis, University of Texas, 1941.

40. *The Rocky Mountain Husbandman*, December 13, 1934.

41. Lea, *The King Ranch*, I, 341-343.

42. Emmett, *Shanghai Pierce, passim*.

43. Manuscript autobiographical material on Henry Rice, Bancroft Library.

44. Haley, *Charles Goodnight*, p. 372.

45. Personal interview with Dr. Rupert N. Richardson, June 14, 1958.

46. John Alton Templin, "A History of Methodism in Denver 1876-1912," unpublished doctor of theology dissertation, Iliff School of Theology, Denver, 1956.

47. Lea, *The King Ranch*, II, Chapter 15.

48. W. P. Webb, editor, *The Handbook of Texas* (Austin, 1952), I, 709; S. E. Buchanan, "A Day at Goodnight College," *Farm and Ranch*, June 6, 1903; Haley, *Charles Goodnight*, Chapter 25.

49. John A. Rickard, "The Ranch Industry of the Texas South Plains," unpublished M.A. thesis, University of Texas, 1927.

50. Typed copy of Thomas S. Snyder's Recollections as told to J. Evetts Haley, November 20, 1933, Snyder biographical file, Barker Texas History Center, Austin; obituary of Colonel D. H. Snyder, *The Cattleman*, VIII (September, 1921), 40-41; "D. H. Snyder—An Appreciation," *Texas Christian Advocate*, January 26, 1922; quotation from "The Snyder Brothers and Southwestern University," *The Book of Southwestern 1873-1923;* letter F. A. Mood to D. H. Snyder, March 26, 1875, Snyder Papers, Barker Texas History Center.

51. Keith, *The Brites of Capote, passim*. Quotation on p. 85.

52. *Ibid., passim*.

53. *The Handbook of Texas*, II, 851.

54. Manuscript autobiographical material on the Murphy family, Bancroft Library.

55. "Captain Charles Schreiner," San Antonio, Texas, *Express*, February 23, 1938.

56. J. Evetts Haley, *Charles Schreiner: General Merchandise* (Austin, 1944).

57. Austin, *Daily Texan*, July 28, 1945.

58. Helena, Montana, *The Helena Independent*, March 11, 1926; Butte, *The Anaconda Standard*, March 11, 1926.

59. J. Evetts Haley, *George W. Littlefield, Texan* (Norman, Oklahoma, 1943), Chapters 13 and 14.

CHAPTER EIGHT. CHANGING TIDES OF FORTUNE

1. J. Evetts Haley, *Charles Goodnight: Cowman and Plainsman* (New York, 1936), pp. 462-463.

2. Interview with William Cooley of Moab, Utah, March 25, 1937, Utah Historical Records Survey by W.P.A., Bancroft Library.

3. Ralph P. Bieber, editor, Joseph G. McCoy, *Historic Sketches of the Cattle Trade of the West and Southwest* (Glendale, California, 1940), pp. 125, 131, 261-262.

4. Personal interview with Dr. Rupert N. Richardson at Austin, Texas, June 14, 1958.

5. Obituary of Colonel Ike T. Pryor, Dallas *News*, October 18, 1937.

6. Typed sketch by Lamar Moore in Western Range Cattle Industry Study files, Colorado State Historical Society, Denver.

7. J. Evetts Haley, *The XIT Ranch of Texas and the Early Days of the Llano Estacado* (Norman, Oklahoma, 1953), Chapter 11.

8. Paul C. Phillips, editor, *Forty Years on the Frontier, as seen in the Journals and Reminiscences of Granville Stuart*, two volumes (Cleveland, 1925), II, 150, 171-174.

9. William Martin Pearce, "A History of the Matador Land and Cattle Company, Limited, From 1882 to 1915," unpublished doctoral dissertation, University of Texas, 1952, Chapter 1.

10. Stuart, *Forty Years on the Frontier*, II, 150.

11. Lincoln A. Lang, *Ranching With Roosevelt* (Philadelphia, 1926), pp. 40-42, 334-337, 348-349.

12. J. Marvin Hunter, compiler and editor, *The Trail Drivers of Texas*, two volumes in one (Nashville, 1925), pp. 743-746.

13. McCoy, *Historic Sketches of the Cattle Trade*, pp. 249-250.

14. *Ibid.*, pp. 308-312.

15. *Ibid.*, pp. 311-314, 434-435.

16. *Ibid.*, pp. 402-406.

17. Haley, *Charles Goodnight*, pp. 266-275.

18. Interview with Charles F. Coffee, Cheyenne, Wyoming (in the middle 1880's), Bancroft Library.

19. Obituary of Colonel D. H. Snyder, *The Cattleman*, VIII (September, 1921), 40-41.

20. *Ibid.*

21. Ellsworth Collings (in collaboration with Alma Miller England), *The 101 Ranch* (Norman, Oklahoma, 1937), Chapter 4.

22. Interview with H. B. Kelly of Cheyenne, Wyoming, at an unspecified time in 1885, Bancroft Library.

23. Typed sketches by Lamar Moore of Lonny Horn and Sam Doss in Western Range Cattle Industry Study files, Colorado State Historical Society, Denver.

24. McCoy, *Historic Sketches of the Cattle Trade*, pp. 375-379.

25. John Clay, *My Life on the Range* (Chicago, 1924), Chapter 22.

26. Lang, *Ranching With Roosevelt*, pp. 92-93.

27. Proceedings, Eastern Montana Stockgrowers Association Convention 1885, quoted in Maurice Frink, William Turrentine Jackson, and Agnes Wright Spring, *When Grass Was King* (Boulder, Colorado, 1956), pp. 93-94.

28. Interviews with Thomas Benton Hord at some unspecified date and place

in Wyoming around 1885 and with Ora Haley, Laramie City, Wyoming, June 30, 1885, Bancroft Library.

29. Interview with the Honorable Hubert Engelbrecht Teschemacher at Cheyenne, Wyoming, at an unspecified date around 1885, Bancroft Library.

30. Interviews with James E. Tuttle at an unspecified place and time (around 1885) in Wyoming; with Fred G. S. Hesse of Cheyenne, Wyoming, February 26, 1885; with A. R. Converse of Cheyenne, Wyoming, March 3, 1885; with Arnold A. Mowry at an unspecified place in Wyoming, May, 1885; and with Worden P. Noble, Shoshone Agency, Wyoming, August 21, 1885—all in Bancroft Library.

31. Clay, *My Life on the Range*, pp. 245-248.

32. Frink, Jackson, and Spring, *When Grass Was King*, pp. 246-248.

33. *Ibid.*, pp. 99-108.

CHAPTER NINE. LAND, LABOR, AND CAPITAL

1. General James S. Brisbin, *The Beef Bonanza: or, How to Get Rich on the Plains. Being a Description of Cattle-Growing, Sheep-Farming, Horse-Raising, and Dairying in the West* (Philadelphia, 1881), Chapter 4.

2. Maurice Frink, William Turrentine Jackson, and Agnes Wright Spring, *When Grass Was King* (Boulder, Colorado, 1956), pp. 401-404, 430.

3. J. Evetts Haley, *George W. Littlefield, Texan* (Norman, Oklahoma, 1943), pp. 137-138.

4. Ralph P. Bieber, editor, Joseph G. McCoy, *Historic Sketches of the Cattle Trade of the West and Southwest* (Glendale, California, 1940), pp. 380-381.

5. J. Evetts Haley, *Charles Goodnight: Cowman and Plainsman* (New York, 1936), pp. 303-305, 323-325, 329-333.

6. William C. Holden, *The Spur Ranch: A Study of the Inclosed Ranch Phase of the Cattle Industry in Texas* (Boston, 1934), Chapters 1 and 9.

7. Tom Lea, *The King Ranch*, two volumes (Boston, 1957), I, 103-110, 144-145, 253-254; II, 471-473.

8. Frink, Jackson, and Spring, *When Grass Was King*, pp. 303-307, 310-320.

9. *Ibid.*, pp. 422-423.

10. Haley, *George W. Littlefield*, pp. 123, 125, 169-170, 198-201.

11. Chester W. Wright, *Economic History of the United States* (New York, 1941), pp. 732-733.

12. McCoy, *Historic Sketches of the Cattle Trade*, p. 85.

13. Holden, *The Spur Ranch*, Chapter 2.

14. Frink, Jackson, and Spring, *When Grass Was King*, p. 10.

15. Holden, *The Spur Ranch*, Chapter 6.

16. Haley, *George W. Littlefield*, pp. 116-117, 171.

17. Buford Elijah Farris, "An Institutional Approach to the Texas Cattle Ranch," unpublished M.A. dissertation, University of Texas, 1949.

18. John Clay, *My Life on the Range* (Chicago, 1924), pp. 124-128.

19. Frink, Jackson, and Spring, *When Grass Was King*, p. 8.

20. Clay, *My Life on the Range*, p. 140.

21. Haley, *George W. Littlefield*, pp. 57-58.

22. Autobiography of Conrad Kohrs, 159 typed pages, Historical Society of Montana, Helena; obituary of Mrs. Conrad Kohrs, Helena, Montana, *Independent-Record*, November 1, 1945.

23. Haley, *Charles Goodnight*, pp. 273, 295.

24. J. Marvin Hunter, compiler and editor, *The Trail Drivers of Texas*, two volumes in one (Nashville, 1925), pp. 923-924.

25. *Ibid.*, pp. 193-202.

26. Haley, *George W. Littlefield*, Chapters 5 and 11.

27. Letter of C. F. Coffee at unspecified period in 1915, Miscellaneous Folder No. 39, Wyoming Stock Growers Collection, University of Wyoming, Laramie.

28. McCoy, *Historic Sketches of the Cattle Trade*, pp. 363-374.

29. Chris Emmett, *Shanghai Pierce, A Fair Likeness* (Norman, Oklahoma, 1953), p. 32.

30. Frink, Jackson, and Spring, *When Grass Was King*, p. 8.

31. Lea, *The King Ranch*, I, 308-320.

32. Haley, *Charles Goodnight*, p. 296.

33. Frink, Jackson, and Spring, *When Grass Was King*, p. 223.

34. Donald H. Welsh, "Pierre Wibaux, Bad Lands Rancher," unpublished doctoral dissertation, University of Missouri, 1955.

35. Hermann Hagedorn, *Roosevelt in the Bad Lands* (Boston, 1921), Appendix.

36. Dan Dillon Casement, "The Abbreviated Autobiography of a Joyous Pagan," dated Manhattan, Kansas, March 14, 1944, sixty-two typed pages in Western Range Cattle Industry Study Collection, State Historical Society of Colorado, Denver.

37. "The Two Buckle Ranch," undated ten-page mimeographed copy of account of ranch, Southwest Collection, Texas Technological College, Lubbock.

38. Interview with William E. Lawrence, Tequesquite, New Mexico, July 23, 1885, Bancroft Collection.

39. Santa Fe, *New Mexican Review*, June 11, 1885.

CHAPTER TEN.   POKER ON JOINT-STOCK PRINCIPLES

1. Newton Bateman and Paul Selby, editors, *Historical Encyclopedia of Illinois and History of Evanston* (Chicago, 1906), I, 30.

2. J. Evetts Haley, *The XIT Ranch of Texas and the Early Days of the Llano Estacado* (Norman, Oklahoma, 1953), pp. 58-63.

3. Interview with Ora Haley, Laramie City, Wyoming, June 30, 1885, Bancroft Library.

4. Interview with A. R. Converse of Cheyenne, Wyoming, March 3, 1885, Bancroft Library.

5. Maurice Frink, William Turrentine Jackson, and Agnes Wright Spring, *When Grass Was King* (Boulder, Colorado, 1956), pp. 142-143.

6. Walter Baron von Richtofen, *Cattle-Raising on the Plains of North America* (New York, 1885), Chapter 10.

7. William C. Holden, *The Spur Ranch: A Study of the Inclosed Ranch Phase of the Cattle Industry in Texas* (Boston, 1934), Chapter 2.

8. Frink, Jackson, and Spring, *When Grass Was King*, p. 212.

9. Chris Emmett, *Shanghai Pierce, A Fair Likeness* (Norman, Oklahoma, 1953), pp. 99-101, 104-105.

10. This account of anti-foreign sentiment is based on the section by W. Turrentine Jackson in Frink, Jackson, and Spring, *When Grass Was King* and two articles by Roger V. Clements: "British-Controlled Enterprise in the West Between 1870 and 1900, and Some Agrarian Reactions," *Agricultural History*, XXVII (October, 1953), 132-141, and "British Investment and American Legislative Restrictions in the Trans-Mississippi West 1880-1900," *Mississippi Valley Historical Review*, XLII (September, 1955), 207-228.

11. Tom Lea, *The King Ranch*, two volumes (Boston, 1957), II, 643.

12. Interview with Orin C. Waid of Cheyenne, Wyoming, at an unspecified date (in the middle 1880's), Bancroft Library.

13. Charles L. Sonnichsen, *Cowboys and Cattle Kings: Life on the Range Today* (Norman, Oklahoma, 1950), p. 29.

14. *Ibid.*, pp. 13-14.

15. General James S. Brisbin, *The Beef Bonanza: or, How to Get Rich on the Plains. Being a Description of Cattle-Growing, Sheep-Farming, Horse-Raising, and Dairying in the West* (Philadelphia, 1881), Chapters 1 and 2.

16. Folders on Malcolm Moncrieffe and W. A. Towers, Wyoming Biography, Archives in Western History, University of Wyoming, Laramie.

17. C. F. Ward, "John S. Chisum, Pioneer Cattleman of the Valley," Roswell, New Mexico, *Roswell Daily Record*, October 10, 1937. See, also, T. U. Taylor, "John Simpson Chisum," in which Chisum's partner's name is identified fully, Barker Texas History Center, Austin.

18. "A Calf Starts a Kingdom," *The Cattleman*, XXIII (December, 1936), 9-13.

19. William Martin Pearce, "A History of the Matador Land and Cattle Company, Limited, From 1882 to 1915," unpublished doctoral dissertation, University of Texas, 1952, Chapter 1.

20. J. Evetts Haley, *Charles Goodnight: Cowman and Plainsman* (New York, 1936), pp. 301-302.

21. Lea, *The King Ranch*, I, 173.

22. Hermann Hagedorn, *Roosevelt in the Bad Lands* (Boston, 1921), pp. 40-43, 479-481.

23. J. Evetts Haley, *George W. Littlefield, Texan* (Norman, Oklahoma, 1943), pp. 67-68, 88, 142.

24. Lea, The King Ranch, I, 99-110.

25. Frink, Jackson, and Spring, *When Grass Was King*, p. 414.

26. Lea, *The King Ranch*, I, 307-321.

27. Interview with Stephen W. Dorsey, Chico Springs, New Mexico Territory, July 27, 1885, Bancroft Library.

28. Haley, *Charles Goodnight*, pp. 326, 331, 354.

29. Lea, *The King Ranch*, I, 132-138.

30. *Ibid.*, I, 355-357.

31. Interview with Alexander Hamilton Swan at Cheyenne City, Wyoming Territory, at unspecified date (in the mid-1880's), Bancroft Library.

32. Biographical material from an unidentified source, written in 1884, biographical files on Swan family, Archives in Western History, University of Wyoming, Laramie.

33. Printed report of First General Meeting of Swan Land and Cattle Company, Limited, July 30, 1883, biographical files on Swan family, Archives in Western History, University of Wyoming, Laramie.

34. Frink, Jackson, and Spring, *When Grass Was King*, pp. 274-277, 307-310.

35. John Clay, *My Life on the Range* (Chicago, 1924), pp. 49-50, 209.

36. Undated memorandum by F. W. Lafrentz and letter from him to Russell Thorp, August 14, 1944, biographical files on Swan family, Archives in Western History, University of Wyoming, Laramie.

37. Clay, *My Life on the Range*, pp. 20-25, 40.

38. Haley, *The XIT Ranch of Texas*, Chapter 4.

39. See advertisement of Merchants National Bank in *Kansas City Journal*, April 10, 1880, and listings of members of Underwood, Clark and Company in directories for the period, as, for example, *Hoye's Kansas City Directory for 1883*.

40. Frink, Jackson, and Spring, *When Grass Was King*, pp. 264-265. The general account of the steps followed in creating new companies is based on the section by W. Turrentine Jackson in this volume.

CHAPTER ELEVEN. THE VANGUARD OF CHANGE

1. Letter by John Thorp, August 26, 1932, files of Wyoming Stock Growers' Association, University of Wyoming, Laramie.

2. J. Evetts Haley, *George W. Littlefield, Texan* (Norman, Oklahoma, 1943), pp. 62-65. Quotation from Pierce is on page 64.

3. Denver, *The Daily Rocky Mountain News*, February 10, 1878.

4. Maurice Frink, William Turrentine Jackson, and Agnes Wright Spring, *When Grass Was King* (Boulder, Colorado, 1956), pp. 355-357, 359-361.

5. Autobiography of Conrad Kohrs, 159 typed pages, Historical Society of Montana, Helena; interview with Ora Haley, Laramie City, Wyoming, June 30, 1885, Bancroft Library.

6. J. Evetts Haley, *Charles Goodnight: Cowman and Plainsman* (New York, 1936), *passim*.

7. Tom Lea, *The King Ranch*, two volumes (Boston, 1957), I, Chapters 1-8 inclusive.

8. J. Marvin Hunter, compiler and editor, *The Trail Drivers of Texas*, two volumes in one (Nashville, 1925), pp. 721-729.

9. Unidentified newspaper account of Nelson Story's career written by his son Byron Story, Archives in Western History, University of Wyoming, Laramie.

10. Interview with Worden P. Noble, Shoshone Agency, Wyoming, August 21, 1885, Bancroft Library.

11. Interview with Morton E. Post of Wyoming (in the mid-1880's), Bancroft Library.

12. Interview with William Van Gasken, Miles City, Montana, October 22, 1885, Bancroft Library.

13. Interview with John Donegan of Montana (in the mid-1880's), Bancroft Library.

14. Haley, *Charles Goodnight*, pp. 316, 326-329.

15. William C. Holden, *The Spur Ranch: A Study of the Inclosed Ranch Phase of the Cattle Industry in Texas* (New York, 1936), Chapter 6.

16. John Clay, *My Life on the Range* (Chicago, 1924), p. 128.

17. The story of this drive constitutes the core of Andy Adams', *The Log of a Cowboy* (Boston, 1903).

18. Lea, *The King Ranch*, I, 347.

19. Haley, *George W. Littlefield*, pp. 111-114, 172, 200-204.

20. J. Evetts Haley, *The XIT Ranch of Texas and the Early Days of the Llano Estacado* (Norman, Oklahoma, 1953), p. 82.

21. *The Trail Drivers of Texas*, pp. 734-736.

22. Clipping, "Fred G. S. Hesse," *Live Stock Markets*, March 28, 1929, and unidentified typed biography, Archives in Western History, University of Wyoming, Laramie.

23. Mary W. Clarke, "Murdo Mackenzie, Scotsman, Makes Cattle History in Western World," *The Cattleman*, XXXVIII (June, 1951), 23-24, 80, 82, 84, 86.

24. Interview with Harry Oelrichs, Cheyenne, Wyoming, March 16, 1885, Bancroft Library.

25. *The Trail Drivers of Texas*, pp. 734-736.

26. Holden, *The Spur Ranch*, Chapter 2.

27. Haley, *The XIT Ranch of Texas*, pp. 98-102.

28. William Martin Pearce, "A History of the Matador Land and Cattle Company, Limited, From 1882 to 1915," unpublished doctoral dissertation, University of Texas, 1952, Chapter two, footnote 85.

29. Letter of John Clay to James A. Robertson, July 15, 1907, Western Range Cattle Industry Study Collection, State Historical Society of Colorado, Denver.

30. Clay, *My Life on the Range*, p. 316.

31. Pearce, "A History of the Matador Land and Cattle Company," Chapter 2.

32. Letter of Harry H. Campbell to William C. Holden, April 26, 1957, Southwest Collection, Texas Technological College, Lubbock.

33. Unless otherwise indicated, all material on the Matador management has been drawn from Pearce, "A History of the Matador Land and Cattle Company."

CHAPTER TWELVE.   CATTLEMAN AND COWBOY:
FACT AND FANCY

1. Harold Bindloss, *The Cattle-Baron's Daughter* (New York, 1906).

2. Andy Adams, *Reed Anthony, Cowman: An Autobiography* (Boston, 1907).

3. Alfred B. Guthrie, *These Thousand Hills* (Boston, 1956).

4. Walker D. Wyman, recorder, *Nothing But Prairie & Sky* (Norman, Oklahoma, 1954), p. 101.

5. Madaline W. Nichols, *The Gaucho: Cattle Hunter, Cavalryman, Ideal of Romance* (Durham, North Carolina, 1942).

6. Edward Shann, *An Economic History of Australia* (Cambridge, England, 1930), Chapter 8.

7. *Ibid.*, pp. 216-217.

8. Warren French, "The Cowboy in the Dime Novel," *Studies in English*, University of Texas (Austin, 1951), XXX, 219-234.

9. "Choosing the Century's Favorite Books: Final Results of a Nation-Wide Poll," *The Literary Digest International Book Review*, II (March, 1924), 261-264.

10. See, for example, James Cloyd Bowman, *Pecos Bill: The Greatest Cowboy of All Time* (Chicago, 1950), for representative stories concerning Pecos Bill.

11. Henry Nash Smith, *Virgin Land; the American West as symbol and myth* (Cambridge, Massachusetts, 1950).

12. Armand W. Reeder, "Roundup of Westerns," St. Louis *Post Dispatch*, book page, June 1, 1958.

13. Irene P. McKeehan, writing in Junius Henderson, et al., *Colorado: Studies of Its Past and Present* (Boulder, Colorado, 1927), p. 163, cited in Percy S. Fritz, *Colorado: The Centennial State* (New York, 1941), p. 420.

14. Joe B. Frantz and Julian Ernest Choate, Jr., *The American Cowboy: The Myth and the Reality* (Norman, Oklahoma, 1955), gives a fuller appraisal of cowboy literature.

15. Quoted in Stuart Henry, *Conquering Our Great American Plains: A Historical Development* (New York, 1930), p. 354.

16. Stuart Henry, "Faults of Our Wild West Stories," *The Literary Digest International Book Review*, I (November, 1923), 34-35.

17. Biographical details concerning Henry's life have been drawn from the sketch of him in *Who's Who in America for 1924-25* and from autobiographical statements in Henry's *Conquering Our Great American Plains*.

18. *The Pioneer Magazine of Texas*, V (April through September, 1924).

19. The comments by all the people cited appeared in *ibid.*

20. "Texas Versus Henry," *The Saturday Evening Post*, CXCVI (June 7, 1924), 34.

21. "The Old-Time Cowboys Defend Emerson Hough," *The Literary Digest International Book Review*, II (July, 1924), 602 and 615.

22. Henry, *Conquering Our Great American Plains*, p. 167.

23. John A. and Alan Lomax, *Cowboy Songs and Other Frontier Ballads* (New York, 1938), pp. xviii-xix.

24. *Ibid.*, p. xxv.

25. *Wyoming, A Guide* (New York, 1941), p. 159.

26. Mahonri M. Young, "Frederic Remington," *Dictionary of American Biography*, XV, 496-497.

27. Ramon F. Adams and Homer E. Britzman (with biographical check list

by Karl Yost), *Charles M. Russell, The Cowboy Artist: A Biography* (Pasadena, California, 1948), pp. 75-80 and *passim*.

28. Philip Ashton Rollins, *The Cowboy: An Unconventional History of Civilization on the Old-Time Range* (New York, 1936), p. 376.

CHAPTER THIRTEEN. THE CATTLEMAN'S ROLE IN
AMERICAN CULTURE

1. James G. Leyburn, *Frontier Folkways* (New Haven, 1935), Chapter 6.

2. Chapter 2, p. 95, by R. M. Hartwell in Gordon Greenwood, editor, *Australia: A Social and Political History* (London, 1955).

3. W. Turrentine Jackson, "The Wyoming Stock Growers' Association Political Power in Wyoming Territory, 1873-1900," *Mississippi Valley Historical Review*, XXXIII (March, 1947), 571-594.

4. Andy Adams, *Reed Anthony, Cowman: An Autobiography* (Boston, 1907).

5. Tom Lea, *The King Ranch*, two volumes (Boston, 1957), I, 157-174.

6. J. Evetts Haley, *George W. Littlefield, Texan* (Norman, Oklahoma, 1943), pp. 207-212.

7. J. Marvin Hunter, compiler and editor, *The Trail Drivers of Texas*, two volumes in one (Nashville, 1925), pp. 959-971. Quotation on page 962.

8. Interview with N. B. Stoneroad, Cabra Springs, New Mexico, July 6, 1885, Bancroft Library.

9. Lea, *The King Ranch*, II, 490-506.

10. *Ibid.*, II, 768-773.

11. Ralph P. Bieber, editor, Joseph G. McCoy, *Historic Sketches of the Cattle Trade of the West and Southwest* (Glendale, California, 1940), pp. 136-137.

12. William Martin Pearce, "A History of the Matador Land and Cattle Company, Limited, From 1882 to 1915," unpublished doctoral dissertation, University of Texas, 1952, Chapter 3.

13. Maurice Frink, William Turrentine Jackson, and Agnes Wright Spring, *When Grass Was King* (Boulder, Colorado, 1956), p. 30, footnote 18.

14. Interview with Dwight Fisk, Cheyenne, Wyoming, February 21, 1885, Bancroft Library.

15. Interview with A. H. Reel, Cheyenne, Wyoming, February 21, 1885, Bancroft Library.

Index

Abilene, Kansas, 2, 16, 33-35, 47, 124, 134, 153, 156, 183, 187, 221, 231, 253, 254, 255, 256-257, 275
Abilene, Texas, 143
Abney, Jack, 201
Accident, role of, 4, 16, 151-152
Adair, John George, 23-24, 63, 84, 86, 120, 189, 203, 206-207
Adair, Mrs. John George, 86, 207
Adams, Andy, 242, 255, 257, 268-269
Adams, Burke and Company, 188
Africa, 88, 194
Agriculture, U.S. Department of, 273
Alabama, 2, 223
Alamo Saloon, 34
Alder Gulch, 183
Alsace-Lorraine, 2, 148
American Historical Association, 256
American Livestock Association, 11, 147
American Nation Series, 68
American National Bank (Austin), 178
Anderson, Miss Eddie, 90
Andover Theological Seminary, 91
Anglo-American Cattle Company, 232
Antecedents, 5
Anthony, Reed, 269
Anthrax, 273
Antoine's (New Orleans), 73
Antonio, merchant of Venice, 219, 220
Argentina, 163
Arizona, 42, 50, 62, 271
Arizona Rangers, 50, 122
Arkansas, 116, 145, 206
Arkansas River, 159
Armour, Philip D., 118, 119
Arnot, John, 42
Art Student's League, 260
Ascasubi, 244
Aten, Ira, 44
Austin, Texas, 124, 186, 230, 235
Australia, 231, 244, 268, 273
Averill, James, 53-54

Babcock, Amos C., 194, 214
Badger, Joseph E., 245
Bales, Catherine Ann, 84
Balganown estate, Scotland, 232, 233-234
Ballard Springs, 236, 237
Bancroft, Hubert Howe, 2, 3, 30, 68
Banks, 157-158, 160, 184-189, 276
Bannack City, Montana, 225
Baptist Memorial Hospital (Dallas), 145
Barton, D. W., 40
Batts, R. L., 30
Baylor University, 142
Beaver Creek, 61
Beaverhead valley, 9
Belle Fourche River, 163
Bernhardt, Sarah, 233
Billier, Fred de, 54
Billings, Montana, 261
Billings County, Montana, 31
Billy the Kid, 50, 153
Bindloss, Harold, 241-242
Blackfoot Agency, 228
Blackstone, 105
Blaine, James G., 198
Blizzards, 154
Blocker, John R., 122, 254
Bloys Camp Meeting, 139
Boers, 244, 268
Boer War, 62
Bog camps, 154
Boice, H. S., 138
Bonnemains, Baron de, 3, 14, 191
Boone, Daniel, 247, 249
Boreman, Adolph H., 192
Boston, Massachusetts, 4
Boston Latin School, 64
Boston tea party, 54
Boswell, Nathaniel K., 50-51
Boyce, A. G., 230-231, 234, 235
Bozeman, Montana, 9, 148, 225
Brands, 161, 181

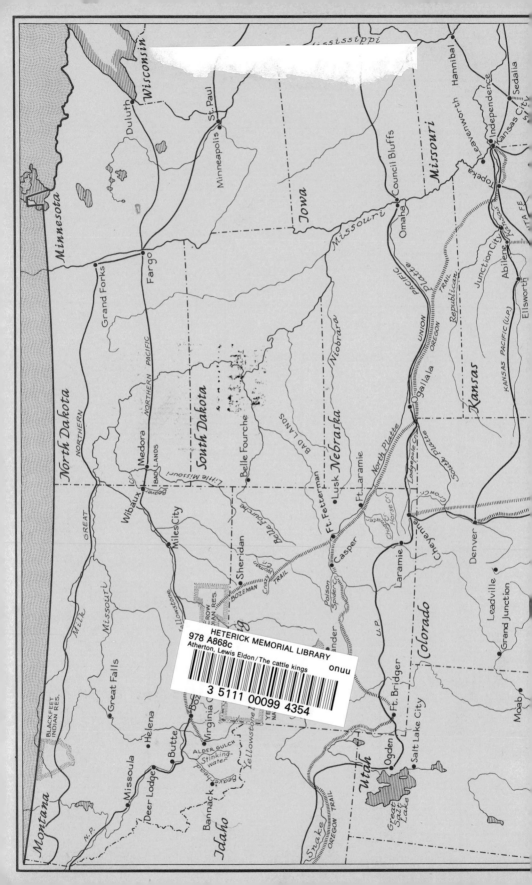